# RACE, CLASS, POLITICS AND THE STRUGGLE FOR EMPOWERMENT IN BARBADOS, 1914–1937

# RACE, CLASS, POLITICS AND THE STRUGGLE FOR EMPOWERMENT IN BARBADOS, 1914–1937

*David V.C. Browne*

IAN RANDLE PUBLISHERS
*Kingston • Miami*

First published in Jamaica, 2012 by
Ian Randle Publishers
11 Cunningham Avenue
Box 686
Kingston 6
www.ianrandlepublishers.com

© 2012, David Browne

**National Library of Jamaica Cataloguing in Publication Data**

Browne, David
    Race, class, politics and the struggle for empowerment in Barbados,
1914–1937 / David Browne

    p. : ill. ;  cm.

Includes bibliographical references and index
ISBN 978-976-637-398-6 (pbk)

1. Barbados – Race relations – 20th century  2. Blacks – Barbados – Economic
conditions   3. Barbados – Social conditions – 20th century   4. Barbados
– Politics and  government – 20th century   5. Working class – Barbados –
Political activity   6. Barbados – History
I.   Title
305.896972981  -   dc 22

Cover and book design by Ian Randle Publishers
Printed in United States of America

Front cover image courtesy of the *Barbados Advocate*

This book is dedicated, with love, to my children – David Jr., Deidriana, Desiree and Damien – and to my mother, Carmen Browne, who believed in the value of a good education. Finally, it is dedicated to the memory of the black working classes of Barbados.

# TABLE OF CONTENTS

# LIST OF FIGURES AND TABLES

# FOREWORD

If Barbados in the nineteenth century, decades after Emancipation, was considered until recently a departure from the West Indian norm, the period between the World Wars added to the tradition of misrepresentation and misunderstanding. While a number of important studies on post-slavery social and economic history has served to integrate the Barbados formation within the wider regional process, this pioneer work by David Browne does precisely the same for the inter-war period. Here we have an excellent study that explores, for the first time, the critical role of the colony in giving definition and direction to dying British colonialism while serving as a theatre for an emerging black Nationalism within the broad discourse of popular democracy in general and Garveyism in particular.

Browne takes us into the institutional networks forged by working-class communities, and reveals with striking clarity their evolving political consciousness which is driven in part by migrants returning from the industrial experience of working on the construction of the Panama Canal. Further, he shows how radical leadership was generated within the bowels of the Panama complex, as well as the local urban and rural context. Men and woman seemed more intolerant of colonialism and determined to demand civil rights by challenging the political power of the planter-merchant elite. The power of the erupting popular political mentality could not be contained by traditional forms of oppression. With enhanced organizational leadership, workers moved their activity to a new revolutionary level in 1937. However, colonial society was already hovering on the brink of political collapse, protected and secured only by means of intense political victimization and military aggression.

Democracy was painfully extracted from the iron grip of plantation elites whose acerbic racial and class mentalities had survived with little social and ideological modification since the seventeenth century. Barbados had secured a reputation within the black communities as the most racially reactionary and institutionally oppressive of Britain's West Indian colonies. The periods between the wars witness the beginning of the end of the old regime. It was a triumph of grassroots politics as workers campaigned for industrial rights and political enfranchisement, while placing at the top of the agenda an end to colonialism. The narrative here is clear and gripping.

Hilary McD. Beckles
General Editor
Forgotten Histories of the Caribbean Series

# PREFACE

Contemporary Barbadian society is very often embroiled in much discussion about 'race' in the form of heated debates in the print and electronic media. But, in the majority of cases, there is a noticeable ignorance on the part of many discussants of the fundamental issues involved in understanding the origin, and the nature, of Barbados's race and class relations, especially during the nineteenth and early twentieth centuries.

The task of researching and writing this book on such controversial issues was accomplished after a close scrutiny of parliamentary debates, Colonial Office correspondence, the dispatches of colonial governors, the reports of police detectives and many other sources, including the oral testimony of working-class people.

This book, I must admit, has a glaring bias in relation to its methodology. It interprets the historical evidence from the perspective of the labouring classes. In short, it is a work that embraces the methodology of 'history from below,' sometimes called 'grassroots history' or 'subaltern studies,' pioneered by many outstanding scholars such as E. P. Thompson, Eric Hobsbawm and George Rudé. This book examines how, in the case of Barbados, the working classes contributed to the development of the island's economy, and to the fostering of social and political change. In short, it examines their struggle for empowerment. In addition, it examines a myth which suggests that the black labouring classes were lazy, docile and devoid of any political consciousness. I would argue that the main impetus for socio-political change in early twentieth-century Barbados was generated by the struggles of the labouring classes, rather than the benevolent and philanthropic notions of the ruling elite. The rebellion of July 1937, in essence, represented the pinnacle of overt political protest, which signalled the end of an era in the island's political development.

It is hoped that this book will assist readers in gaining a better understanding of contemporary racial issues in Barbados. These racial issues all have their roots in the past, and can only be properly understood, and ultimately corrected, by a reference to their historical roots.

I am greatly indebted to the staff of many libraries in Barbados. I wish to thank the staff of the Department of Archives, the National Library Service, the *Barbados Advocate* in Fontabelle, St Michael, and the Barbados Museum and Historical Society. I owe an immense debt to the staff of the Main Library, University of the West Indies, Cave Hill. They were very patient with me, despite my many nagging requests for information.

Special thanks are due to many people, too numerous to mention, whose comments and advice proved to be a vital source of inspiration which kept me going despite the many frustrations. Trevor Marshall, Dr Henderson Carter, Margot Blackman, Ishmael Daniel, and Anthony Reid all read the original manuscript and made useful suggestions. Professor Hilary Beckles has been a source of inspiration from my days as an undergraduate student. My colleagues in the History Department at Queen's College – Jean Wells-Greaves, Farrah Gibbs, Kim Shepherd and Eulodie Coppin-Armstrong – have been a source of inspiration for many years. Miss Nicole Howell must also be praised for her patience in typing the final draft.

David V. C. Browne
Queen's College
Barbados

# INTRODUCTION

B arbados, at the time of the English settlement in 1627, was uninhabited. In fact, the indigenous people disappeared from Barbados about 100 years before the coming of the first Englishmen. It is believed that they were the victims of genocidal raids by early Spanish and Portuguese explorers in search of cheap labour and concubines for their colonies in the Greater Antilles and the mainland of South America. The absence of an exploitable native population in Barbados meant that there was no Euro-Amerindian conflict, which was prevalent in the frontier societies of Spanish America, and indeed, throughout Plantation America.[1] For example, the Kalinago (Carib) peoples, in defense of their homelands and their liberty, were a constant threat to European settlers in the Eastern Caribbean in the seventeenth century. In 1640, a Kalinago attack on the English settlement at Antigua killed 50 settlers and destroyed their homes and crops. Joint military action by a French and English expedition in 1628 succeeded in defeating Kalinago forces in the interior of St Kitts. In 1681, 300 Kalinagos from St Vincent and Dominica routed an English settlement in Barbuda. At the end of the seventeenth century, the Kalinagos in the Windward islands were still holding on to much of their territory and making life very uncomfortable for frontier settlements elsewhere in the Leewards.[2] These conflicts disrupted and, in many instances, slowed the pace of economic development in these frontier communities.[3] Barbados, perhaps because of its most easterly location, and the absence of any conflict between the English settlers and an indigenous population, benefited from a rather early tranquil state of human relations.

The absence of an aboriginal population, and hence a ready supply of cheap labour, forced the English settlers to look outside the colony for a labour force very early in the development of the colony. Scotland and Ireland provided white indentured servants. From 1644 to 1655 some 12,000 prisoners of war entered the island, victims of English civil and political strife.[4] Other groups, such as the Quakers, came voluntarily in order to escape religious persecution. Barbados accepted white indentured servants to a greater extent than any other British-colonized West Indian territory.[5] Their descendants, the 'poor whites,' sometimes referred to as 'red legs' or 'backra johnnies,' still form a small community in the rural districts of St John and St Philip.

When the shift from tobacco to sugar occurred during the 'sugar revolution' of the mid-seventeenth century, there was also a significant shift in the importation of labour, from white servants to black Africans. Between 1643 and 1685, the black enslaved population increased from 5,680 to 46,000 and remained constant until 1705. In 1829, it was 82,902. By contrast, the white population which stood at 37,300 in 1643 had declined to 12,000 by 1705. In 1829, it was 14,959.[6] Whereas the black population had risen at a rapid rate, the white population declined and then remained static. This ethnic composition was to remain a permanent demographic feature of Barbados.

After 1650, Barbados experienced a rapid development of the sugar plantation economy, with chattel slavery as the dominant mode of production. The early settlers immediately built an economic structure centred on the sugar industry and its by-products – rum and molasses – and developed a pattern of social relations which treated the black enslaved population as non-human. They were legally defining them as property. This legal status led to the development of a rabid racist ideology which considered the black enslaved peoples as inherently inferior, pagan, barbaric and lacking in intelligence. It was now easy to justify chattel slavery.[7] Richard Ligon, for example, described the black enslaved in the Caribbean as 'bloody people' who were beastly by nature. Such was the typical perception by the white settlers of the African population in Barbados.[8]

Such ingrained racial attitudes led to the enactment of early slave codes designed to control the 'beast' in the African, and hence, in theory, every facet of his life. As Hilary Beckles has suggested a 'racist, apartheid social order... emerged.'[9] The slave codes were reinforced by the presence of a local militia and the stationing of imperial troops in Barbados. At a micro-level of social relations, each plantation had its own system of punishments, which further kept the enslaved Africans in their place.

But it is the central role that race and colour prejudice played in shaping West Indian communities, and more particularly Barbadian society, that is so striking to this discussion. William Sewell, the New York based abolitionist and journalist, was baffled, during his visit to Barbados in the mid-nineteenth-century, to discover that Samuel Jackman Prescod, who appeared totally Caucasian in features, was rejected by the white community largely because of the knowledge that he had 'black blood' in his veins.[10] Such discrimination existed in all British West Indian territories, but not with the same intensity as in Barbados.[11] In Barbados, racial prejudice was used for more than a justification for the enslavement of the black population. It played a decisive role in the stratification of society, to the extent that the pigment of the skin was used with microscopic precision and detail as the main yardstick to identify social groups and to place them in subjection.

By the beginning of the nineteenth-century, the local plantocracy had created a socio-political and economic order, rooted in race and class prejudice, of which they were proud. They were also willing to defend that order whenever they felt threatened. For example, the suggestion, in 1816, to allow limited political and economic enfranchisement of the Barbadian free coloureds, so as to create an ally against any slave rebellions which may occur in the future, brought out the strongest defence of the status quo during the early nineteenth-century. John Poyer, a white Creole historian, captured the position of the majority of conservative planters in Barbados when he wrote, in 1801:

> In every well-constituted society, a state of subordination necessarily arises from the nature of civil government. Without this no political union can long subsist. To maintain this fundamental principle, it becomes absolutely necessary to preserve the distinctions which naturally exist or are accidentally introduced into the community. With us, two grand distinctions exist resulting from the nature of our society. First, between the white inhabitants and free people of colour, and secondly, between masters and slaves. Nature has strongly defined the differences [not] only in complexion, but in the mental, intellectual and corporal faculties of the different species. Our colonial codes have acknowledged and adopted the distinction.[12]

This most articulate and vehement exposition on the local race relations scene invoked racial theories to justify the segmentation of Barbadian society. If Poyer was so bitterly opposed to a limited enfranchisement of the free coloured joining elements of the planter class, then there was no room to tolerate Samuel Jackman Prescod's attempts to build a liberal democratic society in the early post-slavery society of Barbados.[13] Prescod, a coloured journalist, politician and anti-slavery campaigner, attempted to democratize Barbadian society at a time when the British West Indies was going through the uncertainty of the 'Great

Experiment' of liberating the black population after centuries of enslavement. In place of chattel slavery, the plantocracy of the British West Indies, with the full approval and support of the Colonial Office, endeavoured to put a free labour plan in place, all within an unchanged plantation economy. So whereas, at a theoretical level, some colonial officials wrote of the creation of a new society in the British West Indies, at a practical level, there was little evidence of the democratization of the society or of any change in its socio-economic relations.[14] In short, the racist ideology of slave society survived formal emancipation. The plantation system remained largely intact, with the planter class at the helm. The black population remained politically and economically disenfranchised. All attempts by liberal activists, such as Prescod, to change the status quo, were met by stubborn opposition.

Opposition to political and economic change designed to benefit the Afro-Barbadian population always took the form of invoking the old-fashioned racist ideology of the pro-slavery era. Prejudice and discrimination were given intellectual comfort, for example, largely through the writings of such authors as Thomas Carlyle, Anthony Trollope and James Froude, all claiming to have made pertinent observations of the character of black West Indians. Afro-West Indians were perceived in a stereotypical fashion as lazy, barbaric and savage beings, incapable of self-control, or of wisely exercising political rights. In fact, a popular argument ventilated by the West Indian plantocracy during the post-slavery era was that Afro-West Indians needed to be trained in the 'habits of industry,' and raised in the level of human civilization. This, they argued, could only be achieved by a process of tutelage spearheaded by the plantocracy. These crude perceptions of black West Indians survived into the twentieth century.

But the failure to democratize British West Indian society, and to enfranchise the black population, did not pass unnoticed. Indeed, the plantocracy's opposition to the establishment of a black peasantry in post-slavery society was made in response to an unquenchable quest to obtain land, which would have made the peasantry direct competitors for land, labour and capital. In addition, the attempts to bargain for higher wages and better working conditions, and to obtain political rights, to be educated and to improve life, generally, suggest that Afro-West Indians were not prepared to passively accept their lowly status in post-slavery society. Conflict manifested itself in its most overt form through social and industrial uprisings which plagued Barbados of the nineteenth and early twentieth centuries. The failure of the Apprenticeship System (1834–38) to develop amicable relations between former enslaved peoples and former slave owners resulted in an air of uncertain industrial relations in the immediate post-1838 society in some territories. The 1862 'Vox Populi' riots of St Vincent, the 1876 Confederation riots and the 1895 potato riots in Barbados, and other social upheavals elsewhere during the nineteenth-century, attested to the continuing class conflict in West Indian society.

Throughout the late nineteenth century, then, British West Indian society was a potential breeding ground for rebellion. In Barbados, the plantocracy survived some challenges, especially the 1876 Confederation upheavals and the 1895 potato 'riots,' by firm action on their part. Their survival was almost assured by their long experience in the successful handling of the black population. They had survived previous rebellions, including the 1816 Bussa revolt.[17] As a class, the local plantocracy understood what they had to do in a crisis in order to ensure their own survival. The experiences of these crises brought out not only their bonds of solidarity, but their willingness to use brute force and the law-making powers of the legislature to guarantee their survival. This long, successful history of managing the Afro-Barbadian population was succinctly explained by George Carrington, an absentee planter, in his evidence before the 1897 West India Royal Commission:

> The Barbadian Negroes are most civil as a rule, especially in daylight, in Barbados, to us and to the managers, but you will see the same nigger goes down in a fortnight afterwards to Demarara – he will stand and look at the manager and whistle in his face and 'cheek' him in any kind of way. It is that in Barbados we have such an ample command of the labourer, there is such a lot of them, that they must work and must behave themselves, and it is their home-place; that is why we get hold of them, and they know that they may lose ground. In Demarara they are in such demand that they can do just whatever they like, and they go from one place to another, there is no owner to look after them.[18]

Carrington's testimony captured the mechanism which was used to control the labouring classes under the local tenantry system. It deprived the black workers of ownership of land, but compelled them to work on the estate with little security of tenure, and under the constant threat of expulsion. In essence, workers feared for their very existence, for once expelled from the estate, there were few employment opportunities and therefore slim chances of survival. Carrington could have mentioned how the provisions of the Master and Servant Act, the Vagrancy Act, and other pieces of legislation, worked to keep the black labourer in total subjection.

The economic crises of the late nineteenth-century, which the Royal Commission (1897) investigated, were brought on largely, though not exclusively, by falling sugar prices, rising production costs, falling productivity and outmoded agricultural and manufacturing methods. The local crisis, despite the financial support recommended by the Royal Commission, continued into the twentieth century. The Barbadian plantocracy was able to survive a collapse of the sugar industry partly through the financial support of the Barbados Mutual Assurance Society, and later by the formation of the Sugar Industry Agricultural Bank in 1907.[19] In addition, the superior bargaining position of the planter class – made possible by an abundance of cheap labour, bound to the estate by stringent tenancy regulations and unable to emigrate en masse until the building of the Panama Canal – ensured that wages were kept to a minimum. On occasion, they were reduced. The planter class, through such unilateral action, was able to keep its production costs to a minimum, despite the depressed sugar prices of the late nineteenth and early twentieth centuries. The survival of the sugar industry was thus ensured.

Such depressed economic conditions impacted heavily on the local labouring classes. Their thrift, industry and ability to survive were tested to the limit. This situation was more acute for Afro-Barbadians than for most British West Indian labourers, especially in the larger territories, in that there was little arable land outside of the plantation system available for exploitation in Barbados. Early twentieth-century Barbados, in short, inherited a legacy of poverty, unemployment, underemployment, malnutrition and hunger, from the previous century.

Despite the economic crises, Barbadian society of the 1920s struggled to find what appeared to be an elusive order. The Afro-Barbadian population, for example, demanded economic equality, political rights and social status, while the merchant-planter elite struggled to maintain its dominance. The formation of Plantations Ltd, in 1917, and the Barbados Shipping and Trading, in 1920, ushered in the beginning of a consolidation of the corporate economy through the merger of planter and merchant capital.[20] This process continued throughout the early twentieth century. At the same time, thousands of Afro-West Indians, and indeed Barbadians, were sending remittances, or returning from Panama, and further afield, with cash, and were eager to obtain land to improve their lot. Remittances received through the Barbados Post Office in 1910, for example, totalled £93,361, with £62,102 coming from the Canal Zone.[21] But the merchant-planter elite was unwilling to allow the wholesale economic empowerment of the Afro-Barbadian population. The 1905 Friendly Societies Act, which limited the maximum amount of land which any one society could purchase to a few acres, ensured that there was no widespread acquisition of land – the passport to wealth, social status and political enfranchisement – by the black population. A bitter class struggle which was brewing in the post-slavery period, intensified during the early twentieth century. What were the nature and the outcome of the struggle?

It is this central question which this book addresses. It explores a fascinating period of Barbadian history, that is, the years 1914–37. This period can be perceived as a time highlighted by the beginning of the First World War and ending with the outbreak of the 1937 rebellion. The outbreak of the First World War, on the one hand, resulted in severe hardships for the labouring classes, largely because of food shortages, and the general dislocation caused by the war. On the other hand, the high sugar prices obtained during the war years bestowed a period of temporary prosperity on the plantocracy, who seized the opportunity to put the sugar industry on a sound financial footing. At the same time, the political consciousness of the Afro-Barbadian was aroused by a growing anti-colonial movement spearheaded by more than four local branches of Marcus Garvey's Universal Negro Improvement Association (UNIA), of which many ex-servicemen were members, and by the Workingmen's Association (WMA). In 1919, Clennel Wickham, a First World War veteran, and Clennel Inniss started the *Herald* newspaper, a 'radical' organ which addressed many issues affecting the labouring classes. When the *Herald* ceased operations in 1930 as a result of a lawsuit brought against it by a Bridgetown merchant, Walter Bayley, the radical tradition was revived by Wynter Crawford's *Barbados Observer* in 1934. The 1937 rebellion was the culmination of a struggle, waged at a time of threatening global war and economic crisis, for the control of political power and economic resources.

The book, it must be stressed, is concerned largely with the study of the black labouring classes of Barbados. 'History from below' is a challenging approach to historical research and writing, especially for some West Indian scholars who have been tutored in a secondary school system which emphasized the study of European history and geography, to the exclusion of an intimate knowledge about the Caribbean region. But, more important, the historiography of the region, until the pioneering work of Eric Williams and Elsa Goveia in the 1950s and the 1960s, was dominated by historians whose interpretations of the source materials were not always sympathetic to the region or to its black inhabitants. The majority of these historical accounts relied heavily on the records preserved by a merchant-planter elite, and so was, for the most part, intentionally or unintentionally, biased toward this class. In addition, there is one other consideration relating to 'history from below' and this is that the records preserved by the plantocracy are the records preserved by a minority class. If the history of any epoch is made by all classes in society, it seems that the historiography of the region which neglects any class – and in the case of the British West Indies, the black majority – is deficient, and needs to be addressed.

The nature of the historical records, however, makes it very hard to 'hear' the black working classes. Nevertheless, the task, difficult as it is, is not an impossible one. If the traditional sources are subjected to new techniques in the disciplines of social psychology, anthropology and sociology; perhaps they may become more revealing than previously thought. For example, the extensive research by many European scholars into the role of 'crowds' and the 'collective mentality' of rioting mobs during eighteenth and nineteenth-century European disturbances can be applied to the upheavals of the 1930s in the British West Indies. It is not reasonable to neglect the social history of the black working classes simply because they did not pass on many written records of their thoughts, deeds and actions. After all, the majority lived in a racist society which encouraged illiteracy and made survival a bitter struggle. It is the duty of the scholar to search for the 'invisible mind' of the labouring classes by critical analysis of all existing records, diligent tapping of oral sources, and logical deductions of the thoughts of the lower classes drawn from an observation of their actions and behaviour. It is a unique way of analysing political behaviour contests and social interaction.

In the case of Barbados, this approach has not been explored on a wide scale in the twentieth century. There have been a number of general histories. F.A. Hoyos's *The History of Barbados: From Amerindians to Independence* is a work which has taken the traditional approach of viewing socio-political change in Barbados as influenced largely from 'above.' For example, the central argument of Hoyos is that the conservative merchant-planter elite was jolted into considering socio-political change largely because of benevolent elements of their own class and enlightened members of the black middle class. He sees no role for the black labouring classes.

Hilary Beckles' *History of Barbados: From Amerindian Settlement to Nation State* is another attempt to cover 300 years of history, to satisfy a demand for such literature in secondary schools and colleges in Barbados. The book draws on a wide variety of sources, and, except for a cursory treatment of the politics of the 1950s, is well written, and presented. Beckles argued that social and political change was influenced by the activities of the middle class and working-class Blacks in the post-emancipation period.

Some specific studies, many in the form of unpublished theses, have been produced. Sometimes they focused on the nineteenth and twentieth-century Barbadian history. Ronald Glenfield Parris, for example, in his work *Race, Inequality and Underdevelopment in Barbados, 1627–1973*, suffers from an attempt to cover 300 years of history in a single study. Even though it draws on a wide variety of historical data, it does not deal adequately with any specific period of Barbadian history. The study, to a large extent, is narrative, and lacking in analysis.

Wilburn Will's *Political Development in the Mini-State Caribbean: A Focus on Barbados*, even though it shows evidence of diligent research, does not bring any refreshing approach or perspective to the subject matter. He traces the legacy of Afro-Barbadian participation in the political process, to Samuel Jackman Prescod's attempts at liberal democratic politics of the mid-nineteenth-century. The local attitudes to race and class are seen as products of slavery and British colonialism. More specifically, the period 1914–37, which is of primary interest in this book, is perceived as a 'pre-party era' when Afro-Barbadians' participation in the political struggles of the early twentieth century shook the citadels of plantocratic power.

Charles Henry Kunsman's *Origin and Development of Political Parties in the West Indies* is a monumental study, of which the development of political parties in Barbados is only a small part. In much the same fashion as many other scholars who attempted such a task, the work is lacking in critical analysis and very narrative in outlook. Kunsman, however, produced an abundance of facts and figures on the growth of West Indian political organizations. In the case of Barbados, his major weakness resides in his narrow perception of Barbadian politics as a mere formation of political parties for the contest of political office at annual elections. His assessment of the Democratic League as the first modern political movement in Barbados is based on such a concept of politics. His failure to assess the activities of the WMA and the UNIA ignores the most dynamic forces in modern Barbadian political history.

I propose to adopt a wide concept of politics, which will embrace the motives for working-class actions and behaviour. The formation of political parties and groups, the contest for political office and the issues debated constitute one aspect of the foundation on which local politics was built. In short, politics in early twentieth-century Barbados will be seen largely as a bitter political struggle between the merchant-planter elite and the Afro-Barbadian population for the control of economic resources. Contest for political office at annual elections was only a minor part of the political struggle.

Perhaps the work which has stimulated most interest, while compiling this brief review, is Bonham Richardson's *Panama Money in Barbados: 1900–1920*. The author, among other things, draws a direct link between the social and economic forces which were unleashed during the 1920s as a result of the influx of Panama money and the rising expectations it generated among the black population. Richardson insists that the 'riots' of July 1937 were in part 'an expression of the incompatibility between black Barbadians' rising expectations – hopes financed originally with Panama money – and the anachronistic system of white planter control.'[22] Richardson's thesis is open to debate, for it is very difficult to measure the 'expectations' of a given population, and I am not convinced that Richardson, despite his exciting approach, has provided the answer.

I have highlighted some of the deficiencies in a select group of works on the historiography of the island. In this book, I place much emphasis on the class and race relationships of Barbados. I proceed from the basic premise that race and class discrimination had formed the basis of West Indian society for centuries. Furthermore, since racism had been an endemic feature of our societies, it was most unlikely that it died a natural death when legal abolition came in 1834. Instead, elements of the old system of racism, including the old racial stereotypes of the lazy, barbaric negro persisted, and were fortified, by a vicious system of institutionalized racism.

Chapter one explores the theoretical dimensions of race, class, politics and empowerment. and their application to the race relations climate of Barbados. In addition, an analysis of Barbados's political system and the evolution of its political culture is examined. Chapter two examines the effects of the First World War on Barbadian society and economy; while chapter three looks at the racist ideology and the racial practices of the merchant-planter elite during the early twentieth century. The major part of the chapter will focus on how the racist ideology was used to justify the ruling elite's domination of the economy, the society and the major institutions of the island, including the legislature. Moreover, some attention will be focused on how the racial stereotypes of the white oligarchy were persistently invoked as a means, not only of justifying the subjugation of Blacks, but deliberately to keep them in a filthy environment characteristic of abject poverty.

Chapter four will analyse the role of the black, working-class organizations, mainly the Universal Negro Improvement Association (UNIA) and the Workingmen's Association (WMA), in raising the political consciousness of the Afro-Barbadian population. It culminates with the arrival of Clement Payne on the political scene in March 1937. Some attention is also focused on how the ruling oligarchy, through the surveillance and intimidation of the leadership of these organizations, suppressed them.

Chapter five examines the reaction of Barbadians to the Italo-Ethiopian war of 1935. The analysis is rounded out in chapter six with an assessment of the rebellion of July 1937. The main emphasis is on the role which a heightened racial and political consciousness played in precipitating the upheavals. In addition, the nature of the July 1937 rebellion is analysed, rather than the events simply regurgitated.

# 1

# RACE, CLASS, POLITICS AND EMPOWERMENT: THEORETICAL DIMENSIONS AND METHODOLOGY

The main purpose of this book is to examine the socio-ideological nature of Barbadian society during the period 1914–37, with special reference to the race, class and political relations.[1] This period constitutes the formative years in modern Barbadian political history: a critical phase of political activity that fundamentally shaped the island's political culture in the era before the attainment of constitutional independence. However, the majority of writings on this crucial area of Barbadian history have dealt inadequately with the role race and class relations played in the evolution of the island's unique political culture.

It is important, however, before proceeding further, to define some terms which will be used regularly in this book. The concept of 'race,' for example, has been a highly controversial, and, indeed, confusing term.[2] Despite more than a century of scholarship devoted to the clarification of the concept, it still presents confusion in attempts to define and understand it. A historical review of the controversy surrounding the concept will not be attempted here, since it will serve no useful purpose. However, some clarification of the special way in which 'race' and related terms – racism, racial prejudice, racial discrimination and institutional racism – are employed in the book is necessary.

Race, as a biological phenomenon, can be defined as 'a major group of interrelated people possessing a distinctive combination of physical traits which are the result of inheritance.'[3] This definition emphasizes the different phenotypical features, such as skin colour, eye colour, hair type, body hair and facial structures found among various groups of the human species. It is these phenotypical differences which have been used to point to corresponding differences of genotype in human beings, and to classify them into races.[4]

Unfortunately, these outward expressions, or phenotypes, have been employed by many scholars, including the scientists of the nineteenth-century eugenics movement, to construct their philosophy. Racism asserts that there is a direct link between inherited physical traits and other human characteristics such as personality, intelligence and intellect.[5] Moreover, it has been argued that some races, especially those of the Caucasian stock, possess distinctive attributes which make them inherently superior to all other non-white races.[6] Attempts have been made in some societies to use these attributes as a legitimate basis for making distinctions 'between groups socially defined as races.'[7]

Racial prejudice and racial discrimination are related adjuncts of racism. Racial prejudice can be conceptualized as hostile attitudes directed toward one group by another. The hostility is usually based on generalizations which are held by the dominant group and are readily accepted, and ultimately defended, despite the discrepancies which an objective analysis may expose in such behaviour.[8] Racial discrimination, on the other hand, is a type of social relationship in which one racial group subordinates another by ascribing particular differential treatment to members of that social category.[9] Racism entails more than beliefs; it incorporates actions, whereby individuals or institutions conspire to keep a particular group or groups in subordination. In short, racial prejudice and racial discrimination can be perceived as racism in action.

## FIGURE 1.1
## Interconnecting Links of Racism

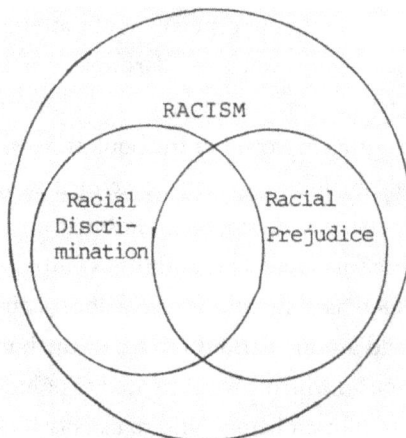

Racism has been classified into numerous varieties,[10] all of which will not be discussed here. However, individual and institutional racism, and overt and covert racism, will be examined, as they bear some relevance to an understanding of the race relations scene in Barbados.

Individual racism refers to the expression of racist attitudes and practices in the behaviour of individuals of a community in face-to-face situations.[11] Indeed, the impact of this type of racist behaviour in any society depends upon the wealth, social status and prestige of the individuals practising it. The very difficult task confronting the social historian who attempts to analyse such behaviour in colonial societies with a tradition of slavery is to determine to what extent such individuals reflected a dominant racial ideology, or exhibited isolated cases of racial prejudice and/or even class snobbery.

Institutional racism relates to the manner in which the various institutions of a society are subtly manipulated by one group in order to control, oppress or discriminate against another group or social category.[12] The policies of these institutions may work to maintain racial inequality without acknowledging the fact. For example, in Barbados the colonial legislature was one such institution, one that perpetuated the dominance of a white minority, elected on a restricted franchise which was deliberately set so high as to exclude the majority of the poor, black population. According to the Representation of the People's Act, 1901, the franchise qualification during the pre-1937 era was set at £50 per annum or the equivalent value in property. The majority of black people of working-class origin who made up the population, and who worked for a few shillings a week, remained disenfranchised. The number of registered voters, for example, stood at less than 3,000 at any time.[13] These voters were largely made up of the conservative, propertied classes and professionals, who never hesitated to invoke the tenets of virtual representation whenever the unrepresentative nature of the legislature was challenged. In fact, the unrepresentative nature of the Assembly was reflected not only in its race and class structure, but also in its occupational structure. During the sessions between 1916 and 1940, 504 seats were filled in the House of Assembly, the majority by white Barbadians. Of these, 33 per cent were legal men, 14 per cent physicians and three per cent civil servants. There was one druggist and one land surveyor; while the occupations of five assemblymen could not be determined.[14] The House of Assembly served, no doubt, as an institution of white control and domination that hardly bothered to represent the interest of the Afro-Barbadian population.

The Established Church, like the Legislature, also served as an institution of white domination. Few Blacks were ever appointed as rectors or parish priests, even though Codrington College produced qualified black priests from its inception. In fact, the established practice of the local Anglican Church was to export ordained black priests to other parts of the Caribbean or West Africa. This practice originated from the export of black Barbadian Clergymen during the mid-nineteenth-century Pongas Mission to West Africa.[15] After three centuries of British rule, it was only in the 1970s that Barbados received its first black Dean of St Michael's Cathedral and black Bishop. It is also worthy of mention that the discriminatory practice of seating Blacks at the rear of Anglican chapels continued into the twentieth century.

The local educational system was also manipulated to perpetuate white supremacy. Most Euro-Barbadians regarded formal instruction, especially secondary and tertiary education, as the exclusive privilege of that group and of a few fortunate Blacks. In 1930, when some members of the House of Assembly reviewed the educational system they agreed unanimously that it needed 'improvement,' but only as far as enabling every child under the age of 12 at least to learn to read and write.[16] The Assembly asserted, further, that if the aim of the local educational system was to produce 'good scholars,' they were already spending too much money.[17] Such thinking occurred at a time when illiteracy was rampant among the black adult population and where more than 14,000 children worked as child labour gangs on the sugar estates.[18] No role was designated, and no opportunity provided, for the use of education as a means of social mobility, at least for the majority of the Afro-Barbadian population.

## Overt/Covert Racism and the Myth of Multi-racial Harmony

The concept of overt and covert racism, popularized by Charles Hamilton and Stokely Carmichael, is used extensively in this book.[19] Overt racism is a race relations situation where open racial conflict and tension exists in the society between the various ethnic groups.[20] Violence, brutality and polarization of racial groups are noticeable features of such societies. South Africa, under its old system of apartheid, was a typical example of a society which displayed all the features of overt racism. Covert racism, by contrast, is a more subtle, and hence less identifiable, form of racism.[21] Racial violence may not necessarily be a common occurrence in such societies, but the actions or inactions of the dominant group usually work in subtle ways to keep others in a deprived position. Early twentieth-century Barbados displayed many features of covert racism.

The subtle disguises of covert racism, for example, existed in Barbados for a long time under the guise of multi-racial harmony, sometimes referred to as 'non-racialism.'[22] According to this notion, among the various ethnic groups of some societies there is an inclination to deny that racial animosity exists, or at least, that race plays an integral part in human relations.[23] In fact, in some societies which boast of multi-racial harmony, even to talk publicly about 'race' is considered to be a potentially disruptive practice which should be avoided. In 1934, George Bernard, made such an observation of Barbadian attitudes to race. He wrote,

> Over the subject of colour prejudice the local tendency is to adopt the
> plan of the ostrich which hides its head in the sand at the approach
> of danger. The existence of such a sentiment is never admitted, and
> its discussion is tabooed by white and black alike.[24]

The origin of the myth of multi-racial harmony can be traced to the early nineteenth century. It was consistently invoked whenever the ability of the merchant-planter elite to govern the affairs of the colony was threatened, or questioned, by the Colonial Office. The white elite would assert their control over local affairs by citing harmony between Whites and Blacks as a true testimony of the accuracy of their confidence. When the 1816 slave revolt broke out in Barbados, the blame was placed on 'misguided men,' misleading reports about immediate freedom, loose statements by William Wilberforce, and mistaken ideas held by the enslaved population of the true purpose of the Slave Registry Bill.[25] The desire of the enslaved blacks to be free, and their dissatisfaction with the slave system, were deliberately ignored as possible sources of discontent. By adopting such a posture, the plantocracy exonerated themselves. In fact, the vast majority of planters who testified before a Select Committee appointed to investigate the slave rebellion spoke glowingly of the excellent treatment meted out to the enslaved population on their estates.[26] Joseph Gittens, the manager of Padmore's estate, St Philip, testified that his 'slaves were in most respects as comfortably situated, and in general as healthy, as most in the island.' Joseph Connell, the manager of Thicket plantation, St Philip, spoke of his enslaved population as being 'perfectly contented and happy.'[27] Indeed, these sentiments were shared by the rectors of the parishes of Christ Church, St James, St Thomas and St Joseph. The findings of the Select Committee were expressed in a similar tone:

> Knowing that the Inhabitants of this colony are influenced by every feeling of humanity as well as self-interest, to use all efforts in their power to promote the happiness and prosperity of their Slave Population, your Committee have no hesitation in asserting, for themselves and their fellow Colonists, that they are at all times ready to adopt such methods for the attainment of these desirable objects, as may be consistent with the safety of their persons and properties.[28]

This curious belief in multi-racial harmony, it must be stressed, continued into the post-emancipation period. For example, in 1875 the planters spoke warmly of a 'peace and contentment which have as a rule characterized all classes of the colony.'[29] Yet the 1876 Confederation disturbances broke out in denial of this boast. In fact, the social upheavals which dotted nineteenth-century Barbados – 1863, 1872, 1876 and 1895 – poured scorn on the plantocracy's echoes of multi-racial harmony.

At the turn of the twentieth century, the concept of multi-racial harmony still persisted among the merchant-planter elite. Sir Harold Austin, in his welcoming address to the Moyne Commission at Queen's Park in 1939, spoke of 'the very best feelings of sympathy [which] exist between the Government and the people of this community.'[30] The irony in his speech was his failure to admit that the 'government' he so glibly referred to was elected on a very limited franchise, and that it used its influence to perpetuate the interest of the white minority at the expense of the black majority population. The rebellion of July 1937 was so fresh in the populace's mind that it probably took a lot of confidence and optimism on the part of Sir Harold, in 1939, to believe the 'very best feelings of sympathy' existed in Barbados. The evidence from the enquiry of the Deane Commission in the latter half of 1937, and the subsequent Report, revealed among other things a deep rift between the two major racial groups.[31] Sir Harold was no doubt aware of those findings. In a few days, evidence collected by the Moyne Commission further disproved the white oligarchy's notions of multi-racial harmony in Barbados.

The idea of multi-racial harmony, in short, was a strategy cultivated by the local merchant-planter elite to appease the Colonial Office whenever their fitness to control the affairs of the State was in question. They used it consistently to justify their dominance of the legislature and to remain politically and economically entrenched in the island. Over a long period of time, the idea of multi-racial harmony in Barbados apparently came to be largely endorsed by the black population itself. Why the victims of white racism accept the oppressors' explanation of their plight is a fascinating discourse.

According to Antonio Gramsci, the supremacy of a social class is manifested by its domination of society as well as by its 'intellectual and moral leadership.'[32] The dominant class achieves social control by influencing the behaviour of the dominated through a system of awards and punishments. Control is effected in an internal way by shaping the personal convictions and values of the dominated into accepting the prevailing norms. In short, the oppressed classes seem to internalize the idea of their domination, based on a fear of the coercive arm of the state and the intellectual leadership of the ruling class. Hegemony, Gramsci insists, can be reinforced by the ruling class's control of the institutions of society and by its economic power.[33] These Gramscian features of hegemony existed in Barbados of the nineteenth and early twentieth centuries, and perhaps played a part in what appeared to be docile behaviour by the black population in the midst of oppression.

The covert nature of Barbados's race relations, therefore, provides a useful place for the application of the conspiracy theory of history, sometimes called the reality principle, as a technique of analysis. This theory maintains that the reality of history lies underneath what is seen publicly and that true history is never hinted at publicly. Therefore, the historian must dig below the surface to uncover the past. The implication is that those in positions of power are constantly concealing their actions in order to keep and expand their power. Even though it is necessary for all historians to probe and dig below the surface to expose what happened in the past, it is erroneous to assume that every public figure is constantly hiding his thoughts and intentions in order to mislead his listeners. Yet it is true that most statements contain a mixture of true feelings and hidden intentions.[34] The colonial authorities in Barbados, ever convinced that the Afro-Barbadian was an impulsive, unpredictable being, deliberately concealed their true feelings and intentions in making certain public utterances in order to avoid alarming him, or ultimately fomenting 'social unrest.' Hence, the need to adopt this historical methodology in order to really unravel the nature of the local class struggle.

## The Influence of Victorian Racial Attitudes

Victorian attitudes to race, superimposed on local prejudices were also very influential in shaping twentieth-century Barbados. These ideas were sharpened by a growing number of anthropological studies with a revived scientific interest in race.[35] During the nineteenth-century, the 'scientific' assertion of black inferiority vis-à-vis other races was formulated and given some intellectual groundings. The heated debates generated in England as a result of the Indian Mutiny (1857) and the Morant Bay Rebellion (1865) acted as further fuel to strengthen the misguided belief that non-whites, and more so people of African descent, were barbaric, lazy, childlike and lacking in culture and intellect.[36] Such racial stereotypes were incorporated into an imperialist-minded Victorian society; even into the educational system.

One way Victorian racial stereotypes were nurtured in the Barbadian value system was through the education received by many local Whites in England's institutions, or at the local 'first grade schools' (grammar schools) which were dominated by white expatriate Principals for a long time. These pupils were socialized in a learning environment of negative racist diatribe which battered the true worth of black West Indians. For example, a widely used textbook of the early twentieth century portrayed the black West Indian as

> ...lazy, vicious and incapable of serious improvement or of work except under compulsion. In such a climate a few bananas will sustain the life of the negro quite sufficiently; why should he work to get more than this. He is quite useless and spends any extra wages which he may earn upon finery. [37]

Such negative descriptions of black West Indians were strikingly similar to the racist sentiments of some nineteenth-century writers. Thomas Carlyle, in his imprudent view of the West Indian islands as tropical paradises, depicted its black inhabitants as perpetual idlers 'with their beautiful muzzles up to the ears in pumpkins, imbibing sweet pulps and juices,' while the sugar crop rotted around them from a lack of labour.[38] Anthony Trollope described the Afro-West Indian's idea of freedom as the desire to 'lie in the sun and eat breadfruit and yams.'[39] James Froude suggested that West Indians 'have no aspirations to make them restless,' and no 'guilt upon their consciences,' because life for them was 'perfect liberty.'[40]

Unfortunately, the educational system perpetuated these racial myths about Afro-West Indians for a long time. Hence, it produced arrogant people who translated their learned value system into action largely in the way they treated the black population. For white Barbadians, this behaviour was institutionalized in the form of one of the most pervasive systems of racial prejudice and discrimination in the British West Indies.

## Barbados and Eugenic Ideas

Amidst the nineteenth-century interest in race, the scientific racism of the eugenic movement emerged in Europe and the United States and spread throughout the world. The modern eugenic movement began with the work of Francis Galton who, in his book *Hereditary Genius*, argued that it is possible to produce gifted people by judicious marriages over several consecutive generations. Galton founded the English Eugenics Society in 1907 and endowed a research fellowship in Eugenics at University College, London. He also suggested that the high birth rate among the poor was a threat to human civilization, and so, it was the duty of the 'higher' races to oppress the 'lower' ones.[41]

Galton's view of science was embraced by many statesmen who believed in racial and class superiority as justification for the suppression of minorities. Through the misuse of scientific data, especially the infant science of molecular genetics, many prominent scientists, scholars and statesmen tried to justify claims to white superiority over all other non-white races.[42] Eugenic ideas found their way into the decision-making process of various institutions worldwide, including those in the West Indies. Some members of the merchant-planter elite in early twentieth-century Barbados, as contemporaries, seemed to be influenced by the eugenic ideology.

The *Agricultural Reporter*, the leading organ of the local ruling class, on September 22, 1919, demonstrated this influence when it glowingly reported the death of distinguished Cambridge scholar, Gordon Kerr Montagu Butler, who was killed in action during the First World War. He was the son of Dr Andrew Butler and Agnata Butler, both of whom had been distinguished academics at the same institution. His brothers, the *Agricultural Reporter* asserted, had become 'Senior Classics' at Cambridge, thereby establishing a record of high intellectual achievement. The *Reporter* concluded that on the birth of Gordon Butler, 'an interesting problem in Eugenics suggested itself.'[43] The *Agricultural Reporter*'s assessment, in essence, echoed Galton's 'hereditary genius' theme, that human intelligence is largely inherited with the environment playing a minimal role in its expression. In the local press, the constant references to the black population as the 'lower orders' and to their 'lack of proper breeding' confirmed the influence of these eugenic ideas among the local white population.

The increasing evidence of 'illegitimate' births in Barbados' vital statistics of the 1920s led the *Barbados Standard* to echo a familiar view of the ruling oligarchy, that such statistics constituted 'social inferiority' among the black population. Illegitimate births were attributed to widespread sexual immorality among the black sector of the population.[44] Many white Barbadians were convinced that such was an inherent personality trait of people of African descent.[52]

This racist ideology was retained as a tool which the merchant-planter elite used to good effect. They argued, for example, that since poor black Barbadians by nature possessed little innate intelligence, there was no justification for spending large sums of money on their physical upkeep, or improvement of their environment.[45] Afro-Barbadians, therefore, were seen as a doomed race whose poverty was of their own making and who were expected to solve their depravity without any assistance from the State. This eugenic idea adopted in Barbados by some prominent members of the legislature, appears remarkably similar to an earlier philosophy of Thomas Malthus, whose works were influential among leading Eugenicists. Malthus considered measures designed to improve the lot of the poor as immoral and 'against the laws of God and Nature.'[46] In his famous 'Essay on the Principle of Population,' he wrote,

> Instead of recommending cleanliness to the poor, we should encourage contrary habits. In our towns we should make the streets narrower, crowd more people into the houses, and court the return of the plague. In the country, we should build our villages near stagnant pools, and particularly encourage settlements in all marshy and unwholesome situations. But above all, we should reprobate specific remedies for ravaging diseases.[47]

Many Barbadian whites shared similar views, and proceeded to set them in motion by a subtle policy of economic neglect, whereby the black Barbadians were allowed to wallow in their own poverty and an unhealthy environment.

In fact, the persistent calls by black activists during the 1920s and 1930s for improvement in social legislation to reduce poverty were met by opposition guided by such convictions.[48] Stanley Clifford Thorne, prominent planter and assemblyman, remarked on one occasion that money spent on the police was better utilized than that spent on education. J.H. Hawkins, an influential medical doctor, insisted that a high infant mortality rate was necessary to check population growth in Barbados.[49] After the Public Health debate of 1924–25, Governor Robertson was shocked to learn that some members of the white community considered welfare and medical assistance to the black population as 'unnecessary.'[50] In short, they did not see it as improper for Afro-Barbadians, especially infants, to die of disease and malnutrition.

The degradation of the Afro-Barbadian population by the white community was persistent and multi-faceted, as every vestige of the African image, even the somatic norm image, was under constant attack. In the columns of the *Agricultural Reporter* and the *Barbados Standard*, but more so the latter, this practice was very evident. Numerous cartoons, in particular, portrayed the physical features of blacks in the most negative and repugnant way. Blacks were always drawn with large, rolling, moonlike eyes and woolly, unkempt hair. The nose was broad and flat with gaping nostrils and the lips were large, protruding, saucer-like structures which took up a large portion of the face. The garb was in a tattered state and in the presence of whites, the blacks carried a stooped, hang-dog posture, subtly implying an innate servility. In addition, the contributions of Afro-Barbadians to any dialogue consisted of incoherent statements which suggested a low level of intellectual ability.[51]

In a cartoon set during the First World War, when a debate raged between merchant and planters over the raising of additional revenue, a white man branded 'MERCHANT' is prostrated by a planter's boot labeled 'STAMP DUTY.' Looking on, quite frightened and agitated, is a black man. The conversation goes like this:

MERCHANT: Here, I say, steady, you're crushing the life out of me!

PLANTER: Never mind old fellar! It's time you should have a share now, We've been seeing old Charnick for some years. Grin and bear it old chap.

SAMBO: (Black man) Hip! Hip! Hoorah! I get off.[52]

In yet another cartoon, a planter is looking up into a black man's breadfruit tree while contemplating the implementation of new Income Tax measures:

PLANTER: No my good man, I should never be so foolish as to order the destruction of a fine tree like this. For I foresee in these trees an excellent opportunity for raising the wind for my forthcoming Income Tax.

QUASHIE: How you meaning. [53]

The graphic illustrations in these cartoons, not only portrayed black Barbadians as graceless and ugly, but lacking the intellectual capacity to grasp contemporary social and political issues which affected them. The references in the cartoons to Afro-Barbadians in the twentieth century as 'Sambo' and 'Quashie' in a way recaptured the 'quashee personality' of racist slave society. It stereotyped black enslaved people as simple, thriftless beings, incapable of independent thought and action.[54]

## White Conservative Elements

Some ultra-conservative members of the white community were adamant that the Afro-Barbadian population should be relegated to the quagmire of society. One writer, in a letter to a local newspaper, was quite blunt:

Here we know full well that the business of the poor is to bear the burdens of the upkeep of the State. That's what they are here for. The poor are the people who are underneath, and the thing that's underneath always bears the weight.[55]

On another occasion, scant regard for the plight of the masses was expressed:

We say, 'keep the masses in their place.' Give them plenty of work and not too much money or leisure and no learning at all. Down with all theories of equal rights.[56]

When the campaigns of the *Barbados Herald* newspaper and the Democratic League called for the abolition of child labour gangs on the estates, and the implementation of compulsory education and school meals for the Afro-Barbadian population, the white population was alarmed. An incensed element of the conservative white community wrote,

To-day an unspeakable radical element of the island is out to lay hands on the most sacred preserves of the Conservative Class. Someone even went so far as to say no children should be allowed to work in the plantation labour gangs. Now really I confess that such an idea reaches the very limit of absurdity. I am strongly of the opinion the people who hold this doctrine do not see what such an action on the part of government would lead to. If you take the children out of the labour gangs you will have to send them to school, and could there be a greater menace to the security of the stern Conservatives, to the welfare of the island, than to have all the children of the masses obtain book learning....A few people stupid enough to say 'Educate the masses' would say anything.[57]

The foregoing analysis has shown how the racial stereotypes of the merchant-planter elite were built up over many generations and became shrouded deep within the mental psyche, perhaps the unconscious mind, of that class. Racism had been an important appendage of slavery, manifested mainly in the form of white slave-owner and black slave. This pattern of racial attitudes and class relations continued unchanged, as master and servant, until the 1930s. In short, the racist ideology of the slavery era survived into the post-colonial society, perhaps because of the persistence of the economic formation in the form of the plantation economy. Emancipation in Barbados was little more than a legal gesture of freedom, simply because the conditions which were designed to maintain black inferiority remained tenaciously intact after 1838 and well into the twentieth century. This book unravels how this was maintained, and then finally challenged, during the early twentieth century.

This task, however, is a very difficult one, because it analyses attitudes and beliefs which were not often expressed openly. Even greater difficulty exists in any attempt to directly link certain behaviours displayed by a dominant white group to the beliefs they were supposed to hold. In Barbados, since little was written down about race relations, and moreover, as prejudice and discrimination manifested itself in a covert form, peculiar difficulties confront the social scientist and the historian where true feelings on many social, political and economic issues were never openly disclosed. Hence, we emphasize the need to resort to the reality principle of history. It must be stressed, however, that here the major concern is to examine *how* the white ruling elite mobilized race and class ideologies in their effort to dominate the society, rather than why they did it. The latter has been adequately dealt with by other scholars.[58]

## Class Relations in Barbados

The notion of social class has been the subject of much debate. In this study the Marxist concept of class consciousness has been adopted as one of the tools of analysis to understand early twentieth-century Barbadian society. For Marx, a class is a socio-economic group determined by a similar relationship of its members to the means of production in the society.[59] The shared interests of the members of one class place them in antagonistic opposition to members of another class. Control of the means of production yields political control directly and, in most instances, indirectly. In addition, a class only becomes an important social agency when it assumes a direct political character; that is, a class 'in itself' becomes a class 'for itself.'[60] This concept conformed well to the Barbadian situation where a white planter class, with a monopoly of the land, and a merchant class, with a firm control of the commercial sector of the economy, exploited a majority black working-class population, who depended exclusively on selling their labour for wages in order to survive. In essence, a constant struggle for economic resources existed between the planter-merchant elite and the Afro-Barbadian population, with the former, among other things, adopting a racist ideology to justify the exploitation of the latter.

But it is the use of 'race' as a concept which poses peculiar difficulties for students of Caribbean history who adopt a rigid Marxist class analysis to critique societies with an extensive experience of black enslavement. Marx never dealt adequately with race in his works. He merely treated it as one other manifestation of fundamental class struggle.[61] In the Caribbean basin where enslavement was a dominant mode of production for centuries, and where 'racism' was an important adjunct of the historical process, it is virtually impossible, and overtly simplistic, to treat racism as a mere manifestation of class struggle.

The intense slavery experience of the British West Indian society, therefore, suggests that it may be useful to consider aspects of Weber's concept of class as a tool of analysis. Weber identifies what he terms 'ownership classes' and 'acquisition classes'[62] based on the kind of services that can be offered on the market. Weber also makes a distinction between classes and what he calls 'status groups.' Class, according to him, expresses relationships involved in production whereas status groups express relationships involved in consumption.[63]

Weber's concepts of class and status groups were constructed in response to the observation of complex industrial societies. Hence, they would appear to have limited application to the agrarian societies of early twentieth-century British West Indies. Nevertheless, his 'status groups' can be employed to explain the presence of some groups in Barbados known for their consumption and lifestyle, and the privileges conferred on them as a result of the acquisition of education. When Fitzherbert King, social commentator and political activist, petitioned the Secretary of State in 1918 for 'increased educational advantages' for the 'middle class,' he never had in mind any group who controlled a substantial amount of economic power. He, in fact, identified a small cadre of civil servants, teachers, printers, clerks and journalists as his middle class, a group who acquired such status largely as a result of their education, rather than their wealth.[64] Police spies who infiltrated the Workingmen's Association and the Universal Negro Improvement Association in the pre-1937 era referred to any teachers, printers or even shopkeepers present, as members of the 'middle class.'[65] Status, in essence, played a very important part in class distinctions in Barbadian society at the particular time, and so cannot be overlooked.

A peculiar class distinction was also highlighted very often in the local print media, where editors and columnists divided Barbadian society into two groups. The 'classes' or 'well to do' referred to the small white elite of merchants, planters and white middle-class professionals, and, the 'masses' referred to the majority of the poor, black working-class people.[66] Sometimes the latter group was alluded to as the 'poorer classes.'[67]

In this book, therefore, the following terms are used: 'Planter-merchant oligarchy,' 'ruling oligarchy,' 'white elite' and, more loosely, 'Euro-Barbadians' refer to the small privileged group of white planters, merchants and senior colonial officials who occupied the upper stratum of society. This group dominated the House of Assembly and the Legislative Council, and was also the embodiment of powerful interest groups such as the Chamber of Commerce, the Barbados Agricultural Society, the Barbados Sugar Producers Association, the Sugar Industry Agricultural Bank and the Barbados Mutual Assurance Society. In addition, there was a larger white middle class of professionals who always identified with the merchant-planter group and at all times expressed the desire to join them through marriage or professional contact. Together these two groups comprised about 10,000 people or seven to ten per cent of the Barbadian population.[68]

A small group of descendants of the white indentured servants, the 'poor whites,' existed on the fringes of Barbadian society in total isolation, mainly in the rural districts of St John and St Philip. They were so proud of their racial purity that they resisted assimilation into the mainstream of Barbadian society, especially with the black population. Indeed, the isolation was so strong that, by the 1930s, the long history of inbreeding, and the subsequent build up of recessive genes in the population, had led to mental and physical frailty in the poor white population.[69]

The terms 'black middle class,' 'black professional class' or, more loosely, the 'coloured class,' refer to the small group of black doctors, lawyers, journalists and small businessmen who through their education and/or professions, formed the elite of the black population. J. A. Tudor, J. A. Martineau, Grantley Adams, Charles Duncan O'Neal, Clennel Wickham, Gordon Cummins, J. E. T. Brancker, C. A. Brathwaite, W. H. Reece, and D. Lee Sargeant, were the most outstanding personalities among this group. As an educated group, who were largely trained in England, and had imbibed the English value system and political traditions, they were looked upon with favour by the Colonial Office as trusted agents and 'sober, responsible' leaders during the 1930s.[70] They spoke on behalf of the labouring classes before the Deane and Moyne Commissions, and dominated the embryonic trade unions and political parties of the 1940s and 1950s. The role of the black middle class is therefore critical to an understanding of the political and constitutional transformation of Barbados after 1937.

The terms 'labouring classes,' the 'black labouring classes,' the 'working classes,' 'Afro-Barbadians,' and 'Blacks' refer to the majority of the population, mainly the 160,000 black-skinned people of African descent. These were employed as wage labourers on the sugar estates, on the wharf as coal heavers, lightermen and stevedores, and as skilled tradesmen and domestics in the sugar factories and homes of the white elite.

In order to fully grasp the class conflict of early twentieth-century Barbados, it is necessary to understand the nature of the relationship which existed between employer and employee. The state of the industrial scene is one important yardstick for measuring the intensity of the local class struggle.

## Industrial Relations in Early Twentieth-Century Barbados

Agriculture, and in particular sugar, was the mainstay of the Barbadian economy during the early twentieth century employing about 34,757 in all aspects of its production. In 1937, of the 65,835 acres of arable land cultivated, 51,886 acres were farmed by large sugar estates, and the remainder by some 18,000 small farmers, 13,899 of whom cultivated less than one acre of land.[71] The sugar plantation, in essence, dominated the Barbadian landscape and, in a largely non-industrial, underdeveloped economy, provided the only means of livelihood for many Afro-Barbadians. In short, Barbados was the quintessential plantation society.

The radius of a mile in any direction outside the immediate vicinity of Bridgetown – Fontabelle, Kensington, Flint Hall, My Lord's Hill, Pine Hill, the Bay Land, Waterford, Bank Hall, Bush Hall was all cultivated in sugar cane and ground provisions, in the period before 1937. The area around Speighstown moving towards Bridgetown were covered with fields of sugar cane. So too were the arable lands near Oistins – Cane Vale, Scarborough, Maxwell, Gibbons Boggs, Silver Hill, Gall Hill, Worthings. The sugar plantation encroached on most rural and urban communities, including Bridgetown. The plantation, in essence, dominated the physical landscape, during the early twentieth century.

The plantation, by extension, also dominated the economic and social system as well. Sugar and its by-products made up 97 per cent of Barbados's exports, and contributed to all its foreign exchange. Tourism, manufacturing and the offshore financial sector were unheard of during this era. The planters' control of the plantation economy was completed by their control of politics through their domination of the local legislature. Barbados, in short, was a typical plantation society, marked by the production of a cash crop (sugar cane), political elitism which bred a shameful brand of political patronage, rigid race and class prejudices and, as George Beckford has argued, 'persistent poverty.'[72]

Before 1937, wages of the labourers on the estates were low. The average wages for men were ls 6d to 2s per day; for women, 10d to ls 3d per day, and for children, 6d to 8d per day.[73] The highest wages were obtained during the crop season when labourers who were paid by the hole could seize the opportunity to accumulate some cash by a concerted effort of steady work. Out of season, referred to in local parlance as 'hard times,' was a difficult period for sugar workers, as they were paid 10d per 100 cane holes dug.[74] Sugar workers generally lived in houses which they rented, but on lands belonging to estates, for which a weekly fee was deducted for rent. This arrangement, the 'located labour system,' gave the plantocracy a monopoly over the labour force and restricted the mobility and the bargaining power of the agricultural labourers.[75]

Apart from employment on the sugar estates, the sugar factories, a small construction sector, a small commercial sector, and private homes, offered some alternatives to plantation life. The wages, even though higher than on the estates, were still low, and the archaic labour laws and the lack of trade unions made these forms of employment just as hazardous as any other kind. Skilled artisans such as carpenters, masons and mechanics received between 1s 9d and 4s 2d per day. Domestic servants, some of whom worked 12 hours a day, seven days a week, were paid from 6s to 8s per week.[76]

The employees of the two foundries in Bridgetown, the Central Foundry and the Barbados Foundry, also worked under the most trying conditions. Low wages, long working hours, long-standing grievances over the calculation of overtime, and a callous attitude of management to the workers, characterized employment at the foundries.[77] These bad employer-employee relations exploded into industrial unrest on many occasions, but reached crisis proportions at the Central Foundry on July 7, 1937, when half the employees walked off the job. Previous to this industrial action, a highly conciliatory letter had been addressed to the Managing Director, requesting a two cent per hour flat rate and a review of working conditions. It was ignored. In another letter to the Deputy Manager, the demands were reduced. He, however, refused to even consider the proposals. Instead, he viewed the cessation of work later as a 'breach of shop regulations' and dismissed the workers.[78] The Deane Commission was harsh in its condemnation of the management's handling of the issue:

> We are constrained to comment on the lack of administrative foresight and sympathetic consideration displayed by the Manager....We are of the opinion that the artisans of the lower grades were deserving of consideration and that the question of overtime pay demanded attention. Had these grievances been investigated immediately, there would have been no occasion for a 'breach of shop regulations.'[79]

The bakers in Barbados were treated no better than the foundry workers in terms of conditions of service. The actual working hours of a baker varied from 11 to 18 hours per day, and in some circumstances, extended to 22 hours. The baking started between 5:00 p.m. and 7:00 p.m. and went on until between 8:00 a.m. and 10:00 a.m. the next day.[80] Some owners adopted the unfair and dangerous practice of locking the bakers in the factory for the entire night, while they returned home to sleep. The proprietor of the Swiss Bakery, when questioned about this practice by the Deane Commission, replied in an unsympathetic fashion, 'I wouldn't want the men to knock off at 4 a.m., because I would have to get out of bed to let them out. I have to leave my bed too early.'[81] In around April 1937, the bakers formed a union and arranged for a 'sit down strike,' but the plans were never put into action, apparently due to a lack of organizational skills and a fear of victimization.

On the waterfront, workers were also subjected to a precarious state of affairs. The lack of a deepwater harbour facility resulted in the arduous task of rowing lighter boats out into Carlisle Bay to load and unload cargo. This activity provided employment for some stevedores, longshoremen and lightermen. Longshoremen were engaged by, and worked under the direction of, a stevedore who was retained by a local steamship agent. The stevedore fixed the rates of pay for the longshoremen and the steamship agent fixed the rates of pay for the stevedores. The stevedores acted as independent contractors employing their labourers.[82] The Deane Commission explained the complicated process:

> The usual method of payment is for the stevedore to hand to his foreman the gross amount of the labourers' wages; the foreman hands this amount with a list showing the payments to be made to each man to the agent, who then makes deductions for money owing to him for loans, drinks, cigarettes etc. and for breakfast usually supplied by a cook shop, and pays the labourers the balance due to them.[83]

This type of paternalistic arrangement was deplored by the Deane Commission as a gross abuse of a system which lacked the necessary checks and balances to prevent the exploitation of workers. For example, on two steamships of 4,000 tons and 5,250 tons loaded in 1937, a Mr Nightengale's books showed a net profit of $420.00 and $831.00 respectively, after deducting three eighths of the profit for his foreman.[84] Another stevedore admitted that he kept no books, but paid his foreman a bonus. Such evidence led the Commission to conclude that the profits of the stevedores were 'abnormal and excessive.'[85] Indeed, the conditions under which the waterfront workers toiled was a source of discontent, especially after the First World War. The pressing need to improve working conditions led to the waterfront strikes of 1919, 1927 and 1937.

The above scenario reveals a grim picture of a potentially explosive industrial climate in early twentieth-century Barbados. A striking feature of the labour relations scene was the gross exploitation of the black labouring classes by a white employer class. As a group, the black labouring classes even though they functioned under the most trying conditions, had few avenues for redressing their grievances. Trade unions were illegal, political organization was scoffed at, and spokesmen for the working classes, such as existed in the UNIA and the WMA, were viewed with suspicion and subjected to police surveillance. This anti-black working-class feeling was backed up by a series of rigid legal codes, mainly in the form of the Master and Servant Act and the Better Security Act, 1920.

## The Located Labour System

The Master and Servant Act 1891, a modification of the original 1840 legislation, was based on an archaic, almost feudal, system of paternalism and servitude. According to the arrangement, priority was given to claims for wages up to £5 by domestic servants and agricultural labourers. The employer, in turn, was legally liable to provide food, clothing and shelter in the form of employment to his servants. If he refused or neglected his side of the bargain, he was liable to penalties under the Offences Against the Person Act.[86] Theoretically, this arrangement may seem to be based on a spirit of mutual benefit to both parties, but in an overpopulated island with its labour-intensive economy, and where low wages and bad working conditions were the norm, it was very difficult for the labouring classes to seek redress. The repulsive side to this type of paternalism was the built-in provisions in the legislation and the judicial system, against any worker who demanded higher wages or absented himself from work or, even worse, encouraged other workers to strike. Such action was regarded as a breach of contract meriting dismissal, victimization, blacklisting or even prosecution in the magistrates' court.[87]

For example, on the complaint of Darrell Greenidge of Farm Pantation, St George, William Gittens, a located labourer, was fined 8s and 2s costs for absenting himself from his stipulated duties of five days 'without lawful authority or excuse.'[88] Hubert Carter, a located labourer of Moncrieffe plantation, St John, was fined $5, payable within 14 days, or the alternative of a week's imprisonment with hard labour, for absenting himself from work for five days. Frederick Belgrave, a carter of the same plantation, received the identical punishment for a similar offense. A similar fate met Robert Weir of Halton plantation who had the audacity to transfer his services to Sunbury plantation without first notifying his former employer. He was fined 10s and 2s costs, payable within 14 days, with the alternative of a month's imprisonment.[89]

## The Better Security Act, 1920

The Attorney General, C. P. Clarke, while commenting on another piece of legislation, the Better Securities Act of 1920 – an Act which imposed severe penalties for striking workers in the essential services – gave as his sole reason for the Bill the fact that it was a transcript with slight 'modification of sections 4 and 5 of the English Imperial Conspiracy and Protection of Property Act, 1875.'[90] He argued that the English Act had saved that country 'one or two catastrophes'[91] and so the local one could perform a similar role in Barbados. The local Act in part read,

> Anyone employed by the Water Department, or by any employer who is under a duty to supply light to any place, who breaks his contract of service maliciously, knowing the probable consequence to be the deprivation of the inhabitants of their water or light, is liable on summary conviction to a fine of £20 or three months' imprisonment...[93]

The harsh penalties contained in the Better Security Act were stimulated by a growing concern about strikes and rumours of strikes in the island immediately after the First World War. In addition, the UNIA had emerged as a vibrant organization at about the same time, with the stated intention of getting a better deal for the black labouring classes. This stated intention was viewed as a serious threat to the economic interest of the ruling classes and, in the process, increased their distrust of the labouring classes. Governor O'Brien vigorously advocated the need to nip 'trouble' in the bud, while endorsing the comments of the Attorney General on the Better Security Act. He wrote:

> Legislation of this nature was considered desirable in consequence of a strike of the employees of the Water Works Department at the pumping station of Bowanston which was, fortunately, quickly settled, but which, if persisted in, would have had the effect of

cutting off the water supply at short notice from the greater part of the island. [93]

There is no evidence to suggest that the provisions of the Better Security Act were invoked in Barbados before 1937. In fact, the Act was legally designed to deal with unrest among workers in the essential services (defined as light and water) but, unfortunately, it was interpreted by all workers, and by their spokesmen in the WMA and the UNIA, as applicable to all categories of workers. These organizations campaigned vigorously for the repeal of the Act, and the WMA even attempted to send a delegation to England to protest against the legislation.[94] WMA activist, Willie Brathwaite, during the heat of the 1927 dockworkers' strike, spoke out against the measures:

> They had got together and pass a worthless and pernicious bill to bring us back to slavery. You cannot tell your wife nor child not to work for a pay which is inadequate to demands, if you do, unlimited power is given to the Police and Magistrates to do whatever pleases them. We are determined to put down this ridiculous legislation. The very Reverend who teaches you Christianity is the one who led the few men in prayers when the Bill pass into law. If you were to study the serious-ness of this island one of these mornings we all would wake up in jail....[95]

Another spokesman, Edwin Turpin, referred to the Better Security Act as 'iniquitous,' 'dangerous and pernicious.'[96] Its presence on the statute books of Barbados proved to be a haunting spectre for workers, which succeeded in keeping them in line. This fear was most potently expressed in a petition by 78 employees of the Waterworks Department, addressed to Governor Mark Young. It read, in part,

> The position is this, Your Excellency, that as employees of the waterworks department, we are subject to the same discipline as other Government employees, who get the benefit of uniform, books, etc. We get none of these things, and although our salaries are exceedingly small, yet some of us are compelled to pay house rent and to maintain a family. Such men as plumbers, labourers and chauffeurs, skilled and unskilled labour may be called out for duty at any hour of the day or night, and further, failing to execute promptly our duty, there

is an act on the statute book, we are told, which involves a penalty
not exceeding twenty pounds or imprisonment of three months.[97]

The majority of the black working class were forced to eke out a living on
the sugar estates under the most trying conditions and at the whim of legislative
encirclement by outmoded labour legislations. On the tenantries in the rural
districts, squalor and disease plagued the communities. Those who were
displaced from plantation labour migrated to Bridgetown in a frantic search
to obtain a limited number of jobs as porters, coopers, seamstresses, hawkers,
shop assistants and domestics. In fact, as late as 1937, there were about 2,000
domestics in the area of Bridgetown and its suburbs.[98] Wages were low, and
unemployment and underemployment were high in this urban space.

## Urban Squalor

The haphazard drift of people into Bridgetown during the early part of
this century created some of the most overcrowded, dilapidated and poverty-
stricken urban slums in the British West Indies. Any analysis of housing in
the districts of Carrington's Village, Cat's Castle, Chapman Lane, Ellis Village,
Suttle Street and Greenfield, in the first half of the twentieth century, would
reveal a most horrible existence for its black inhabitants.

Carrington's Village Tenantry covered an area of approximately 37 acres,
on which 1,026 dwelling houses stood. Seven hundred and eleven houses were
owner-occupied, of which 58 were overcrowded and needed enlargement,
289 were unfit for human habitation, 325 needed repair, and only 44 were
structurally sound. Of the 315 rented houses, 20 were overcrowded and needed
enlargement, 146 were unfit for habitation, 127 needed repair and only 22
were structurally sound. There were 1,030 separate families occupying these
houses, with a total population of 3,607.[99]

Cat's Castle stood on 6¼ acres, with 179 separate dwelling houses, of
which 62 were owner-occupied and 117 were rented. Of the 62 owner-
occupied houses, nine were overcrowded and needed repair, 19 were unfit for
habitation, 31 were in need of repair, and only three were structurally sound.
Of the 117 rented houses, eight were overcrowded and needed repair, and
only three were structurally sound. Two hundred and sixty six families lived
in the 179 houses. The average rent was 60 cents monthly for a house plot,
and $2.60 for a house.[100]

Suttle Street Tenantry, consisting of one acre with 26 buildings, was considered one of the worst slum areas in Barbados. Twenty one buildings, which contained 76 families, had a total population of 140. Of the 21 buildings, 14 were considered unfit for habitation, one was owner occupied and six were in great need of repair. The average rent for a single house was $2.60 per month, flats $3.75 and single rooms $1.00 per month.[101]

This morbid tale of overcrowding existed in other areas of Bridgetown inhabited by Blacks, such as in Nelson Street, Emmerton Lane, Garden Land, Phillips Tenantry and Ellis Village. In these districts no proper sewerage systems existed and in some areas buckets of excreta were thrown into the sea as a disposal method. In Chapman Lane, a lack of proper drainage resulted in constant flooding and the formation of stagnant, mosquito-infested pools during the rainy season. The haphazard layout of the villages did not provide for proper ventilation or the acquisition of a comfortable living space for their inhabitants. In Suttle Street, there were no proper kitchen facilities and so cooking was done in the passageway on oil stoves. For the majority of city dwellers, cooking was done on coal pots. Kerosene oil lamps provided the only source of light at night. These open flames, in the mainly wooden, ramshackle and overcrowded structures, were no doubt fire hazards. Overcrowding in Bridgetown was described by a Committee appointed by the Governor as a 'grave social evil, threatening public health, weakening morals and destroying the promise of the future.'[102]

The unhealthy environment in which city folks were forced to live, and the lack of employment opportunities for many of them, created a feeling of frustration, hopelessness and, no doubt, alienation. It was this feeling of hopelessness which probably stimulated the UNIA, the WMA and the Democratic League into action. Clement Payne's arrival on the scene in 1937 exploited this fertile ground for discontent, which was harnessed into meaningful political action.

Whereas Blacks existed in squalor on the plantation tenantries and in urban communities, the Whites practised a residential exclusion, prominently displayed by their presence in old plantation Great Houses or in secluded areas such as Highgate Gardens, Belleville and Strathclyde. Belleville, for example, denied hassle-free access to Blacks, even the residents of nearby Carrington's Village. When Blacks ventured into Belleville, they were expected to avoid walking on the same side of the road as any white person. In addition, on encountering any white residents of the district, they were required to display all the signs of servility such as tipping the hat, bowing politely or initiating respectful pleasantries.

During a personal exchange, senior citizen Tony Hinds reported an incident that occurred when he was a nine-year-old. One afternoon, while he traversed the district of Strathclyde on his way to Bank Hall, he received a severe beating with a stick from a black watchman who reminded him that he should never venture into the area 'when the white people playing tennis.'[103] Perhaps the most alarming case of racial discrimination occurred in 1925, when a black women delivering milk to the residents of Strathclyde was kicked by one of the white inhabitants, for no other reason than that she dared to enter the district. A Police Magistrate lamented,

> This is a most outrageous case.…It is the sort of thing that can only happen in Strathclyde. Strathclyders think that Strathclyde is some heaven into which one cannot enter unless they are admitted by an Archangel. I cannot acquiesce to that. This woman was attacked by the watchman and then, for no reason by Mr R. Innis. I am satisfied that he did kick her.[104]

## Political Relations in Barbados

In this book, much attention is paid to the conflict which existed between the various classes in Barbadian society, as forming the essence of local political activity. This conflict centred on a constant struggle between the two main ethnic groups over the nature and distribution of political power and the control of economic resources. In the melee of political activity, the aim of the well-entrenched white elite was to maintain complete control over the organs of economic and political power. On the other hand, the black population – that is, the black labouring classes and the black middle class – attempted to capture political power, or at least to use recruitment to political office as a means of redressing longstanding grievances.

It is important, however, to understand the structure of government in Barbados during the early twentieth century, in order to grasp the nature of Barbadian political contests and activity.

The Government consisted of a nominated Legislative Council of nine members and a House of Assembly of 24 members elected annually by a limited franchise. The executive functions of the Government were vested in an Executive Committee consisting of the Governor, the Colonial Secretary, the Attorney General, a member of the Legislative Council and four members of the House of Assembly.[105] The members of the Committee from both Houses of the Legislature were traditionally drawn from among prominent members of the planter-merchant class and were allowed to exercise considerable influence on the Committee. During the early twentieth century, the Executive Committee was dominated by such prominent white figures as H. B. G. Austin, W. B. H. Massiah, S. C. Thorne and A. S. Bryden.[106]

The powers of the executive government in theory resided in the Governor in Executive Council. In practice, the Executive Committee managed government property, introduced money votes, drew up plans for public works and handled other such matters associated with the running of government.[107] In short, the Executive Committee was the principal arm of government. But the Legislature, and in particular the House of Assembly, controlled the purse strings, and never hesitated to remind the Committee of this fact, especially by their procrastination on public work programmes. Despite their politely worded messages promising 'to cooperate in every way with the Executive' to further the development of the island, these words were seldom translated into reality by increased expenditure, especially if this was to benefit the black population.

The Legislative Council was a nominated Upper Chamber with the constitutional privilege, and the power, to reject measures emanating from the Lower House. It was supposed to be a chamber in which elder statesmen and retired civil servants would avail themselves of an opportunity to share their long-accumulated knowledge and experience in public life and public enterprise for the enlightenment of the population.[108] This virtuous intention was not always achieved, as the Council had become largely a dumping ground for retired, conservative members of the planter-merchant community who considered it their exclusive privilege to sit uninterruptedly in the Legislative Council until they were too old to be useful. For example, in 1933, G. Laurie Pile, at age 78, had been sitting in the Legislative Council continuously from July 4, 1905. John Hutson, a former Chief Public Health Inspector and Poor Law Inspector, at age 76, had been sitting from October 1, 1925. A. S. Bryden, a leading Bridgetown merchant and prominent member of the Chamber of Commerce, at age 74, had been sitting from November 6, 1925. E. B. Skeete, at age 78, had been sitting from May 21, 1928.[109] Other prominent, long-serving members of the Legislative Council during the 1920s and 1930s were S. C. Thorne, H. W. Reece, E. T. Grannum, J. O. Wright, A. P. Haynes and T. W. B. O'Neal.

Probably the classic example of the domination of the Legislative Council can be cited in the service of Sir W. K. Chandler, Master of Chancery and Judge of the Assistant Court of Appeal, who sat from October 29, 1884, until his retirement in 1929. After 16 years as President of the Legislative Council, he had amassed a fortune as a planter, a director of many companies and Master of Chancery. In many cases these men began their political careers in the House of Assembly and then switched to the Legislative Council.[110]

Governor Mark Young attacked this abuse of unlimited tenure in the Legislative Council in a confidential dispatch to his superiors in 1933. He suggested that future appointments should be for a term of five years, and any member should only be eligible for re-appointment for two periods of five years.[111] Any further extensions should only be given in the most exceptional circumstances. Governor Young's superiors at the Colonial Office approved the plan and attempted to put it in place in the form of amendments to the Letters Patent and Royal Instructions of 1937.[112] These proposed amendments created a storm in the white community, however, and they were dismissed as an unjustified attack on white privileges. Political mobilization in the form of strongly-worded statements of protest and boycotts were forwarded to the colonial Governor by both Houses of the Legislature.[113] In addition, the full influence of the Chamber of Commerce, the Agricultural Society and the Voters Association, with the signatures of the island's leading citizens, were thrown in as added evidence of the strength of opposition to the amendments.[114] For example, accompanying the petition of the Voters Association were the signatures of such leading merchants and planters as A. Del. Innis, Robert Challenor, A. S. Bryden, Robert Arthur, C. R. Armstrong, J. M. Kidney, Hubert Boyce, D. Laurence Johnson, H. Bourne, Charles MacKenzie, W. W. Watkins and Bruce Weatherhead.[115] At a meeting of the Chamber of Commerce held on May 6, 1937, A. Del. Innis, President, and J. Niblock, Vice-President, along with ten other prominent businessmen signed a petition which was submitted to the Secretary of State.[116] At a meeting of the Agricultural Society held on May 7, 1937, a strongly-worded petition regarded the amendments as an 'infringement of the constitutional principle constantly affirmed and maintained in this island…which should not have been changed without obtaining the opinion of the Legislature.'[117]

The Secretary of State, W. Ormsby-Gore, in reply to the Legislature put their unfounded concern into perspective when he wrote,

> I regret, however, that the objections which have been taken to the change in the term of office of the Legislative Councillors are still maintained among that section of the community from which the members of the Legislative Council are usually selected, more particularly as I cannot but feel that these objections are based on apprehensions for which no real grounds exist.[118]

What the opposition to the amendment of the Letters Patent demonstrated was a remarkable show of solidarity by the merchant-planter elite in the face of what they perceived as a threat to their privileges as councillors. It also revealed a strong desire to protect the entrenched privileges and status of the local oligarchy.

At the parochial level of government, the same close watch over the possible erosion of white privileges was very evident among the merchant-planter elite. The Vestry system, established by the early settlers immediately after the settlement of Barbados, was from its inception dominated by the Plantocracy. At the beginning of the twentieth century, it had had a long history of domination by the white power structure. Parochial affairs were administered by 11 Parish Boards, elected annually on a narrow franchise, under the provisions of the Representation of the People Act, 1901 (No.2). The Rector of each parish church was the ex-officio chairman of the Vestry. Its functions included the appointment of Guardians for the care of the sick and poor, of Commissioners of Health for the control of sanitation, and of Highway Commissioners for the upkeep of roads. To provide funds for these purposes, rates were levied on lands and houses, and taxes on trade establishments and vehicles, in the individual parishes.[119]

More specifically, the main function of the Vestries was the administration of poor relief through the annually appointed Guardians of the Poor. From the Vestry funds, these Guardians maintained the Almshouses, of which there was one in each Parish, and appointed Inspectors of the poor. Medical Officers were responsible for the notification to the relevant authorities of cases of poverty or sickness, and the circumstances surrounding any patient desirous of relief.[120]

Planter-merchant control of the parochial system of government remained one of the most revealing aspects of the deep-rooted nature of the white power structure. The Vestries were in the forefront of the opposition to expenditure on Afro-Barbadians during the early twentieth century, especially in the areas of education, housing development and public health. For example, the attempt to centralize public health administration through the appointment of a Chief Medical Officer in 1928 was met by such opposition from the Vestries as to appear out of proportion to the simple matter of the appointment of an officer to administer healthcare. But the real fears of the Vestrymen were rooted deep within the merchant-planter class's inability to contemplate a loss of power in such a vital area, and a ceding of control over local medical affairs to a central authority.[121]

In addition, the Vestry system provided some Euro-Barbadians, who were unable to obtain positions of leadership in other areas of public life, the opportunity to exercise some power in society. The fears, therefore, were based on a feeling of insecurity.

From the domination of both chambers of the Legislature and the local Vestry system, the tentacles of planter-merchant class control extended deep into Barbadian society, through to the membership of committees and boards of key institutions. Such boards were the Education Board, the Railway Board, the Board of Health, the Central Poor Law Board, the General Hospital Board, the Agriculture Board and the governing bodies of the various schools. For example, A. S. Bryden, in addition to being a businessman, a member of the Chamber of Commerce and the Voters Association, was a member of the Legislative Council, a member of the General Board of Health, the Board of Agriculture and the Central Road Board.[122] J. R. Phillips was a member of the Legislative Council, the General Hospital Board and the Board of Health.[123] Fellow Councillor A. P. Haynes was a member of the General Hospital Board and the Railway Board. S. C. Thorne, until 1930, represented St Thomas in the House of Assembly, then became a member of the Legislative Council, and a member of the Agriculture Board, the Central Road Board and the General Hospital Board. H. Jason Jones, prominent businessman and parliamentarian, was also a member of the Education Board and the Central Road Board. B. G. Yearwood, representative for St Joseph in the Lower Chamber, was also a member of the Hospital Board, the Central Road Board and the Victorian Emigration Society. Other prominent members of the merchant-planter elite, such as G. C. Mahon, Dr W. B. H. Massiah, Dr N. L. Boxhill and Sir F. J. Clarke, dominated these boards as well.[124]

Close scrutiny of the minutes of these various institutions would reveal the 'watch dog' attitude of these men to the affairs of the island. Their occupation of critical areas of decision-making enabled them to influence the direction and the pace of political, social and economic development. In short, through the control of all facets of Barbadian life, the merchant-planter elite formed a powerful interlocking directorate of immense power, that extended throughout Barbadian society and affected every facet of local life. It is clear how dispossessed the Afro-Barbadian could have felt at the time. In fact, the oral testimony of black working people emphasized this reality: the need for empowerment.

In this case empowerment is defined as the ability of a people to design and participate in processes and events that shape their lives. In short, it is a means and a process that entails the right to participation at all levels of society, the right to knowledge, including education, the right to access all kinds of resources, the right to employment, the right to liberty, happiness and social services. The foregoing discussion has highlighted the oppressed state of the majority of the black population and their quest for justice. The struggle for justice would be a struggle for empowerment.

# 2

# BARBADOS AND THE GREAT WAR, 1914–18

The assassination of Archduke Franz Ferdinand of Austria in the Bosnian capital of Sarajevo on June 28, 1914, ignited a global conflict commonly referred to as the Great War or the First World War. All the major European nations which had aligned themselves from the late nineteenth-century into the Triple Alliance, made up of Austria-Hungry, Germany and Italy, and the Entente Powers or Allies, consisting of Russia, Britain and France, devoted large portions of their national budgets preparing for such a conflict.[1] Statesmen and Generals created elaborate military plans for such a war, but no one had even imagined the pain and turmoil which this conflict was about to bring upon the world.

As soon as the news of the Sarajevo murders reached Vienna, Austria declared war on Serbia in 1914. Germany entered the war to help Austria. Russia joined to assist Serbia. France then entered to assist Russia. Germany invaded Belgium in the tactical manoeuvre called the Schlieffen Plan, to conquer France by avoiding the Maginot Line and encircling Paris. Britain entered the war by sending an expeditionary force to assist Belgium. The major European powers were now embroiled in a great 'tribal' war that was to have global repercussions.[2]

The theatre of this war not only encompassed an Eastern and a Western Front in Europe, but, embraced the Mediterranean, the Middle East and Africa. German U-boats roamed the sea-lanes of the world, attacking Allied shipping, including British merchant ships.[3] Great naval battles fought between Britain and Germany made shipping so precarious that exports of primary products from the various colonial dependencies were severely restricted, thereby putting pressure on their fragile economies. In addition, imports of vital manufactured goods into the colonial empires were also restricted and this led to tremendous hardship and material deprivation.[4] Never before in human history had a war caused so much dislocation, loss of life and human misery. Moreover, the dawn of human inventiveness in terms of military weapons proceeded with the invention of poison gas in 1915, the tank in 1916 and the submarine and torpedo shortly after. The world had changed forever. Barbados and the wider Caribbean, being colonial dependencies of England, did not escape the vagaries of this Great War.

The shortage of basic imported foodstuff immediately led to rationing in Barbados. T. S. Garraway and Company, a British export giant, for example, informed the colonial authorities of the prohibition of the export of condensed milk to Barbados. Similar restrictions were placed on medicines, clothes and steel products.[5] These restrictions had a tremendous negative impact on the local population, especially the poor working classes who were already reeling under the pressure of low wages, deplorable housing conditions and malnutrition. Afro-Barbadians were now admonished in the name of loyalty to the British Empire to make further sacrifices. The Colonial Secretary, T. E. Fell, while reflecting on the outcome of the war, captured the suffering and sacrifices of the local population in a dispatch to his superiors:

> I want also to tell you that I have felt and appreciated the fact that during these three years people on small salaries, and people of the labouring class of this island, owing to the increased cost of living, have seen hard times, but they have thoroughly played the game. During these terrible years I have never felt any anxiety whatsoever that the people in Barbados would embarrass the Government, or bring discredit upon themselves at such a time.[6]

During the war years much emphasis was placed by the colonial authorities on improving the yields of local agriculture in order solve the shortage of certain basic supplies. Increased agricultural production was facilitated by the passing of the Vegetable Produce Act, which made it compulsory for all estates to devote a portion of their lands to the production of ground provisions. The control of reaping and sale of produce was organized by a committee appointed under the same Vegetable Produce Act.[7] The duration of the First World War was a difficult time for the local population marked by widespread malnutrition, and unfortunately, high death rates. The local death rates from 1916 to 1918 were 32.2., 28.8 and 25.9 respectively.[8] Yet these tribulations did not dampen the loyalty of the local population to the cause of the Allies.

## Barbadian Support for the British War Effort

There was much enthusiasm generated among all sections of the local population in support of the war effort of 1914. The Barbadian legislature, for example, led the way by voting a generous sum of £100,000 for the British war effort.[9] A sum of £5,621.10.4 was also donated as a contribution from the 'people of Barbados' to the King George Fund for Sailors.[10] In addition, a 1915 Act imposed an export tax of 2s 6 d per ton on sugar and 10 d per gallon on molasses, and, later a Stamp Act and a Postal Surtax Act, raised additional revenues which were all earmarked for the war effort.[11] Indeed, no other colonial legislature in the British West Indies responded as promptly, or as generously, as the Barbadian legislature, to support the British during the First World War. Apart from the monetary contributions, numerous messages from both houses of the legislature and from individual citizens, reminded the government of Britain of the enduring loyalty of the people of Barbados.

Many business houses and their staff also threw their full weight behind the war effort. A contribution of £200 towards the King George Fund for Sailors was made by the Barbados Fire Insurance Company. A 'Bill of Exchange' for £150 was donated by the Barbados Foundry Limited and £50 by the West India Rum Refinery Company Limited.[12] A handsome grant of £2,000 was donated by the Barbados Mutual Assurance Society. Contributions to the Belgian Relief Fund were made by the staff of Knights & Co., C. S. Pitcher & Co., L. W. Sampson & Co. and Laurie & Co. Ltd

Some individuals, in an admirable display of loyalty to the British Empire, made personal contributions to the war undertaking. Alexander Ashby in his final settlement left his entire estate of approximately £38,421.5.11 to the Colonial Bank of London to clear any outstanding debt and then to remit the remainder to the Secretary of State for War to be used by the British Government, 'for any purpose, either directly or indirectly, connected with the war.'[13] Ashby also made another contribution of £5 to the Belgian Relief Fund. E. F. S. Bowrie, L. G. G. Taggart, Captain W. Jordan, Captain H. Miller and P. A. Shepherd together contributed £24.92 to the same Fund. G. E. Hinkson, a former Sergeant-Major in the West India Regiment, relinquished one quarter of his 'military pension as a gift toward expenses of the war.'[14]

Various voluntary organizations also emerged throughout the island to raise funds to defray the expenses of equipment and the transport of young

Barbadian men from the colony to the war zones of Europe and North Africa. These included the Citizens Contingent Committee, the Barbados Recruiting Committee, the Red Cross Fund Committee, the Prince of Wales Fund Committee, the Motor Ambulance Fund Committee and the Belgian Relief Fund Committee.[15] An advertisement in a local newspaper in 1916 captured the patriotic spirit of Barbadians for the war effort:

MEN ARE WANTED
FOR
THE BARBADOS CITIZENS CONTINGENT

This is a unique opportunity for young men to prove their loyalty to their King, and the Island of their birth. The committee hopes that they will be able to send at least 50 more in March. The money is there. WILL MEN COME FORWARD? Men are as much needed at the Front TO-DAY, as when the war commenced.[16]

Another newspaper, the *Barbados Globe*, was so overwhelmed by the generous response of its readers to its appeals to support the war effort that it was moved to write in appreciation:

From the very outbreak of hostilities appeals of the sort have been flowing in upon us, and while we may not have been able to take on every application, we have taken on most of them, and as we have already expressed it, the responses have been magnificent.[17]

Apart from the generous monetary contributions made by individuals, business houses and volunteer organizations, 811 young men were enlisted to serve in the Barbados Contingent of the British West India Regiment as of 1916. Eventually, over 1,000 served their King and country on the battlefields of Europe and the Middle East. The local recruitment committee pledged to send 328 men each year, and to bear the cost of £5,070 annually to transport the men from the colony to the various war zones. Patriotic young men of Barbados willingly placed their lives on the line.

## Discrimination in the Army

But even before these young men from Barbados could leave their homeland, the spectre of racial prejudice haunted them during the sifting process associated with recruitment. The first 2,000 volunteers of the 'working classes' who were interviewed by the local Recruitment Committee were considered, not for combatant duties, but for labour duty.[18] On the other hand, young men of the 'better class,' referred to as 'representatives of the classes,' who were drawn from the Volunteer Force and the Cadet Corps of The Lodge School and Harrison College, were trained with the hope of 'eventually becoming junior officers' in the British West India Regiment.[19] In fact, this latter group, like many others in the West Indies, objected strongly to serving in the same regiment as black Barbadians of humble working-class origins.[20] The intention of the local Recruitment Committee from the outset was to deny black working-class soldiers any chance of being promoted, or of occupying positions of responsibility in the West India Regiment. This practice did not find favour with the soldiers of African descent.

The discrimination process which started at home continued on the battlefront and embraced the majority of West Indians. No distinctions were made by the British military officers concerning the Barbadian recruits, even those who were led to believe that they were 'a special class'; they were all simply treated as natives.

This disregard stunned the 'better classes' of Barbadian coloured soldiers. For the most part, they were confined mainly to menial, non-combatant jobs, just like their black working-class counterparts. For example, of the 397 Barbadian non-commissioned officers serving with the Mesopotamia Expeditionary Force, 101 were motor-boat drivers, 81 were guards, 71 were clerks, 23 were carpenters, 16 were camp police, 12 were blacksmiths, 11 were pitters, six were telephone operators and 76 were of 'miscellaneous employment.'[21] This general breakdown could be applied to numerous other black recruits serving in the British West India Regiment, and even the West Africa contingent.[22] The majority did not perform any combat duties thereby giving them the dignity of meeting the enemy on the battlefield. In addition, they were further incensed at receiving less pay than European soldiers and being overlooked during promotion in favour of less experienced and less qualified white European non-commissioned officers.[23] By Army Order No. l, 1918, for example, only British soldiers received increases in salaries. When West Indian soldiers sought an explanation for the discriminatory policy, they were rebuffed by a ruling of the War Office which stated that they could not obtain the increases because they were 'Natives.'[24]

This insult created widespread discontent among black soldiers of the West India Regiment. Twelve Barbadians stationed in Egypt petitioned the local Recruitment Committee in an angry tone:

> We have been deceived. We would like to think the deception was not intentional. The fact remains conditions are not as we expected and it is to you (J. Chancellor Lynch) and other gentlemen of like position to whom we look to retrieve our wrongs.[25]

Chairman Lynch sympathized with them, for they were from an early contingent which was 'specially chosen,' that is, from among the 'classes,' whom the Committee expected to rise in the ranks of the British West India Regiment. The European Officers, however, had different plans for them. On December 6, 1918, another angrily-worded petition, with the signatures of 180 black sergeants stationed in France and Italy, requested of the Secretary of State for the Colonies an explanation for the lack of salary increases to black soldiers and a refusal to promote them to 'any rank in the British Army.'[26]

A petition of ex-soldiers, for example, sought a conference with the colonial Governor, Charles O'Brien, and the main complaints were stated as follows:

(a)   Lack of local support resulting in 'invidious treatment.'
(b)   Lower Scale of Separation allowances.
(c)   Extreme reluctance of the Imperial authorities to grant the Barbados contingent increased rates of pay which were accorded to British troops.
(d)   Failure to pay a War Bonus to local returned soldiers.[27]

## War Veterans as Political Activists

Probably the most volatile situation of the war was precipitated by the mutiny of black soldiers at the Cimino Camp, Taranto, Italy. Discontent was brewing from the inception of the war, over bad living conditions, low wages and racial discrimination which black soldiers had to endure.[28] Secret meetings were held by the Sergeants of the British West India Battalions to protest against the conditions. According to the spies who had infiltrated these gatherings, the events took on a political flavor and an association called the Caribbean League was formed. The headquarters was to be situated in Kingston, Jamaica, with sub-offices in each of the British West Indian islands. Definite plans were being formulated for future political activity in the West Indies once the war was over.[29] In fact, a black sergeant of the 3rd Battalion vented his anger and frustration when in making a speech he said *inter alia* 'the black man should have freedom and govern himself in the West Indies and…force must be used, and if necessary bloodshed, to obtain the object.'[30]

The Caribbean League was aborted, however, by the firm action of the military establishment in Italy. Some of the ringleaders were transferred to other regiments, a few were demoted, and the intimidating presence of an extra machine gun company reminded the others of the possible consequences, should they persist in their activities.[31] A violent confrontation was averted, but the bitterness persisted much longer, as the embryo of a political movement was formed.

No vibrant branch of the Caribbean League was ever established in Barbados. However, it can be argued that the attempt at mutiny in the Cimino Camp and the general feeling of disappointment throughout the British West India Regiment spilled over into the West Indies after the war.[32] One way it manifested itself was in the various forms of non-violent resistance to British rule, mainly by a proliferation of humble petitioning once the soldiers were demobilized. As W. F. Elkins wrote,

> The revolt at Taranto was the modern advent of mass resistance by West Indians to British rule. The soldiers of the British West India Regiment began the national liberation struggle that eventually led to the demise of open colonial rule in most of the British Caribbean.[33]

It is being suggested that the maltreatment of black soldiers by the British military authorities was the foundation of the protest by demobilized veterans in Barbados, and perhaps, throughout the British West Indies. Clennel Wickham, himself a war veteran, echoed this sentiment:

> There is no doubt about the changed outlook which the War has brought to the mind and tempers of colonial peoples. To the natural impulse to growth which such a lopping off of excrescence, as the war occasioned, brought to the mind must be added the individual experience of the various soldiers. Most of the men who served, returned to their homes with their sense as well as their senses quickened. They were no longer content to be considered children

in the Empire, they wanted to assume the dignity and responsibility of grown ups.[34]

The degree of discontent by the black soldiers of the British West India Regiment, and the willingness to translate that discontent into political protest, cannot be overstated. The Returned Soldiers Committee of Barbados, which was established with the sole intention of aiding returning veterans, was bombarded with numerous complaints similar to those of the Egyptian contingent.[35] Even the *Barbados Globe* and the conservative *Agricultural Reporter* were moved to take up the issue. The *Globe* published a petition bearing the signatures of 43 Barbadian non-commissioned officers, setting out in great detail their grievances.[36] The *Globe* wrote,

> In the battlefield, coloured West Indians tell of how they were treated by the English Tommy – that being regarded as inferior by those who should have known better, he was often insulted by a class of soldiers whose respectability and intelligence stood at considerable discount.[37]

The Agricultural Reporter wrote in a similar tone:

> Men of the British West Indies Regiment who have returned to Barbados have intimated, both officially and unofficially, that they have a great many grounds of complaints against the authorities both local and imperial. We are fully convinced that these men have a great many good grounds of complaints.[38]

It seems reasonable to suggest, however, that when the Allies secured victory in the war, both local and imperial authorities were uninterested in entertaining the complaints of ex-servicemen. This feeling of neglect led to much bitterness, as well as a feeling of despair and a sense of betrayal. Louis Sebro, a returned veteran, remarked on one occasion, 'If we can fight for King and Country, we should be allowed to have a voice in our Government.'[39] This retort personified a widely held political expectation shared by many ex-servicemen and political activists.

The British government, however, never had any intention of giving black Barbadians a share in government in return for their participation in the war and their loyalty to the British Empire. Perhaps some black Barbadians got carried away in the tide of multi-racial enthusiasm generated for the war effort, and misinterpreted this to mean that the local race and class barriers were being broken down. Perhaps Clennell Wickham's episode at St Cyprian's Church, which will be discussed in the next chapter, was conceived in a similar miscalculation on his part. He most likely felt that his faithful service during the war, and the medals attesting to his bravery, were passports to civil liberties and a dismantling of the racial barriers. Many ex-servicemen who harbored similar thoughts were painfully jolted into reality when they were ignored and neglected, and Britain more than ever tried to keep her empire intact. Ex-servicemen, after much disappointment, channelled their energies into social and political protests by joining the local UNIA or the WMA, and petitioning the Colonial Office with their grievances. Governor O'Brien wrote to Viscount Milner, Secretary of State, complaining:

> It is a fact that a certain amount of unrest exists among the coloured population of Barbados and that the returned soldiers of the British West India Regiment and the repatriated coloured seamen have formed generally speaking a discontented group.[40]

He went on to stress that the complaints related mainly to concerns about pay and an idea held by ex-servicemen of being deliberately neglected by colonial authorities, and persecuted by 'cowardly civilians,' even though they fought faithfully for 'King and Country.' O'Brien thought it was a good sign that the general population was unsympathetic to their cause. At the same time, he identified divisions in the ex-servicemen's protests. The 'better class' coloured man, he insisted, was too loyal to the Crown and too deeply religious to favour concerted measures against authority. In addition, the most 'respectful' of the group, were so afraid of one another as to 'admonish reckless speakers.'[41] In essence, he identified petty divisions among the Afro-Barbadian population which he considered to be a hindrance to their progress and which would have prevented them from embarking on any unified political action. The ex-servicemen, therefore, were a discontented group who should be ignored. However, despite this negative perception of ex-servicemen, as far as inciting the local population was concerned, O'Brien was kept on his toes by a consistent flow of petitions, even from the merchant seamen as well. Their protests contained similar grievances to those of the ex-servicemen.

Despite the conservative demands of these requests, the colonial authorities, and the merchant-planter class, viewed the protests of the veterans as alarmist propaganda which could upset the social peace of the island and provide fodder for political agitators. Even more alarming to the authorities was the potential of ex-servicemen to challenge the State if they should obtain firearms during any social upheaval. After all, they were trained in combat and their loyalty could not be predicted in the light of their constant complaints.

The colonial authorities therefore took steps to minimize the possibility of such an occurrence being initiated by war veterans in Barbados. In a secret dispatch, Governor O'Brien was urged to update local legislation relative to the storage of arms, because of the 'existence of unrest among the native population.'[42] The Secretary of State also enclosed a copy of the Firearms Amendments Ordinance, 1919, of Grenada, as a model piece of legislation on which to base the local bill. The Barbadian legislature, however, assured him that all arms and ammunition were stored safely, and the initiative had already been taken to update the Firearms Amendment Act (1915) by the Ammunition Bill (1919), to take care of such an eventuality.[43]

On anticipating the full demobilization of ex-servicemen in around March 1919, O'Brien was once again advised to take steps against a possible uprising in Barbados. The Ceylon Scheme of 1915, formulated from the British experience gained in putting down 'riots' in Ceylon, was discussed extensively by the local security officials and put in place. This elaborate scheme set out detailed instructions for the rapid deployment of the militia and the police to deal with unrest in 'Bridgetown and the estates.'[44]

This fear of unrest in Barbados was further accentuated by the arrival of news that 400 Blacks, many of these demobilized soldiers, had rioted in British Honduras on July 23, 1919.[45] Similar reports were coming in of 'disturbances' by black seamen at Cardiff and Liverpool, England.[46] On July 28, 1919, reports of rioting in the 'Black Belt' of Chicago was also received with much alarm. From June 1919 to the end of the year, there were approximately 25 race riots in various urban areas of the United States.[47] Closer to home, in Trinidad, Cipriani's Workingmen's Association, with which some Barbadians were in close contact, was agitating for social and political reforms. A series of strikes occurred there during the year, culminating in a highly confrontational series of industrial disputes at the Port-of-Spain docks in December 1919.[48] The local authorities were very much distressed at these happenings and the possible effects they could have on Barbados. The First World War, it seems, had thrown up some anxieties which they had never anticipated.

During the Great War of 1914–18, Barbados gave unstintingly of her resources, both in men and money. The generosity of the Government and people during this difficult period which confronted the British Empire had been acknowledged on numerous occasions by the authorities. Suffice to say that the First World War had a tremendous impact on Barbados, and confirmed the remarkable loyalty of Barbadians; it also opened up a lot of discontent in Barbadian and the wider West Indian society. The indignity suffered by war veterans was channelled into political protests on their return to the West Indies. War veterans returned with a heightened sense of consciousness and political organization, and were not prepared to accept the injustices with any passivity. The political agitation of the post-war era, which has featured so prominently in shaping the political systems of the Caribbean, and indeed Barbados, will be examined in subsequent chapters.

# 3

# RACIAL ATTITUDES AND CLASS CONFLICT IN BARBADOS, 1918–37

A great deal of fanfare and pageantry organized by Governor Charles O'Brien greeted the war veterans returning to Barbados in the first half of 1919.[1] Among the First World War veterans was Clennel Wickham, an intelligent, ambitious man, whose political consciousness had been stirred, apparently by his experiences in the British West India Regiment, and by an ardent love for Fabian socialist literature. In an ostentatious display of his military uniform and his medals, he visited the St Cyprian's Anglican Church to praise God for his safe return to Barbados. But he made the mistake of sitting, without invitation, in one of the front seats of the Church. This action created a furore among the predominantly white congregation who demanded his immediate removal. Their request was only achieved after a good deal of protest from Wickham.[2] He had been a regular member of the Sunday School class as a boy, and, until his departure for the war, would have been aware of the discriminatory practice of pew renting. and seating blacks at the rear of the Church. He expressed surprise that this entrenched racial practice of the slavery era continued well into the twentieth century, especially after black Barbadians had participated in a war which was fought to save the world from tyranny and to promote democracy. Wickham remarked that 'the sheep were still separated from the goats'[3] and vowed never to return to St Cyprian's Church. Perhaps, he was naïve to expect a fundamental change in the race relations situation of Barbados to occur overnight, after centuries of use, when no mechanisms were ever put in place to foster the change.

Nevertheless, this incident not only highlighted the continuing presence of discriminatory practices in the Established Church but, in a way, indicated the type of confrontation which was likely to occur between people who were not prepared to accept the prejudices of the pre-1914 era and the entrenched system of racism in the island. The white congregation of St Cyprian's, a chapel-at-ease located in suburban Belleville, Bridgetown, displayed the signs of an unbending attitude toward any relaxation of established racial practices. The perpetrators of these obstinate attitudes did not appear to have recognized the changes which were being forced upon the old order as a result of the Great War. The exposure of hundreds of black West Indians to conditions in Europe during the war, and to discrimination in the British West India Regiment, created a group of veterans who were not prepared to accept racial discrimination passively on their return home.[4] Such discernment on the part of returning veterans was best exemplified by Wickham's defiance of the St Cyprian's congregation. This incident, and the general state of poverty among the black population, acted as the stimulus which spurred him into a career of 'radical' journalism in the *Herald* newspaper the same year.

The local oligarchy, and in particular Governor O'Brien, expressed much concern about the apparent unstable industrial climate in the West Indies, and further afield, in the period immediately after the War. They feared the possible effects on Barbados. But, even more, they were convinced that a domino-like effect of unrest occurring in England, North America and elsewhere in the West Indies was bound to reach Barbados. If the neighbours' political houses were on fire, they argued, then it was necessary to wet the local one by firm action, so as to prevent a social and political cataclysm at home.

The formation of a local UNIA division in 1919 conjured up additional fears that foreign 'agitators' were misleading the highly excitable black population. But Governor O'Brien, while he shared these concerns of the ruling elite, was particularly worried about the combat experience of the demobilized ex-servicemen and seamen. During his private meetings with members of the merchant-planter elite, he bombarded them with hysterical references to the potential security risks which disgruntled ex-servicemen posed, and urged the ruling elite to provide employment for these men as a matter of priority.[5] Even before the war had ended, Governor Probyn, O'Brien's predecessor, anticipating some possible discontent among ex-servicemen, embarked on a similar policy of urging the ruling elite, both privately and in the press, to provide employment for them as a matter of precedence during their demobilization.[6] In addition, he spearheaded the establishment of a Returned Soldiers Committee to aid ex-servicemen on their return to Barbados; but the legislature's insensitive refusal to provide adequate funds resulted in the ineffective functioning of the committee.[7]

Probably the only suggestion designed to assist ex-servicemen which the ruling elite embraced with any enthusiasm was emigration. A small, overpopulated island with a 'superabundance of labour,' they argued, should pursue emigration like a 'safety valve' to relieve undue population pressure, and so avoid any possible social turmoil as a result of overcrowding and the lack of opportunity. Moreover, they reasoned that mass emigration could remove the burden of responsibility for providing jobs from the shoulders of the merchant-planter elite. In addition, the ruling elite quite cleverly recognized the potential that emigration offered for relieving the island of what they considered a source of trouble – the war veterans.[8]

The legislature, therefore, sponsored the emigration of 153 ex-servicemen to Cuba.[9] Private emigration agents were encouraged to recruit ex-servicemen as a matter of priority and the veterans were encouraged to avail themselves of 'the excellent offers in Cuba.' On August 8, 1919, Emigration Agent G. S. R. Archer, shipped 109 returned soldiers to Cuba with the full approval of the Assembly.[10] Indeed, the idea of an emigration scheme on the 'scale of Panama' was pursued with much vigour. But as the traditional outlets for West Indian emigration closed after the First World War, the local oligarchy's dream of shipping their problem overseas were shattered. Nevertheless, they pursued the policy with much tenacity throughout the 1920s and 1930s, culminating in the ill-fated Vieux Fort project of 1937.

The fears of rebellion instigated by ex-servicemen and ex-seamen were not realized in Barbados during the early twentieth century. It seems reasonable to suggest that the merchant-planter elite, and in particular Governor O'Brien, had overreacted to the grievances of these men.

It is important, however, to reflect on the political actions and the thoughts behind the actions, especially the patterns of expenditure pursued by the merchant-planter dominated legislature during this period, even as the Great War took place, in order to grasp the nature of the class struggle in Barbados.

The generosity of the local legislature to the Allies' war effort, referred to previously, occurred against a background of abject poverty in Barbados. Barbados was a British dependency and one may be tempted to argue that it was merely performing its duty to the Mother Country. But the island did more than its fair share for the war effort, and this must be emphasized. If the priority of a government is to look after the welfare of its citizens first, then, as a ruling class, the merchant-planter elite failed miserably in its duty to the Afro-Barbadian population. It is being suggested, however, that the neglect of the Afro-Barbadian population during the First World War, and even after 1918, cannot be explained solely in economic terms. Some analysis of the racial attitudes and practices of the ruling class is vitally necessary in order to gain a full understanding of the transformation of Barbadian society.

Before the outbreak of the Great War, increasing evidence of malnutrition among the black population was being brought to the attention of the ruling elite. Public Health Inspector John Hutson, in his report of 1913, made reference to the increasing presence of Vitamin B deficiency diseases such as pellagra and beri-beri among the Afro-Barbadian population. He suggested that special attention should be devoted to the cultivation of peas and beans of all kinds to supplement the low protein diet 'on which the labouring classes now exist.'[11] This advice was completely ignored, as more and more lands, including the acreages under cotton were put into sugar cultivation in order to capitalize on the artificially high sugar prices being offered as a result of the war. For example, the acreage planted in cotton dropped from 3,970 acres in 1913 to an average of 1,078 by 1916 (see table 3.1). Before 1914, approximately 7,000 bales of cotton were exported annually, but in 1916 only 3,500 bales were exported.[12]

## Table 3.1
## Drop in Acreage of Cotton Cultivated 1913–16

| Year | Acreage |
|------|---------|
| 1913 | 3,970 |
| 1914 | 2,985 |
| 1915 | 3,323 |
| 1916 | 1,078 |

Source: Probyn to Long. October 22, 1917 in Dispatches from Governors to Secretary of State, December 1916 to December 1920. Department of Archives.

**Table 3.2**
**Sugar Production in Barbados 1914–20**

| Year | Tons |
|------|------|
| 1914 | 29,404 |
| 1915 | 29,847 |
| 1916 | 73,581 |
| 1917 | 69,367 |
| 1918 | 57,191 |
| 1919 | 64,628 |
| 1920 | 48,212 |

Source: Noel Deer, *The History of Sugar Vol. I* (London: Chapman and Hall Ltd, 1949).

**Table 3.3**
**Average Price of Raw Sugar in London 1919–20 (in shillings per cwt)**

| Year | Price |
|------|-------|
| 1914 | 11/7 |
| 1915 | 14/4 |
| 1916 | 24/3 |
| 1917 | 31/6 |
| 1918 | 33/0 |
| 1919 | 38/5 |
| 1920 | 58/0 |

Source: Noel Deer, *The History of Sugar Vol. I* (London: Chapman and Hall Ltd, 1949).

On the other hand, increased acreages devoted to sugar cultivation, along with excellent rainfall during the war years, resulted in a dramatic increase in sugar production. Sugar output grew from 29,404 tons in 1914 to 73,581 tons in 1916 (see table 3.2). Sugar exports, in essence, reflected the increased acreages devoted to the planting of sugar cane. The amount of produce exported from January to September 1916 was 46,347 tons of sugar and 62,767 puncheons of molasses, as compared with 26,565 tons of sugar and 51,566 puncheons of molasses in 1915.

Provision growing, in the meantime, was given little priority by estates, despite the legal provisions of the Vegetable Produce Act. With the reduction of food imports as a result of the war, a food crisis engulfed the island. Food shortages had become so acute that the Executive Committee, mainly at the instigation of the Governor, suggested the passing of a Vegetable Produce Bill to ease the food crisis.[59] The planter class grudgingly adopted the measure, and expressed much joy when the Act was hurriedly amended at the end of the war. The problems of squalor, disease and malnutrition among the black population continued unabated.

From 1883 to 1914, the average price of sugar on the London market fluctuated between 7 s 0 d per cwt and 19 s 0 d per cwt, but from 1915 it rose steadily from 14 s 4 d per cwt to as high as 58 s 0 d in 1920.[14] In May 1920, raw sugar sold in London for as high as 146 s per cwt Barbadian planters, capitalizing on the high prices during the war years, recorded capital accumulations of £500,000 each year, a period of unprecedented prosperity, which was last seen more than 100 years before when sugar sold for as high as 72 s per cwt.[15]

This newfound wealth encouraged some estate owners to resort to much speculation. For example, in 1920 alone, 24 estates, comprising 6,766 acres, were sold for £990,650 or an average of £146 per acre.[16] This newfound wealth did not 'extend to the whole community,' but instead was employed mainly to fuel the spirit of land speculation in the island, to clear estates of long accumulated debt and to improve machinery in the sugar factories.[17] Afro-Barbadians, except for moderate salary increases, derived few benefits, and were accorded no improvement in their physical environment, in spite of the temporary prosperity. The planters, it can be argued, showed good business sense by seizing the opportunity to improve the financial position and the productive capacity of the island's most vital industry. However, it must be noted that not even a small percentage of the capital was devoted to the upliftment of the black population or to enhance the infrastructural development of the island. In short, the merchant-planter elite missed the opportunity to rid the island of some of the squalor and disease.

## Deliberate Neglect of the Afro-Barbadian Population

This wilful neglect of Afro-Barbadians by the oligarchy during the war years was deliberate. It continued after 1918 and throughout the early twentieth century. For example, in 1923, a Reserve or 'Calamity Fund' had been established by the Treasury. By March 31, 1925, the balance of credit invested in the Fund, including interest, stood at £136,652. In the financial year 1925–26 the Fund had shown a surplus of £70,000 and was described as experiencing 'a very favourable situation.'[18] Despite this healthy financial position, no conscious effort was made to initiate capital works programmes, or policies to generate employment for the Afro-Barbadian population. The pleadings of the Governor-in-Executive Committee to reduce the level of poverty among the black people went unnoticed. The legislature, nevertheless, was satisfied with the state of the island's finances and sufficiently proud of its management to state boldly:

> The House are pleased to note that the financial position of the colony is very satisfactory and that there is a considerable estimated surplus and will consider the appropriation of it when the question comes before them.[19]

The 'question' apparently never appeared before them, for despite the fluctuating fortunes of the Barbadian economy, the policy of socio-economic indifference toward the Afro-Barbadian population continued throughout the early twentieth century. In 1936, the said Reserve Fund was again in a healthy position, but the legislature's promises to relieve the suffering among the black population were never translated into reality.[20] Instead, the merchant-planter elite boasted openly about their shrewd management of the island's finances. Repeated requests from the Governor, the UNIA, the WMA, and journalist Clennell Wickham,[21] to devote some attention to the social and economic advancement of black Barbadians did not touch the social conscience of the ruling class enough to prod them into action.

The same parsimonious attitude to the spending of the financial resources of the island, however, was never observed in relation to the interests of the ruling elite, especially pertaining to the survival of the sugar industry. The onset of any crises, the majority of which were brought about mainly by falling sugar prices in the traditional London market, was met by prompt capital infusion. In fact, the formation of the Sugar Industry Agricultural Bank in 1907, from the original sum of £80,000 donated to the island as a result of the recommendations of the 1897 Royal Commission, is indicative of the ruling elite's commitment to the preservation of the industry. Whereas in other British West Indian islands similar assistance was whittled away among individual estates in the form of short-term assistance, the establishment of a bank by the Barbadians proved to be a wise decision.[22] The bank provided credit to sugar estates during the most trying times in the life of the industry and averted bankruptcy on a huge scale. In 1921, it was indebted to local banks in the amount of £67,000, and had received withdrawals by estates the same year, over a three-month period, of about £106,000. There were also due to the bank loans, made on the 1920 crop, of £249,000.[23] Of the £538,302 loaned against the 1921 harvest, £462,107 was still owed at the end of the crop. £221,311 was outstanding at the end of the 1922 crop season.[24] This state of affairs placed the bank in a rather precarious financial position. The management of the bank threatened to make no financial advances to estates on the 1923 crop.[25]

The plantocracy, recognizing the vulnerable financial state of the bank, became alarmed and determined to reverse this trend. By a frantic, yet coordinated piece of lobbying, the bank was saved when the colonial Governor was instructed to raise a loan on the foreign money market to be put at the disposal of the bank. He succeeded and it was saved.

The strategy of the merchant-planter elite to save the sugar industry was pursued with much vigour at the highest level of local society, and even in the international arena. When Major E. F. L. Wood, Under-Secretary of State for the Colonies, visited the island in 1922, a powerful delegation presented a somber case for the revival of the sugar industry. They argued that horrible and catastrophic rebellions, marked by widespread destruction of property and lives, would inundate Barbados should the sugar industry be allowed to collapse. Major Wood received the deputation in the most cordial fashion and, perhaps alarmed at the somber attitude of the planters, promised to place the problems of the local industry before the Secretary of State.[26] No representation on behalf of the plight of the black labouring classes, however, was presented to Major Wood. Even the conservative *Agricultural Reporter* was compelled to lament this neglect:

> It should be noted that the Governor of Barbados, although time afforded, never extended to representatives of the Middle Classes, or to the Masses, the Labour Classes, any opportunity of making representations to Mr Wood on behalf of these nacoms of the

community. As a matter of fact, Mr Wood has been brought into contact only with members of the Oligarchy. In these Democratic days no good can result from such a narrow and offensive course of action.[27]

Again, in October 1929, when the West Indian Sugar Commission visited the island, the Barbadian plantocracy seized the opportunity, through the Barbados Sugar Producers Association and its affiliate members, to put their case in the most organized and forceful manner. In fact, no opportunity was ever missed to lobby any visiting British official who was willing to listen to them. In addition, they petitioned the Colonial Office on occasion, in the most earnest way. A 1935 petition forcefully highlighted the low sugar prices obtained on the London market and the inability of Barbados to maintain the 'social and educational needs' of the population. It wrote of a 'singularly dangerous situation' which faced the island should the industry decline.[28]

Later the same year, the legislature refused to wait on visiting officials or resort to humble petitioning of the Colonial Office. Instead a delegation comprising S. C. Thorne, G. D. Pile, G. D. Leacock and the Director of Agriculture, Dr J. S. Saint, visited England to put the case of the sugar industry before the British Government.[29] Once more, working-class representation was strikingly absent from the delegation. Clennell Wickham was compelled to ask, in one of his columns about the London meeting, 'Will labourers' difficulties be revealed?' [30]

It is very difficult to determine the extent of white Barbadian influence on the direction of British policy in the West Indies. It is clear, however, that they often pursued what they wanted for the island with vigour, especially in relation to the financing of the local sugar industry. This feat was usually achieved by presenting the financial woes of the industry in the gloomiest terms, and, then to associate any major downturn with the threat of instantaneous rebellion among the black population. Financial anguish existed at times, but the difficulties of the sugar industry were often conveniently exaggerated in order to gain the British Government's sympathy and attention.

## Declining Fortunes and Racial Stereotypes

Shortly after the Great War, the market for West Indian sugar started to shrink, as the conditions which created the artificial shortages, and ultimately the high prices, disappeared. Those planters who bought up sugar estates during the boom period found themselves in a very difficult position. The *Barbados Globe*, while commenting on this short duration of land speculation, wrote of the 'mushrooming millionaires of yesterday' being transformed into the 'paupers of today' in a short space of time:

> Others again rushed wildly in for widening their landed possessions, and bought out at fairy prices all who had the sense to feel content with what they had amassed. Syndicates were hurriedly formed to the exclusion and frequent surprise of some close friend and relative, money was raised and injected, and it looked twelve months ago as if Barbados would soon be owned and held by a favourite few.[31]

When the price of sugar fell, over £60,000 was lost by some planters who had hoarded sugar in the hope of capitalizing on higher prices in the near future.[32]

Prolonged drought during the 1920–21 period worsened the situation, and bankrupted estates were being sold, resulting in a deteriorating unemployment situation.[33] In addition, the cost of living reached its highest peak since 1914, especially during August 1920, when the retail price of 25 basic commodities in common household use stood at an average of 220 per cent higher than the retail prices prevailing in August 1914.[34] The labouring classes, who depended heavily on a fixed weekly income, were hardest hit. The re-introduction of the Vegetable Produce Act was suggested by the Governor-in-Executive Committee as a possible solution to the hardships which faced the labouring classes as a result of these sharp increases in the cost of living. This suggestion, however, was vigorously opposed by the planters, who argued that the sad plight of the black population was due to their laziness and a tendency to indulge in praedial larceny, rather than to price increases.

This racial stereotype was clearly highlighted as the debate on the amendment to Vegetable Produce Bill itself occurred in the House of Assembly in July 1920. A lot of emphasis was placed on the alleged increasing incidences of lawlessness and praedial larceny in the island, rather than on the main objectives of the Bill, that is, to improve the food situation in the island. Instead, some members of the House pounced on the opportunity to put, in the same Bill, harsh penalties such as corporal punishment for men, and hair cropping for women convicted of crop larceny. Dr Boxhill, G. Elliott

Sealy, T. Chandler, Edmund Baeza and H. Graham Yearwood were the most vociferous advocates of these forms of punishment.[35] No sympathy was to be extended to the offenders as the debate took on a tone more reminiscent of seventeenth-century slave society than twentieth-century free labour society. The outspoken, conservative elements in the Assembly got their way with the punitive measures.

But the cropping of women's hair, a punishment which was discontinued in British prisons in the nineteenth-century, caught the attention of the Secretary of State. In a dispatch, he reminded the Assemblymen that the practice was a primitive and degrading punishment to inflict on women.[36] He insisted that the penalty should be removed from the local Act. His insistence, however, only served to incur the wrath of the conservative elements in the legislature, the majority of whom openly expressed their disagreement. Their resentment of the Secretary of State's concerns was best expressed in the attitude of Dr Boxhill:

> The Secretary of State probably thinks that it is a case of cutting
> long plaits hanging down to the ground which will not grow again
> in a few weeks, and even if it is an indignity it can be concealed.[37]

Clennell Wickham, writing in the *Barbados Herald*, was quick to pick up the racist sentiments expressed in Dr Boxhill's speech:

> The inference is clear. The indignity of hair cutting practised on a
> woman of Negro origin is nothing at all. It is mere fun. One of the
> characteristics of Ulotrichian origin is short woolly hair. Such hair by
> cropping is rendered very little shorter. Hence the indignity would
> be less than if practised upon a person of European origin whose
> hair is longer. This statement is insulting, most insulting indeed.[38]

The hostility directed at the Afro-Barbadian population by some members of the House of Assembly cannot be overstated. For example, Edmund Baeza, in his contribution to the debate, suggested that some 'more cruel methods of punishment than flogging would be the best thing to be done.' He insisted that the notion being held by some benevolent citizens that it was cruel to flog Afro-Barbadians for praedial larceny was a 'maudlin sentiment' which should not be tolerated, in that the circumstances in Barbados demanded that 'we have got to be cruel to be kind.'[39]

## The Print Media Supports the Merchant-Planter Elite

These unsympathetic attitudes of the Assemblymen were upheld by supporters of the ruling class in the local press. The *Barbados Standard* wrote of the 'hooligans' and 'creatures' who raided potato fields at night, and 'the canaille (pack of dogs) of the country districts who terrorized this once peaceful island.'[40] The *Agricultural Reporter*, in a similar tone, stressed the need to rid the island by 'safe and healthy emigration' of the 'social scourge of loafers and vagrants' and of 'the habits of idleness' cultivated by the black population.[41] The *Barbados Globe* argued that the harshest measures possible should be meted out to the 'heartless vermin' who 'have no real human existence and hence cannot lay claim to the consideration demanded for human folk.'[42] It recommended the use of the cat-o'-nine-tails as a psychological deterrent against those convicted for praedial larceny:

> There seems to be some good in the policy recently adopted for exterminating a certain form of crime, viz. praedial larceny, by imposing short sentences when convicted and applying the 'cat.' The short sentence sends the culprit home to be seen and his wounds caused by the lash attended to by those around him....[43]

The advocacy of such brutal forms of punishment by the ruling class is frightening to even contemplate. Governor O'Brien, who at times had shown some sympathy for the deprived state of the black labouring classes, was also carried away in the wave of hostile feelings. He wrote to his superiors at the Colonial Office complaining about a 'loafing class to whom steady work is abhorrent' and who brought up their 'offspring to regard theft and imprisonment as of no importance.'[44]

Such an unbending spirit, it seems, provided the justification for some of the most cruel and excessive forms of punishment for what would appear at times to be minor offences. For example, on August 3, 1919, Beresford Moore, an 11-year-old of Whitehall tenantry, St Michael, received 12 strokes with a tamarind rod for stealing sugar cane valued at l d from George Sealy.[45] Gordon Alkins, 13 years old, received eight strokes for stealing 'a small quantity of cocoa' from a lighter.[46] Henry Brathwaite, eight years old, received ten strokes for stealing three ears of corn.[47] Francis Johnson, nine years old, an assistant herdsman of Haggatt Hall plantation, received eight strokes with a tamarind rod for stealing a green sugar apple valued at a penny.[48]

Crime, and the penalties imposed on criminals in any society should always be considered in relation to the unique customs, mores and traditions of the particular society in which they occur. In addition, the historian must be careful when passing judgment on the penalties imposed for crime in any society to pay particular attention to the value of the existing currency vis-à-vis the purchasing power of goods and services at the particular time. The above-mentioned offences were committed by very young children, who in the majority of cases, as the Courts heard, lived a life of severe material deprivation, neglect and illiteracy. Yet there is no indication that any attempt was made by the judiciary to understand how this deprived social environment impacted on the behaviour of these juveniles. The young offenders were simply regarded as common criminals and, in some cases, received punishments which did not appear to be commensurate with the crime.

But of course, the judiciary was dominated by members of the merchant-planter elite, or aspirants to and sympathizers of the oligarchy, who shared similar perceptions of the black population, and their judgements reflected such convictions. It is very difficult for any group, or even an individual, to overtly oppose the accepted beliefs and practices of the ruling class of any society. The socialization process places tremendous pressure on individuals to conform, in most instances, to the tide of public opinion on any major issue espoused by the ruling elite. In Barbados, the dominant racist ideas which influenced the dispensation of justice were formulated and espoused by a white oligarchy and reinforced by the local press, which had tremendous influence over local public opinion. The juvenile offenders, one can argue, were caught up in a forceful wave of racist thinking, which advocated the stamping out of crime and lawlessness among the black population as a matter of urgency, through harsh penal measures.

The racist remarks directed at the Afro-Barbadian population by the merchant-planter elite, and amplified by the local press, therefore, provided the justification for the tightening of the screws on the black population. The *Barbados Globe* kept up its rhetoric about 'wicked lawlessness, which must be put down' immediately.[49] The *Barbados Standard* not only expressed concern at the number of robberies in Bridgetown and its suburbs, but called for the infusion of new blood into the Police Force, and an updating of the law to provide for a 'practical Vagrancy Act.'[50] The *Agricultural Reporter* joined in the attack, but directed its attention at the Chief Executive, Governor Charles O'Brien:

> For ourselves we wish to join in the protest raised against the abominable and disgusting behaviour indulged in daily on the highways of this City by a steadily growing army of lewd women and idle, dissolute vagabond men that infest it…there is, in our opinion sufficient power vested in the Executive by the Legislature to enable the situation to be grappled with and fully remedied.[51]

A similar concern was expressed by the powerful Chamber of Commerce who implored the Colonial Secretary to investigate the matter.[52] The outcome resulted in stricter legislative control for the black population, in the form of an amendment to the Vagrancy Act (1897 – 3) and the Vagrancy (Amendment) Act (1919 – 13). It gave the police sweeping powers to deal with anyone 'lying or loitering in any highway, yard, or other place between 6 p.m. and 5 a.m.' The Attorney General stressed that the Act brought into the category of idle and disorderly such 'daytime loafers as give cause for suspicion.'[53]

Such sweeping powers in the hands of the Police alarmed the Colonial Office. When Viscount Milner sought an explanation of the circumstances which led to such a far-reaching Vagrancy Act, his main query was played down. Instead he was bombarded with tales of crime, lawlessness and idling in the City as justification for the punitive statutes. In addition, Governor O'Brien assured him that there was no chance of the Police ever abusing their power because the criminals were well known. The Secretary of State was warned that the only fear in Barbados 'would be if the consent of His Majesty was withheld; it would result in an exaggeration of the situation.'[54] Milner agreed, and endorsed the newly amended Vagrancy Act.

There was, however, a feeling among some sections of the white population that the revised Vagrancy Act did not go far enough. The *Barbados Standard* called for an extension of it, with two stipulations: that 'every reputed thief shall be called upon to give a satisfactory account of his whereabouts to the Police on the occasion of every robbery' and that special powers should be given to the Police to deal with every 'habitual loafer' who idled in the city.[55] The *Standard* proceeded to advocate drastic measures which, if enforced, would have led to a virtual police state, for unemployed blacks:

> We therefore think that the proposed amendments may be...
> extended so as to include every able-bodied person who tends to
> become an habitual loafer on the public highway or in the villages
> of the island. If after due warning by the Police, these are found
> pursuing their daily vocation of irresponsible loafing they should
> be arrested and placed before the magistrate, and if unable to prove
> their means of honest livelihood, work should be found for them in
> road-making or cleaning drains...if they refuse this work and persist
> in returning to their old habit, then they may be allowed to try their
> hand at the picking of Oakum at Glendairy.[56]

This attempt at the wholesale curbing of the fundamental civil liberties
of the Afro-Barbadian population, under the guise of suppressing anti-social
behaviour, was supported again by other newspapers. The *Barbados Globe* wrote
of 'an exceedingly dangerous condition of things which must be put down.'[57]
The *Agricultural Reporter* wrote of a 'typical spirit of lawlessness and rudeness
which is fast spreading amongst the masses of this country' and which must
be checked, not only by firm policing of the unemployed, but by 'emigration
to suitable fields.'[58]

Only the *Barbados Weekly Herald* demonstrated any sympathy for the
sad plight of the masses. On one occasion, Clennel Wickham described the
*Barbados Standard* as a 'villifier of the masses' who

> ...has been most persistent and consistent in declaring that our
> population was largely made up of shiftless, and congenitally lazy
> citizens, who shirked work even though it was impossible for them
> to obtain some and showed preferences for, to them, the congenial
> task of pilfering from their neighbours, to that of earning an honest
> penny by the sweat of the brow.[59]

The *Barbados Herald* called on the colonial authorities to 'make provisions
at once for a reduction of the evil' by introducing 'a broader and better system
of elementary education and technical training' as well as emigration. These
programmes, the *Herald* insisted, should be financed by a fair and equitable
system of Income Tax, rather than the existing system of *ad valorem* duties
which targeted the goods used most frequently by the poor.[60]

In response to the planters' persistent requests to control idle youth, the
Assembly debated the Habitual Idlers Bill in 1919, instead of trying to rid the

island of poverty. According to the Bill, a habitual idler was defined as a person 'who has no visible lawful means of subsistence and who, being able to labour, habitually abstains from work.'[61] Section 5:2 of the Bill, in a noticeable shift away from the traditions of British Law, insisted that the prosecutor should not be bound to prove a person has no visible lawful means of subsistence, but rather the accused person should have to prove that he has a lawful means of subsistence. Even H. G. Yearwood, one of the most conservative members of the legislature, in his contribution to the debate on the Bill, exposed the travesty of justice contained therein:

> I am afraid I cannot vote for this section because it practically would mean that any man charged before a police magistrate with being a habitual idler will be presumed to be guilty, before he is tried, and he will have to prove his innocence. That is fundamentally and absolutely against all British law, a man is charged and it is the duty of the person who is making the charge to prove that it is brought home.[62]

Similar comments on the Bill were made by Dr Massiah, G. C. Williams and C. P. Clarke. But the dominant tone of the debate, especially in the contributions of Edmund Baeza and Stanley Robinson, suggested that the pressing need for collective security in the island relegated the infringements of individual liberties to a position of lesser importance.[63] The Habitual Idler Act was passed by an overwhelming majority in the Lower Chamber, despite the queries raised by some Assemblymen as to the inadequacies of the Bill. It took a concerted campaign by Clennel Wickham in the *Weekly Herald* to force the Legislative Council to throw out the Bill.

The 'idlers' who were stigmatized with so much emotion by the merchant-planter elite were the large groups of unemployed youth unable to find work as a result of the lack of imaginative policies from the said ruling class. The punitive legislation for the further suppression of these people was framed in misconceptions about Afro-Barbadians and fuelled by a rabid racial prejudice.

A widely held belief suggested that the gangs of idle youths provided the breeding ground for criminal activity. Every criminal act, or violent confrontation with the police, was attributed to vagabond idle youths. For example, when, in March 1919, a scuffle broke out between the police and residents of Golden Square, in which stones were thrown and firearms discharged, the usual rhetoric of disorder and lawlessness emerged with a vengeance.[64] The discharge of firearms signalled a dangerous trend which alarmed the white elite. This potential for trouble had to be curbed. The Assembly, therefore, passed the Peace Preservation Act 1919, No. 6, a transcript of the Peace Preservation Ordinance 1897 of the Gold Coast, as an appropriate response. It gave the Governor-in-Executive Committee power to proclaim any district to be free of arms except those authorized by a Proclamation. Magistrates, in turn, were given the authority to issue warrants to search for arms in any locality, after the proclamation was read.[65]

In any society, a close observation of the letter of the law is usually a useful indicator of the spirit in which the legislation was conceived by the lawmakers. In early twentieth-century Barbados, the Habitual Idlers Act, the Vagrancy Act, the Peace Preservation Act, and other similar forms of legislation reflected the concerns and the anxiety of the colonial officials and the merchant-planter elite. This legislative encirclement of the Afro-Barbadian population was achieved by a formidable ruling class who felt insecure because of what it interpreted as potential unrest, and attempted to protect its interest by resorting to its control of the legislature as a device for entrenching its rule.

Apart from its law-making powers, the oligarchy also built up a well-organized and disciplined police force. This force kept all suspected 'agitators' and subversive elements under close surveillance.[66] A Volunteer Force provided backup services, should any social upheavals occur. The increased presence of island constables throughout the 1930s provided a useful policing presence at the micro level of society in the rural districts of the island. By 1934, there were 700 Parish and Island Constables.[67] The constables were trained, among other things, in the detection and the prevention of cane fires. Plantation watchmen were urged to be vigilant in the exercise of their duties.[68] In addition, being a British dependency, the ruling class were no doubt aware of the Mother Country's commitment to the stability of the island and so would have quelled any upheaval if the need arose. In short, the Afro-Barbadian population faced a phalanx of a security apparatus which set out to control every facet of their lives.

## True Colours Revealed at Private Meetings

Further probing below the surface of the planter-dominated legislature is essential in order to grasp fully the feelings and attitudes which motivated the white elite to formulate measures to keep Afro-Barbadians in line. Such an understanding can be gleaned from a critical observation of the behaviour of members of the merchant-planter elite in the relaxed atmosphere of their homes, private boardrooms, exclusive clubs and organizations such as the Bridgetown Club and the Yacht Club, and committee meetings among their own kinfolk. In fact, an individual's true behaviour is usually more apparent in his micro-environment of close interpersonal relationships among immediate family, friends and associates of the same racial and class status, than in the macro-environment of the society's accepted value system and behavioural code. In essence, members of the merchant-planter elite who gathered at private luncheons, and in exclusive clubs, were more revealing of their true feelings toward the black population there, than in any formal setting such as the legislature. It is the tapping of these sources which are most revealing of the merchant-planter elite's racial prejudices and class snobbery.

Such an opportunity presents itself for the historian when, on July 30, 1919, at a private luncheon held at his residence; the Governor informed some of the island's leading planters of a situation which concerned him. He said changes had been brought about all over the world as a result of the First World War, and these were most evidently expressed in the demands of the labouring classes throughout the West Indies. He mentioned the presence of an organization (UNIA) in one of the West Indian islands designed to 'stir up trouble by pitting black against white' and he did not like it.[69] Governor O'Brien then attributed the feeling of apprehension among the local black labouring classes to 'agitators,' to profiteering by merchants, to dissatisfied war veterans, and to a local press which highlighted the apparent bad treatment of blacks at Cardiff and Liverpool during the race riots there. He concluded by appealing to the planters to put their 'house in order' by encouraging amicable relations with their employees, by assisting with a large-scale emigration scheme, and by initiating public works projects to assist the unemployed.[70]

Much apprehension can be detected in O'Brien's remarks. He no doubt feared an escalation of any local discontent into open social turbulence, and so his suggestions, especially the emigration scheme, were designed to reduce the level of discontent in the society. The representative group of planters shared his concerns, but baulked at the suggestion of initiating public work projects, probably because of the expenditure which would have been involved. They indicated a willingness, however, to discuss the matter 'at a later date.' The only suggestion which received a favourable response was the idea of mass emigration.[71]

In December 1919, after much delay, Governor O'Brien returned again to the same theme in an address to a representative group of the island's leading merchants and planters. Representing the merchants were George Manning, H. B. G. Austin, F. O. Swan, and J. R. Bancroft. Representing the planters were G. L. Pile, A. P. Haynes, E. W. Mahon, Dr C. E. Gooding and Dr T. W. Hawkins. Together, this representative group of planters and merchants, with their business and family ties, constituted a very powerful and influential interest group. O'Brien began his speech again, by stressing his acute care, in all his public utterances, to avoid any remarks 'that could encourage labour in any demands.' The strength of the local constabulary and the Defence Force, efficient though they were, was never designed to be distributed throughout the island and so, in the event of any disturbances, they would be heavily taxed to guard the Armoury, the Wireless Station, the Water Supply, and the Railway, the latter two more so, owing to the length of their lines. The Railway would have caused some concern, after a number of attempts were made to derail trains. And with lines running from Bridgetown to isolated rural districts, it was difficult to protect them against saboteurs.[72] The Volunteer Force, with the greater number of members residing in and around Bridgetown, and in full-time employment, did not provide a comforting thought. O'Brien called again on the employers 'to put your house in order; do not wait until trouble arrives to do so.' He concluded on a note of warning which is worth quoting in full, for it expressed the underlying fear and tension which existed in Barbados at the time:

> It is easy to say no trouble can come to Barbados. If you are satisfied that the labouring classes are, as stated by the Sec. of State, as well now as under pre-war conditions despite the largely increased cost of living, you have anyway no reason to fear criticism. If, on the other hand, labourers cannot earn a sufficiency to maintain themselves and their families throughout the year, surely it is advisable to put the matter on a sound business footing. You have had good years for your industry and it is not surprising that the labouring classes here as elsewhere should desire to benefit from the better times.[73]

O'Brien was offering suggestions to defuse what he perceived as an impending clash between labour and capital and, possibly, even deeper social and industrial unrest. A dockworkers' strike in Port of Spain, Trinidad, in early December 1919, and a riot in Tobago, were extensively covered in the local press.[74] Around the same time, there were disturbances in Jamaica, in the Bahamas and in St Lucia. These events coincided with similar signs of unrest at home, and the local authorities were becoming alarmed. During February 1919, the porters and lightermen of Gardiner Austin & Co. Ltd went on strike. This was followed by the coal heavers' and lightermen's strike at Laurie and Co. Ltd. An increase in pay per trip led to a reluctant resumption of work on both occasions.[75] In January 1919, a lightermen's strike petered out, due to a lack of organization, without any improvement being achieved. In February, stevedore labourers formed a 'league' and went on strike. They demanded a working day from 7:00 a.m. to 5:00 p.m. and a pay increase of $2 per day.[76] In August, railway drivers struck after a rejection of their application for a 'living wage.'[77] The *Barbados Globe* was moved to comment:

> Barbados is just now passing through an epidemic of strikes among most branches of labour; it began on the wharf amongst the Lightermen and Steamship labourers, then it was extended to the coal-heavers and coal-carriers; now the infection has reached Mr Chase's staff of street-sweepers and rumour has it that a few days ago the labourers on a St Michael plantation had also struck. This claim is for an increase of wages, and the success of the one is an inspiration to the other to hold out for what they deem to be just and fair.[78]

The *Globe* concluded on the usual theme of perceiving Afro-Barbadian labourers as unproductive, impulsive and prone to making unreasonable demands. The white employer class had always argued that such character traits demand that a tough anti-worker stance should be adopted at all times. This fixed perception, no doubt, stood in the way of progress between workers and employers in Barbados, but more particularly, it fuelled a dominant ideology which perceived black labourers as mere 'hewers of wood and drawers of water,' incapable of independent thought and action. This potentially unstable industrial climate, according to the merchant-planter elite, required close monitoring at all times.

But coupled with the strikes and rumours of strikes, potato raids and cane fires caught the attention of the local authorities. A potato raid was classified as a situation 'where three or more persons are concerned in making a raid on a field of provisions.'[79] According to this definition, there were then a considerable number of potato raids in Barbados during the early twentieth century, probably a continuation of those which occurred during the late nineteenth-century. In June 1917, a series of potato raids in the parish of St Lucy and in the Speightstown area forced the local authorities to offer a reward of £25 for information leading to the arrest of the perpetrators.[80] On the night of March 1, 1918, the Belle estate in St Michael was raided by a 'riotous mob' of 80 or more of the 'lower class' who made a violent assault on a constable as he attempted to intervene in their nocturnal activities.[81] On October 27, 1921, three men entered Mount Standfast Plantation, St James, and carried off 650 pounds of Indian corn fodder.[82] At Porter's estates, also in St James, 14 men stole '200 holes of potatoes' and fired four shots at the watchman.[83] On June 22, 1921, 20 men stole an acre of provisions from Rock Hall estate, St Peter. Laurie Cummins, the watchman, was forced to jump to safety in a dry well to avoid three shots which were fired at him.[84]

Some of these raids appeared to be organized, and the use of firearms on some occasions led the ruling classes to fume about armed gangs which threatened life and property. They insisted that the potato raids were the acts of seditious elements and should be firmly stamped out. G. D. L. Pile recommended the 'cat' as the only suitable punishment, as 'prison life was too easy.'[85] H. W. Reece, a coloured Assemblyman, was perceptive enough on one occasion to warn the House of Assembly to make some distinction between armed raiders who stole estate crops for the market and those who stole to satisfy genuine hunger. He called for leniency in punishing the latter type of offenders.[86] To a large extent his advice was ignored and the relentless cry for the harshest penalties possible continued quite unabated.

The *Agricultural Reporter* took a similar position, insisting that the potato raiders were the 'lawless, idle vagabonds who were found in the thousands throughout the island.'[87] The *Barbados Standard* referred to them as a 'riotous mob' and a 'common herd' who deserved 'the cat.'[88] The *Barbados Globe*, in a similar tone, had this recommendation:

> We believe in the healing influence for good of the cat, and, as often perhaps as any of our contemporaries, have strenuously advocated its use when the culprit happens to have already passed beyond the stage of reform.[89]

The constant reference to the apparent scourge of lawlessness, violence and immorality among the black population of Barbados was never viewed in relation to the economic depression after the war, and the attendant ills of unemployment, underemployment, and, ultimately, frustration and alienation. Furthermore, even though the black labouring population depended largely on a fixed wage for its existence, no attempt was made in the post-war era to grant wage increases which were commensurate with the increased cost of living. Instead, members of the white oligarchy resorted to the usual racial stereotype of the lazy, thriftless negro, in order to rationalize the local situation. George D. L. Pile, prominent planter and Assemblyman, for example, was a vociferous critic who always pontificated about the black labouring classes 'who would not work for as much money as they could earn.' He went on to suggest that Afro-Barbadians were inclined as a habit to work only four days a week instead of five, even when work was available.[90] Dr T. W. Hawkins, prominent medical practitioner, Assemblyman and planter, reiterated Pile's view that 'there was a majority of the community who did not work and would not be persuaded to work.'[91] F. O. Swan testified to the granting of 'adequate' wage increases in the post-war era and so, in his opinion, there was no distress among the black population. He affirmed that many poor people travelled by train and he did not know of any 'dissatisfaction' in Barbados. If any trouble should start in the island it would come from the idlers on the wharf. He recommended their wholesale arrest as a solution to the problem of idling.[92] E. M. Mahon, a prominent merchant, summed up the racial attitudes of the ruling elite when he asserted, *inter alia*,

> What the labouring population insisted upon was their leisure and, make the wages what you will, the people take their leisure. They would work for a certain sum. They would be willing to forego the balance of their possible earnings for their holiday.[93]

The merchant-planter elite no doubt perceived the black population as an unambitious, simple-minded and pleasure-seeking group. According to this stereotype, their main intention was to work as little as possible, or, at least, only to earn enough to maximize their idleness, and to pursue crime. There is a striking similarity here between this perception of Afro-Barbadians and the racial stereotypes of the Victorian era. However, an objective analysis of early twentieth-century Barbados would reveal that the black labouring classes did not opt to work four days a week, but rather were forced to do so by a plantation system which came under severe strain as a result of the post-war depression.[94] The sugar industry, therefore, did not always offer steady employment. Shipping had also slowed down when Lamport and Holt Line and the Canadian National Steamship Company discontinued their services to persons from the port of Bridgetown, thereby aggravating the unemployment situation there.[95] In addition, the war bonus of $2.00 per trip earned by stevedores and lightermen was discontinued after 1918. The economic depression and the rise of unemployment demanded not only a sympathetic outlook, but the prudent use of financial resources. The ruling class failed to adopt this approach.

Yet, despite this bleak economic outlook, the official statistics reveal a steady increase in the number of Friendly Societies, and the savings in them by Afro-Barbadians. At December 1937, for example, 199 Friendly Societies existed in Barbados, with a membership of 54,484 and a total contribution of £69,429. The majority of the funds invested in these societies came from remittances sent by relatives abroad and pittances saved from meagre salaries.[96] These figures did not include the funds saved by individuals in private 'meeting turns,' in the Government Savings Bank, or in other forms of private savings. Despite the economic downturn in the country, the labouring population displayed signs of thriftiness. This evidence certainly suggests no proof of inherent thriftlessness among the black population, yet the myth persisted with vigour among the ruling elite. To justify minimal wage increases for the labouring population, the myth of the lazy negro was invoked more than ever. Colonial Secretary Francis Jenkins echoed this ideological conviction on one occasion:

> Every old Barbadian who has to do with labour will tell you that if you increase the local rate of wages you decrease the amount of work in proportion. That is, I think, true of every African and not peculiar to Barbados. If an African can earn enough to keep himself for a week by working for three days he will not as a rule, work for six.[97]

Jenkins's pronouncement reveals a kind of thinking which assists one in understanding why the representative group of merchants and planters at the December 1919 meeting opposed wage increases with such vigour. The opposition was based on deeply ingrained stereotypes of Afro-Barbadians' apparent laziness, rather than a mature, objective analysis of the socio-economic conditions in Barbados.

There had been much discussion, also, by the island's leading planters and the local print media, that profiteering by merchants and shopkeepers, rather than low wages, was largely responsible for the deprived state of the labouring classes.[98] A heated debate over the issue prompted the Governor to set up a Profiteering Commission in 1920, comprising prominent citizens E. B. Skeete, F. A. C. Collymore, E. S. Hailey, R. J. C. Clinkett and John R. Bovell.

## The Profiteering Debate

The terms of reference of the Commission were to investigate whether profiteering existed on the island and, if so, what measures should be taken to deal with it. After 37 meetings and the submission of numerous memoranda, the Commission reported that no evidence of profiteering existed on the island.[99]

It should be stated, however, that due to the largely, unregulated mercantile section and the underdeveloped state of the colonial bureaucracy, it was difficult, or even impossible, to detect any concealed evidence of profiteering. It is even more difficult, therefore, for a present-day researcher to determine the level of profiteering, if any existed, especially in the light of the near inaccessibility of certain documents of the corporate sector. However, one thing is certain, concerning the profiteering debate, and it is the fact that the accusation was apparently deliberately fomented by some estate owners against the mercantile community, probably in an attempt to remove the blame for the deprived conditions of the black labouring classes from their shoulders.[100] The heated debate continued after the Commission submitted its report and so Governor O'Brien instructed the Colonial Secretary, Francis Jenkins, to investigate the allegations as well. He also claimed that he found no evidence of profiteering, even though he observed the prices of some basic items were higher in the rural shops than in urban areas. He attributed this to the cost of freighting. The price of food, Jenkins observed, had gone up by 100 per cent, and clothing by 300 to 400 per cent, since the end of the World War, yet wages had only risen by 25 per cent.[101] Jenkins recommended moderate wage increases as vitally necessary for alleviating the hardships among the labouring Afro-Barbadian population.

The suggestion, initially, was received with much suspicion, and ultimately outright resentment, by the white employers. They argued that any increase in wages would raise their cost of production, and, possibly lead to social unrest. Several planters reported their personal objections directly to the Governor, on occasion.

It is interesting to reflect on the fact that the planters drew a direct link between social unrest by the black population and the championing of wage increases by the colonial authorities. The Colonial Secretary indicated that he was warned by some planters at the July 30, 1919 luncheon, and particularly by G. L. Pile, 'never to give utterances to such views as these in public,' for he would be 'stirring up trouble, setting class against class.' Moreover, he was cautioned to 'remember Pope Hennessy.'[102] At a meeting of the Executive Council, September 2, 1919, it was again reported:

> As regards the bettering of the position of the poorer classes with
> relation to their ability to buy food and clothing, the conclusion was
> reached, after prolonged discussion, that there was no action which
> the Executive could take in the matter.[103]

The Council proceeded to arrive at a rather hopeless conclusion, as far as Afro-Barbadians were concerned: that 'if the executives were to range themselves on the side of labour in a demand for higher wages the effect would be to precipitate trouble.'[104] It appeared as though the ghost of the 1876 Confederation 'riots' still haunted the memory of the plantocracy. Such ideas made a mockery of their boast of multi-racial harmony in Barbados. Instead, they exposed the dominant, racist views which perceived the black population as highly impulsive and therefore incapable of understanding the dynamics of the economic impact on society. Such a limited intellectual attainment, the white elite argued, meant that Afro-Barbadians were incapable of thinking for themselves, or articulating their grievances. As a result, they were prone to anti-social behaviour and easily misled by the 'irresponsible rhetoric' of agitators. This erroneous conviction on the part of the merchant-planter elite formed the basis of their opposition to the presence of local and foreign political activists in the island. They were branded as mere 'troublemakers.' In addition, the oligarchy was convinced that the local legislature should remain the exclusive domain of white domination simply because few Blacks possessed the intellectual capacity to take their place in the honourable Chamber.

## Epidemics, Public Health and Planter Class Indifference

The pursuit of their own narrow class interest appeared to have blinded the local merchant-planter elite to the realization that some programmes were difficult to implement along strict race and class lines. The outbreak of epidemics, for example, affects all classes, and in the area of public health, the folly of this policy was blatantly exposed on numerous occasions.

The effort to control infectious diseases during early twentieth-century Barbados necessitated some expenditure to prevent epidemics and to upgrade existing legislation. Both measures were usually opposed or ignored by the planter-dominated legislature. For example, John Hutson, Public Health Inspector, devoted the major part of the period 1913–19 to humbly requesting the legislature, with little success, to pass pieces of legislation for the control of typhoid fever.[105] The Chamber was only awakened to the seriousness of this threat to public safety when there was a typhoid outbreak in 1920 and a rise in the number of cases in 1925. Even then the legislature was reluctant to adopt the measures.

In fact, Dr Hutson's entire professional career was met by the legislature's opposition to the upgrading of public health and the centralization of public administration. In the *Official Gazette*, April 24, 1924, he presented his final official report entitled 'Ten Years Sanitary Progress.' More than 40 recommendations were made to the Assembly for the improvement of Public Health between 1913 and 1921. These recommendations included measures such as the registration of the causes of death, an isolation hospital for Bridgetown and St Michael, the canalization of the Constitution River, the building of a modern sewerage system in Bridgetown, the control of flies, and the control of milk supply. The most frequent entry accompanying the majority of the proposals was 'no action taken' or 'adopted some years later.'[106] It is very ironic that Dr Hutson labelled his report as 'Sanitary Progress' for there was none. In the meantime, the slums of Bridgetown remained harbouring grounds for disease pathogens. The milk shops and dairies were described by two visiting health experts as fly factories and 'germ disseminators of the most pernicious kind.'[107]

Probably the most embarrassing episode for the local oligarchy was Dr Hutson's appearance before the London-based British Colonial Advisory Medical and Sanitary Committee in 1922. His testimony related the sad account of his inability to get even the minimum of health regulations approved by the Barbadian legislature, despite the deplorable state of the island's medical and health facilities. The Committee listened in horror as he related tale after tale about the poor state of public health in Barbados. The Duke of Devonshire wrote to Governor O'Brien in disbelief, expressing concern at the fact that, in a colony 'with such an ancient history of British influence and settlement, there should be so scant an appreciation of the vital importance of good sanitation to the health and welfare of the community....'[108]

The Committee saw the typhoid outbreak of 1920 as the 'inevitable outcome of inadequate sanitary control.' The average burial rate of 34.2 per 1,000 for the years 1919–22 was seen as a 'matter of grave concern.' The death rate of children under five years of age, which, for the years 1919–22, averaged 43.95 per cent of the total death rate, represented a 'grievance and sad mortality which would be a reflection on any British Colony.' The Committee noted that Barbados's infantile mortality rate was the highest they encountered in dealing with the medical reports of the 'colonies and Protectorates.' They recommended the need for a centrally controlled and directed administration of sanitation for the colony.[109]

The Colonial Advisory Medical and Sanitary Committee, in essence, could not comprehend how 'Little England,' with its long history of connection with England and its large number of medically-trained Assemblymen, could have been so neglectful of such a vital area of concern to all in society. After all, Dr N. L. Boxhill, representative for St George, was a medical doctor, a Police Medical Officer and a member of the General Hospital Board. Dr Briggs-Clarke, representative for St John, was also a Police Medical Officer for District C, and Dr W. H. B. Massiah, representative for St Lucy, was a Police Medical Officer for District E and a member of the Executive Committee.[110] These men were not only prominent doctors who were trained in English institutions, but occupied positions of influence and were responsible for advising the government on improving medical facilities and public health in general. But they did not. This lack of initiative in this direction puzzled the Colonial Office, in that the Public Health Movement in Britain, and in Europe, had demonstrated more than a century earlier that a clean environment was necessary to prevent the outbreak of epidemics. It was even more shocking to learn of the ignorance these medical men had shown in that regard, for the very medical principles on which public health rested in the metropolis were ignored by local medical personnel.

Despite the embarrassing revelations by the Duke of Devonshire and the Colonial Advisory Medical and Sanitary Committee, the ruling elite insisted that the condemnations were an unjustified interference in Barbados's affairs. The *Barbados Globe*, in its defence of the oligarchy, described the Committee's conclusions as 'unjustified.' It argued that the Committee was made up of all 'absolute strangers' to the island who received their information from one Health Officer (Dr Hutson) and a Colonial Secretary.[111] Under such circumstances it was bound to arrive at the wrong conclusions. When the St Lucian *Voice* highlighted the findings of the Committee, an affronted *Barbados Globe* could not understand how the St Lucian editor could have used the 'notorious official despatch' as a source of evidence. It argued further that since St Lucians visited Barbados on a regular basis for medical treatment, the *Voice* was quite misguided to endorse so readily the 'piffle' of the Advisory Committee.'[112]

Who, then, was responsible for the deplorable state of the public health in Barbados and for the fact that it impacted most on the black labouring classes? The white oligarchy denied that its refusal to vote adequate funds for public health was responsible for the lack of proper medical facilities and the attendant rise in death rates, infant mortality rates and infectious diseases. In fact, the plantocracy removed any moral responsibility for the unfortunate state of public health from their shoulders. A dispatch from Governor O'Brien listed nine recommendations by the Executive for the upgrading of public health; all of which were rejected by the Vestries. Among these were the registration of the causes of death, the effective disposal of sewage and excretal matter, the regulation of milk supply, the control and treatment of venereal diseases, the control of midwives, the control and treatment of tuberculosis, the medical inspection of school children, the appointment of health visitors and district nurses and the improvement of maternity and Baby Welfare work.[113] The majority of these recommendations, O'Brien advised, would not involve any substantial expenditure by the Legislature; only the need to put in place the necessary legislation. Yet they were ignored and rejected.

Despite the failure to implement these improvements, the responsibility for poor sanitary conditions and for the ultimate outbreak of diseases and high infant mortality rates was placed on the shoulders of the Blacks themselves. The ruling elite argued that black Barbadians were dirty, unkempt in appearance, kept their surroundings filthy and neglected their children. It was argued that the scant, unclean and 'stomach sickening attire of some Bridgetown idlers' was responsible for the disease and squalor there, rather than the overcrowded, rat-infested slums of Suttle Street, Nelson Street, Cat's Castle and Emmerton.[114] In short, Afro-Barbadians created their own environment of destruction. This eugenic ideology of the ruling elite provided the justification for the economic neglect of the black population. Members of the merchant-planter elite insisted that it was the inherent nature of the local Afro-Barbadian population to live in squalor, and so no amount of improvement would change them. They had to express a desire to change on their own, before such assistance could be given.

This view was clearly expressed by Governor W. C. F. Robertson, and approved by the local legislature, during an address at the opening of a legislative session in 1928. He said,

> The success of the measures taken by any Government for the amelioration of the conditions of life of the people it governs in a large degree depend on the existence among those of a desire for improvement....[115]

He went on to quote from a report on agriculture in India, in which it was stated that no improvement in agriculture could have been made there 'unless the cultivator has the will to achieve a better standard of living, and the capacity in terms of mental equipment and physical health to take advantage of the opportunities which science, wise laws and good administration may place at his disposal.'[116] Robertson proceeded to apply this assessment of the Indian peasant to the Afro-Barbadian population. He returned to the over-burdened theme of the 'lazy negro,' citing reports of Government Departments and conversations with private employers, as the source of his evidence.[117] However, one can detect in the views of Robertson and the Assembly the strong influence of eugenic ideas and the Social Darwinist ideology, which placed the responsibility for the poverty of the black population on their own apparent bad habits, laziness and certain inherent, undesirable personality traits. But more importantly, there was the belief that such people were hopeless and should be allowed to wallow in their own misery rather than receive any assistance from the State. So that, in the draft reply of the Legislative Council of 1928, it agreed to 'give the most careful attention to any measures' submitted for the advancement of the Afro-

Barbadian.[118] However, such vaguely-worded promises were never translated into reality, since the Governor and the Executive Committee, dominated by members of the merchant-planter elite, shared similar views. Therefore, no concrete policies designed to improve the lot of Afro-Barbadians ever emanated from the core of the local decision-making apparatus. The black population, it seems, found itself between the devil and the deep blue sea.

The influence of eugenic ideas among sections of merchant-planter elite was, however, most avidly highlighted during the Public Health debate of 1925. A local Public Health Commission was set up in response to the severe criticism which had been made of public health by the Colonial Advisory Medical and Sanitary Committee. The Commission, one can argue, was conceived to procure some time under the appearance of investigating the situation. Two prominent members, J. W. Hawkins and A. J. Hanschell, however, exposed its true intention when they argued *inter alia* that the birth rate and the death rate in Barbados was 36 and 28 per 1,000 population and for England 22 and 19 respectively. Relying exclusively on these statistics, they argued that births out-numbered deaths in both places by the same eight per 1,000 population and since 1,000 corresponded to one square mile in Barbados and two in England, no backwardness in sanitation could be responsible for the high infant mortality rates in Barbados. They insisted that the island was twice as densely populated as England with a poor black population which was reluctant to emigrate permanently. They concluded:

> It simply shows that births in Barbados are very high, which is no sanitary fault and cannot be prevented in a tropical island like Barbados except by moral education, and the prevention of the most unfit from having children, if that is practicable.[119]

The opinions expressed by Hanschell and Hawkins were strikingly similar to the views of the eugenicists of the late nineteenth-century. A remarkable similarity can be seen in their dubious use of population statistics to prove their 'scientific' theory. Moreover, the association of Barbados' tropical climate with its population growth hinted at a possible influence of outmoded nineteenth-century theories which linked the rate of population growth with climatic conditions. The mention of moral education for Afro-Barbadians was a mere high-and-mighty insinuation which can be traced back to the post-emancipation era, and which usually linked false notions of black immorality, especially illegitimacy, to high infant mortality rates. Furthermore, the suggestion of preventing the 'most unfit' from conceiving children, seems similar to the kind of social engineering (possibly forced sterilization) which was practised in a later era in Nazi Germany. Crucial moral questions had to be addressed, such as the criteria which would have been employed to determine who were fit or unfit to bear children. In addition, what method would have been used to prevent pregnancies or to terminate them would have been vitally important.

The influence of nineteenth-century Social Darwinism was also very much alive in the minds of some white Barbadians. This theory declared that natural selection should be allowed to run its course in human society. Individuals differed in their fitness to thrive in society, and passed on their degree of fitness to their offspring. Government, therefore, should never intervene to help the poor and weak, because such action could encourage defective traits to pass from generation to generation and interfere with the natural evolutionary process.[120] Social Darwinists, for example, argued that the mass poverty which existed in the industrial cities of the USA during the mid-nineteenth-century and the earlier twentieth century were of the inhabitants' own making, because of immorality, laziness and bad genetic stock. While the Social Darwinists opposed central government assistance to the urban poor, they gave millions to big business and industry. They argued that the principle of the survival of the fittest should be rigidly applied to human society.[121]

The views of local adherents to Social Darwinist principles were very evident whenever the need to control the island's rapid population growth was given any consideration. The most popular solution advanced was the insensitive policy of economic neglect, if an emigration scheme could not be put in place. Hawkins wrote,

> The island is saturated to its full with population, and as no scheme of emigration has succeeded and the outlets to America and Cuba are practically shut, the death rate must be high in proportion to the high birth-rate, in order to keep the population down to its present saturated point. The universal law of nature, 'the survival of the fittest,' will in spite of good sanitation, send to the wall as many of the weakest as will nearly equal the number of births. The weakest are mostly the infants and particularly the illegitimates. This law must

act more rigidly in Barbados than in countries not so saturated and where there is room for increase.[122]

The subtle hints at some form of social engineering by Hanschell and Hawkins during the Public Health Commission of 1925 were eventually exposed in the most blatant fashion four years later, before the visiting West India Sugar Commission. On the issue of the island's high infant mortality rate, Dr Hawkins testified:

> **Dr Hawkins**:…Unless we can have this very high infant mortality we would have a greater population than the island could support, assuming that it can support its present population. If you do not have this high infantile mortality the island would be over-populated and would be poorer than it is at present. Fifty per cent of those infants die before they are five years old, and with that 50 per cent dying, the island's population is still increased.

> **The Chairman**: As a substitute for emigration, you have a high infantile mortality? (Laughter)

> **Dr Hawkins**: Instead of the island being put to the expense of having to bury that surplus population of infants, it would pay some place which is badly in need of a big population, like Demerara, to make use of that surplus. It is a good infantile; in many cases it is not the refuse of the island. The refuse of the island consists of the people whom we cannot get rid of. We would be glad to get rid of those whom we consider as the grown up rascals.[123]

Hawkins proceeded to pontificate in the most emotional way about the 'grown-up rascals' of the Afro-Barbadian population with the customary bias typical of the white oligarchy.

One should observe the central role which emigration played in his plan for population control. It was all part of a widely-held belief that emigration should act as a safety valve to relieve population pressure at home. Such a heavy reliance on an outward-looking policy remained a fundamental part of Barbados' planning throughout the pre-1940 era, and, in a way could have detracted from the need to examine the dynamics of the local economy in order to generate opportunities for the advancement of Afro-Barbadians.

After quoting the vital statistics of 1925 verbatim, Hawkins concluded on a shocking note:

> ...Hence it shows that the excessive death rate is only due to the infants. The mothers are not able to raise them and there is nowhere to put them. Like animals, there is nowhere to pasture them and you may as well let them die when they come.[124]

Melville Inniss, a UNIA activist, went on the attack at a meeting of the Westbury branch of the organization when he heard of Hawkins's comments. He saw in Hawkins's remarks a subtle, genocidal attempt 'to reduce the race' with much the same intention as biblical Pharaoh of antiquity in his dealings with the Israelites.[125] The vicious inferences of Dr Hawkins were quite clear. This strategy of neglect, and indifference, so manifest in the policy of Hawkins was also propounded with regularity by other white Barbadians. For example, on March 6, 1912, Governor Probyn called a conference on infant mortality with the parish Medical Officers, the Poor Law Inspectors and members of the Central Poor Law Board from across the island. Among the suggestions he made were the appointment of parish nurses to advise and care for pregnant mothers, the implementation of a nursery programme and the distribution of free milk to needy children in the island.[126] All of these proposals were unanimously rejected by the participants, except the one which dealt with the need to provide for a more careful registration of the infants' deaths. The medical officers insisted that such programmes would constitute a waste of parochial funds and so should not be implemented. Probyn backed down in the face of such formidable opposition.[127]

As already mentioned, this lack of interest in the general welfare of the Afro-Barbadian population cannot be explained solely in economic terms. Indeed, many proposals which appeared to require little or no capital expenditure were opposed and rejected with no logical or sensible reason given. One can only suggest that the opposition was influenced by the race and class prejudices of the white minority. The attempt to eradicate the hookworm parasites (ankylostomiasis) during the 1920s is another example of the indifference meted out to the local black population by the white elite.

The scourge of ankylostomiasis was first brought to the attention of the local authorities in 1913, when Dr Wickliffe Rose, Director of the Rockefeller Sanitary Commission, visited Barbados and found the agricultural fields heavily infested with the parasite.[128] In 1916, Dr George Paul of the same Rockefeller Commission visited the island and arrived at a similar conclusion. His efforts to solicit the help of the International Health Board were delayed by the outbreak of the First World War. Again in 1918, Dr H. H. Howard of the Rockefeller Anti-Hookworm Campaign visited Barbados. He started a 'Demonstration Campaign' in an area of St John of about four square miles with a population of 4,000 people. With the proper disposal of excreta and improved sanitary conditions, the parasite was under control immediately in the experimental district.[129]

The details of the minimum requirement for the disposal of excreta were obtained from Dr Howard. The Chief Public Health Inspector, excited by the success of the St John experiment, circulated a chain of memoranda to the Commissioners of Health in each parish, urging them to support the initiative and to indicate the extent of their willingness to assume the expense of carrying into effect the measures. Dr Howard, in turn, offered to conduct the eradication of the hookworm free of cost if the eleven parochial boards approved the scheme.[130] The responses were described as 'lethargic' and proved to be very disappointing on the whole.

The Commissioners of Health for Christ Church argued that the parish-wide scope of the project rendered the scheme 'impracticable.' This conclusion was arrived at without a proper survey being carried out. The Commissioners for St John replied in a similar tone, citing the impossibility of ascertaining the outlay of such a scheme and their unwillingness to assume any expense for putting it into effect. St Lucy's Commissioners suggested that 'the matter was under consideration' and St James and St Andrew thought 'more information was required.' The Commissioners for Bridgetown, St Michael, St George, St Thomas, St Peter and St Joseph did not bother even to reply.[131] The lack of cooperation and interest shown by the parochial boards forced Governor O'Brien to express regret that Dr Howard's generous offer could not be accepted.

## The Appointment of a Chief Medical Officer

The only major proposal which was put in place to upgrade health regulations, and to centralize health administration, was the creation of the post of Chief Medical Officer in 1928. This was done only after severe demands from the Colonial Office. The merchant-planter elite, however, put a series of devices in place to limit his power and so nullify his impact on the state of public health. The post, for example, was non-pensionable and inadequately paid, hence making it difficult to attract well-qualified officers for a long time.[132] In addition, the duties were deliberately confined to the granting of medical advice (which could be ignored) and the submission of annual medical reports. Moreover, some of the duties previously performed by the Poor Law Inspectors and the Public Health Inspectors were transferred to the Chief Medical Officer. The holder of the post, therefore, became an overworked individual, bogged down by the heavy demand to produce annual reports, but without the power to implement sanitary policy. One of the first officers to hold the post resigned in disgust at his lack of authority to upgrade the health regulations and to centralize the health administration. He wrote,

> The position of the Chief Medical Officer is devoid of all executive potentiality and is also beset by multitudinous political, Parochial and legal inhibitions thus being rendered entirely impotent of any advisory or progressively constructive influence.[133]

Another officer, Dr J. F. C. Haslam, assumed duty on January 15, 1933, and immediately observed difficulties which the office holder faced. He wrote, on another occasion,

> His sole statutory relationship to the eleven parochial sanitary authorities is that of an inspecting and reporting officer employed and paid by an outside authority. The Chief Medical Officer is not even on the permanent establishment of the Central Government. For these reasons and being without any executive authority he is unable to frame and carry through for the colony a consistent sanitary policy but must strike by means of personal influence and unfailing tact to guide and coordinate the activities of eleven independent lay boards.[134]

The legislature was responsible for the deliberate curtailment of the Chief Medical Officer's authority. No means existed by which the Chief could force any of the 11 sanitary boards to act on his advice except by an order or direction made by the Board of Health. The Order then had to be confirmed by the Governor, approved and sanctioned by both Houses of the Legislature and published in the *Official Gazette*.[135] In short, the tardiness of the parochial boards was difficult to deal with, and it would have taken an extraordinarily energetic Chief Medical Officer to resist such an entrenched system of plantocratic power. The majority of individuals who held the post in the pre-1940 period were expatriate Englishmen who seemed unprepared to risk alienation in a foreign land. Many of them therefore resigned, rather than face what appeared to be unmitigated frustration.

Public health, however, remained in a deplorable state throughout the 1930s and, as late as 1939. Governor Mark Young wrote in disgust to his superiors:

> Health administration is in need of radical reform. The present system puts practically all the responsibility and the power into the hands of the annually appointed Commissioners of Health of each parish. The Chief Medical Officer has no authority over them, and the General Board of Health practically none.[136]

The tendency to deliberately ignore the health and sanitation needs of the Afro-Barbadian population bore a striking similarity to the Malthusian-type neglect of the 'social undesirables' practised in other parts of the world. In early twentieth-century Barbados, this idea was conceived in a false notion which considered any expenditure designed to improve the condition of blacks as 'unnecessary, impolitic and calculated to create unrest.'[137] The black population, according to this notion held by members of the merchant-planter elite, should fend for themselves without any assistance from the State.

So whenever policies were enunciated, or even suggested, to change this state of affairs, they were met by a torrent of camouflaged racist notions about lazy negroes, and emphasis was placed on the pressing need to be prudent with scarce financial resources. For example, when black political activists of the UNIA and the WMA called for the abolition of child labour on the estates, and the implementation of compulsory education, the plantocracy argued that if child labour gangs were sent to school they would have to be fed, and the 'finances of the colony could not stand the strain.'[138] In essence, these physically and emotionally underdeveloped juveniles were expected to support themselves, as no notion of welfarism or charity had touched the social conscience of the merchant-planter elite. In short, reference to the economic cost of educating the children was a mere excuse to justify inaction. The real motive, inspired by racist notions, was to keep the black population in a servile role in society. White Barbadians, largely because of their racial stereotyping, did not see widespread illiteracy among the black population as a waste of human resources. Blacks were inferior, and the local educational system helped to keep them in their place.

A similar response greeted the suggestion of substituting fresh cow's milk for condensed milk supplied to school children during the 1930s. The Legislative Council opposed the idea on the grounds that it posed a risk of spreading infectious disease in contaminated milk, that it was too costly, and that there was no certainty of it generating employment despite increased expenditure.[139] The Legislature was known to have previously opposed legislation designed to ensure hygienic conditions during milk production. There was, therefore, not much genuine concern in their anxiety about contamination. The rejection of the milk scheme because of its possible ineffectiveness in reducing unemployment seems like a noble concern, but on serious analysis, one would discover that this position was only taken as an added justification to reject the scheme in the first place. Unemployment had always been highlighted as a grave social problem throughout the period after the First World War, but it was always ignored and treated in the most cursory way. The sudden distress with the state of unemployment in the island must be viewed with suspicion.

When, in 1932, for example, C. A. Brathwaite raised the issue of unemployment in the House of Assembly, the familiar response by the majority of white Assemblymen was to remind him of the 'high cost' involved, and the need for a supply of more 'facts and figures' on unemployment.[140] The legislature was aware of the promptings of the Governor-in-Executive Committee to address the desperate situation of the unemployed. In addition, from 1929 when the Employment Agency was established, despite its shortcomings, statistics on the number of applicants seeking jobs were available, which could have indicated the nature of the problem on the island. The Employment Agency, it is true, was set up to take some sting out of the criticism that nothing was being done for the unemployed. Under such dubious origins, and without a sense of direction, it hardly performed the duty that an employment agency should perform. However, its very presence provided an alibi for the ruling class. The agency remained largely a statistical gathering centre, a function which it did not even perform efficiently.[141] Yet the local legislature persisted with it, and unemployment continued to be a neglected area and a grave social problem. Stanley Clifford Thorne summarized the indifferent mood of the white Assemblymen when he exclaimed on one occasion 'unemployment my eye!'[142]

The constant reference to the moral insensibility of the merchant-planter elite vis-à-vis the welfare of the Afro-Barbadian population is so important that its repetition serves only to underline its relevance to the discussion. The survival of the black population in early twentieth-century Barbados was precarious largely because of the policy of neglect and indifference. The masses were born into a miserable state of poverty, which offered little hope of acquiring material wealth if they survived beyond the age of five. For with an infant mortality rate fluctuating between 270 and 400 per 1,000 births, many infants were spared the horrors of Barbadian life. Yet the merchant-planter elite felt no moral obligation to reverse this trend. Those who survived grew up to live a life of severe deprivation. The educational system helped to reinforce the institutionalized system of racism, and encouraged illiteracy among the black population. There were few avenues for social mobility, except for a very few privileged Blacks. The black population was forced to contend with the drudgery of plantation life with its low wages and harsh industrial climate. Strict labour codes regulated the industrial climate to such an extent that the bargaining power of the labouring classes was almost non-existent.

At the end of his poverty stricken life, when the Afro-Barbadian was too indigent to care for himself, he ended up in the local district hospital, popularly known as the almshouse, to pass away the twilight of his years in the most humiliating way. The almshouse itself was an institution designed exclusively to meet the needs of the large number of destitute black people. This reality was exposed on many occasions when the Overseas Settlement Committee attempted to settle impoverished white widows of black Barbadian seamen in Barbados. Governor O'Brien wrote, on one occasion,

> The difficulty with a woman married to a negro is that she is so cut off from association with people of her own colour in Barbados owing to the prejudice of the white inhabitants. If Mrs. Campbell become a charge on the Vestry her only refuge would be the Almshouse where there is no accommodation for Europeans and the conditions would be, I think, unsuitable.[143]

In essence, from the womb to the tomb, the majority of black Barbadians lived a life of abject poverty which denied them the least chance of enhancing their own personal development. The merchant-planter elite, on the other hand, dominated society through its ownership and control of the land, the vital import-export sector and the political machinery. This domination existed in the State, even in the Church, and in almost all aspects of local life. Their monopoly of power, and the intermarriage of elitist merchant-planter families, created a powerful ruling class with remarkable bonds of solidarity. They guarded their wealth, status and privileges with some jealousy, for the ruling elite had understood its antagonistic relationship with the Afro-Barbadian population.

The racist ideology of the ruling elite, in fact, was embodied in a complex system of racial stereotypes which made it easy to justify inequality between white and black Barbadians. It was argued that the wants and needs of Afro-Barbadians were so few as to make wage increases counter-productive, by aiding them in the satisfaction of their limited needs by working less. Any accumulation of capital, it was believed, was spent in pleasure-seeking pursuits. On the other hand, Afro-Barbadians were prone to keeping their surroundings unclean and neglected their offspring. In addition, they were impulsive, lacking in intelligence, easily excited by cheap political rhetoric, prone to violence, anti-social behaviour, cheating, lying and stealing to support their idle habits.

The measures advocated for the control of what were perceived as an 'impulsive' Afro-Barbadian population were indeed insensitive and harsh. They were predicated on a racist feeling of white superiority which insisted that blacks were to be kept in their place by punitive penal codes, firm laws and vigilant policing. Stereotyped as mere 'hewers of wood and drawers of water,' this pre-determined, inferior destiny of Afro-Barbadians was sealed by a policy of economic neglect, because the financial resources of the colony were allocated to ensure the continued dominance of the white elite.

The plantocracy, in essence, refused to allocate any substantial monetary resources that would contribute to the eradication of poverty among the black masses. In fact, they stuck to macro-economic models which slavishly tried to balance revenue and expenditure in terms of government expenses. Whenever calls for the social upliftment of the masses in regard to education, sanitation, healthcare, slum clearance and welfare were made, the planters always referred to the high cost of initiating these measures, and the burden of recurrent expenditure. In short, the constant mention of the high cost of initiating social progress for the Afro-Barbadian population was only a convenient excuse to neglect them in the first place.

Another example of the plantocracy's stinginess is brought home most forcefully during the Income Tax debate of the early twentieth century. When the market for sugar experienced difficulties after the Great War, colonial Governor Charles O'Brien moved to introduce an Income Tax regime. In 1918, the Executive Committee sent a Bill to the House of Assembly who immediately played 'battledore and shuttle cock' with it. The Bill, after considerable debate and opposition, was passed only reluctantly three years later.[144]

It is not difficult to comprehend why a legislature dominated by the white ruling elite would pussyfoot with the Bill. They reasoned that any income tax measure could only be a burden on the class of people who owned the most capital – after all, the black working classes worked for a mere pittance, as has been mentioned before. The planter elements in the legislature were not prepared to allow a situation where they would be taxed in order to finance the maintenance of institutions to support the black inhabitants of the society, especially the black labouring classes. After much pressure from the Executive, the House of Assembly reluctantly passed the Income Tax measure, but placed the burden of the tax on the 'professional and salaried classes.' In this way they exonerated the planter-merchant community from their fair share of the financial burden. By Income Tax Act Section 6 (2) the tax structure rendered it 'both highly unreliable and often extremely inequitable in its incidence.' In addition, the legislature increased the *ad valorem* duties imposed on items which were consumed largely by the working classes, thereby putting a heavy burden on the meager wages with which this class was already finding it difficult to eke out a living.[145]

Afro-Barbadians, it must be noted, did not accept their fate passively. Every action has its consequences, and they did respond to the oppression they faced. This response will be dealt with in the next chapter.

# 4

# WORKING-CLASS POLITICAL ORGANIZATIONS IN EARLY TWENTIETH-CENTURY BARBADOS: UNIA AND WMA

In 1932, in the heat of a public meeting in the urban community of Westbury Road, Bridgetown, working-class political activist Melville Inniss urged his listeners to appreciate the fight Marcus Garvey had put up to improve the lives of Blacks in the diaspora.[1] Another activist, Kenneth Wood, reminded his audience of the discriminatory employment practices so prevalent in the business houses of Bridgetown. He called on the working classes of Barbados to unite.[2] These statements and numerous pronouncements by grassroots activists during the early twentieth century preached about widespread poverty and other social ills among the black section of the population. A close examination of the utterances of these men picks up the defiant mood, and indeed the concern about improving the state of civil society in Barbados at the time. In a way, the issues raised reflected the nature of the conflict which existed in early twentieth-century Barbados between the two dominant classes in the society. These activists, no doubt, were aware of the danger they faced in confronting an entrenched merchant-planter class. Their aggressive activism, in short, captured the reality of the intense political struggle in Barbados during the early twentieth century.

The manner in which Afro-Barbadian activists attempted to wrest political power from the dominant merchant-planter elite manifested itself in various forms of campaigns. For example, in the press, and more particularly in the *Barbados Herald*, the educated and intellectually inclined Afro-Barbadians such as Clennel Wickham, Clement Innis and Erskine Ward, provided a theoretical framework for the working-class struggle. When the *Herald* became defunct in 1930, Wynter Crawford continued the radical protest in the *Barbados Observer*. Some learned activists presented petitions to the Governor and the

Colonial Office. In addition, a variety of social and cultural clubs, served as centres of recreation as well as outlets for political discussion and debates, and hence, contributed to the sharpening of political awareness among the black population. The UNIA and the WMA, resorted to a number of highly confrontational methods of political activity, such as holding mass political meetings and public demonstrations, and making attempts at industrial activity. Finally, there was another group, mainly the black middle-class members of the Democratic League, who confined their agitation largely to recruitment to political office in the annual elections to the House of Assembly. In a political system, activism can take many forms. In Barbados, it ranged from such 'low-key' activities as humble petitioning and pamphlet writing to high levels of political activity such as public meetings, demonstrations and recruitment to political office.

## Figure 4.1
## Political Activity in Barbados

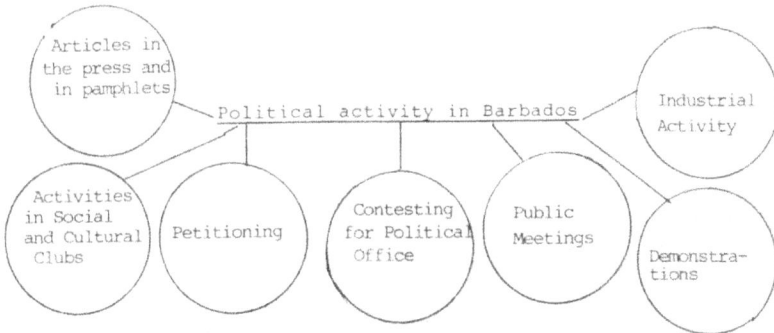

The central theme of this chapter dispels the notion that the attempts to bring about political change in Barbados were solely the efforts of expatriate colonial officials and benevolent members of the local elite. Instead, I will argue that the success of Afro-Barbadian political activity was due to intense political struggle in their kindred organizations, and the establishment of links that extended into the larger society. In short, their political struggles took on an all-pervasive character.

It must be stated, however, that the intensity of political activity in any political system depends on the nature of the political system itself, and the attitude and/or tolerance of the ruling classes to change.[3] In early twentieth-century Barbados the merchant-planter elite responded in a truculent and scornful manner to the varied forms of working-class political activity in the island. The ruling elite constantly resorted to an ideology which gave them comfort by dismissing all form of protests by black activists as the rhetoric of 'hotheads' bent on disturbing the tranquility of the island.

However, on scrutiny, one can identify various strands of political ideologies which these activists promoted. For example, there was an extreme radical socialism contained in pamphlets such as 'The West Indian Organizer,' 'Negro Worker' and 'Resist the War Plans of the MacDonald Government.' This literature was smuggled into the island by 'foreign agitators.' Even though it is difficult to ascertain the extent to which it was circulated, the fact that UNIA and WMA activists mentioned it during their campaigns, suggests that it had an impact, however small, on some sections of Barbadian society.[4] Marcus Garvey's Pan Africanism formed the main plank on which the activities of the WMA, and more so the UNIA, were based. Black middle-class activists such as Clennell Wickham, Charles Duncan O'Neal, and the vast majority of the members of the Democratic League, espoused a mild form of Fabian Socialism. It was couched in the principles of State Welfarism.[5] A strikingly similar strand of political ideology, labelled Asquithian 'liberalism,' could be associated with Grantley Adams.[6] Adams claimed that he rooted his political beliefs in the tenets of State Welfarism and an incorporation of a gradualist constitutional approach to political change.

## Figure 4.2
## Political Scene in Barbados

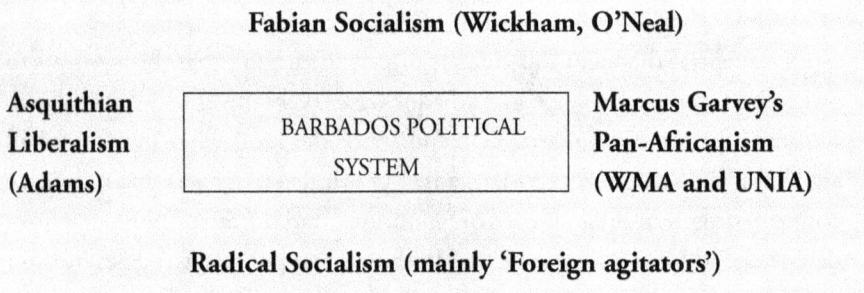

**Fabian Socialism (Wickham, O'Neal)**

| Asquithian Liberalism (Adams) | BARBADOS POLITICAL SYSTEM | Marcus Garvey's Pan-Africanism (WMA and UNIA) |
|---|---|---|

**Radical Socialism (mainly 'Foreign agitators')**

One should be wary of the political labels which these activists attached to themselves, for their proposed programmes did not always coincide with the theoretical formulations and policies of the doctrines elsewhere, as in Europe. For example, Adams's claims to be a Liberal, even though he was very vague on what he meant by 'liberalism,' were nowhere similar to the liberalism of the late nineteenth-century European theorists. The Fabian Socialism of the Democratic League was similarly just as vague.

This apparent confusion over the meaning of political labels was very evident during the political battle between Clennell Wickham and Grantley Adams during the 1920s. Clennell Wickham and Clement Inniss provided the earliest evidence of popular post-war protest in the *Barbados Herald* newspaper, which highlighted the grievances of the underprivileged. Clennell Wickham, in his column 'Men and Matters,' proved to be a constant thorn in the flesh of the ruling elite. His attacks on oligarchical rule, the deprived living and working conditions of the labouring classes, high infant mortality rates, poor nutrition, and the use of child labour on the estates, constituted a biting indictment of local white rule.[7] The ruling elite, however, fought back through their conservative organ, the *Agricultural Reporter*. A war of words soon started between the *Herald* and the *Reporter* when Grantley Adams joined the latter as a leader writer in 1925. He became engaged in heated debates with Wickham. Much emphasis has been accorded by Adams's biographer to these debates, which were dominated to a large extent by arguments over the merits and demerits of 'socialism' and 'liberalism.' The debate, however, was not as acute as it appeared at the time, for Adams's claim to be a convert to 'Liberalism,' and Wickham's to 'Socialism,' were made at a time when the practice of these ideologies was still in its infancy.[8] The debate about the Russian Revolution, for example, was remote and sterile within the Barbadian context, in that the revolution was still in its infancy in the 1920s. There was therefore no model of socialism to use as a guide.

In short, there were certainly no inherent differences in policy, or goals, between the Democratic League, of which Wickham became a member in 1924, and the Progressive League of 1938, of which Adams became leader. These organizations, it appears, were not inclined to transform the system of production in Barbados from private to public ownership. The Progressive League, later to become the Barbados Labour Party, was able to capture political office, but its policies did not stray very far from its original strategy of constitutional and parliamentary reform. The Democratic League was never able to hold political office as a way to implement its policies, and so it is much more difficult to judge how it would have performed. However, an examination of the performances of Charles Duncan O'Neal, C. A. Brathwaite, and other

League members who sat in the House of Assembly between 1925 and 1936, reveals no hint of any fundamental differences between the Progressive League and the Democratic League.[9] As Keith Hunte wrote,

> ...The long-drawn-out debate between Liberals and Socialists in the 'twenties' of this century was unnecessary. Their immediate goals were the same....Much time was wasted in hair-splitting on political ideologies that were not pertinent to the local situation.[10]

It is very difficult, then, to understand and to explain the disunity which existed between Adams, on the one hand, and Wickham, O'Neal and the Democratic League, on the other hand. During a 1929 political meeting held at the offices of the *Agricultural Reporter* on High Street, Bridgetown, in support of the candidature of A. J. Hanschell, Adams spoke of his intention to organize a 'Progressive Association' on his return to the island in 1925. He was immediately challenged by Thomas O'Neal, the brother of Duncan O'Neal, to explain why he did not join the Democratic League which was in existence at the time. Adams's retort revealed his outlook at the time. He was interested in a Progressive Association rather than a 'revolutionary Association.'[11] His reply caused quite a stir in the vociferous audience in the hall.

The incident, and the verbal exchange, disclosed Adams's perception of the Democratic League as a radical organization not in tune with his liberalism. It seems reasonable to speculate here, however, that if Adams, with his skills as a debater and a writer, had joined up with the Democratic League in a concerted attack on the white oligarchy, the pace of political change, and ultimately the toppling of the plantocracy, could have been achieved long before the 1940s. This did not occur before this period, largely because Adams aligned himself with the dominant merchant-planter elite during the period before 1937. His support no doubt did much to convince the white oligarchy that he would help to maintain the status quo. The role Adams played during the 1927 dockworkers' strike, and in the libel case against the *Herald* in 1930, attests to the support which he provided for the plantocracy in their struggle against the working classes. Perhaps his links with the local oligarchy could have slowed the pace of political change in the island.

During the 1927 dockworkers' strike, stimulated by long-term grievances over pay and conditions of work which went back to 1918 when the war bonus of $2.00 per trip was discontinued, O'Neal – with little funds and moral support except from the *Herald* and the Workingmen's Association – found himself locked in battle against the wrath of the white elite. No support came from the black middle class, not even those who were members of his Democratic League. In fact, many of them thought O'Neal had gone too far in support of the strike as a means of addressing the workers' grievances. Adams, writing for the *Agricultural Reporter*, blasted him as a 'Bolshevik' and a 'dangerous agitator.'[12] The strike collapsed after a few days, mainly due to the manipulation of the strikers by the Chamber of Commerce, and the inherent weaknesses in the infant labour movement which O'Neal was trying to build.[13] Samuel Hall, speaking at a WMA meeting, captured the dilemma which the striking workers faced when he argued that the lack of a 'grocery' prevented the dockworkers from putting up a more determined fight.[14] In other words, the threat of starvation, accentuated by the workers' dependence on a weekly wage, weakened their will and capacity to challenge the mercantile establishment of Bridgetown. O'Neal was even more direct in his assessment of the dockworkers' strike: 'Beware of the middle class Negro...the last time you went on strike you had to return to work owing to starvation.'[15] O'Neal was referring to the black middle-class members like Grantley Adams who actively supported the merchant class, or like some others whose silence during the strike and on issues facing the working classes gave solace, encouragement and consent to the white oligarchy to crush the infant labour movement.

The demise of the *Herald* newspaper in 1930 was but another instance where an outlet for the grievances of the working classes was stifled with the help of Adams. It occurred because of a libel case brought against the newspaper by a white businessman, Walter Bayley. Adams represented the plaintiff in a famous case that brought racial tension to the forefront of Barbadian society. The case generated island-wide interest, mainly as a result of what was perceived as a personal vendetta against Wickham and the *Herald* by Adams.[16] The drama of Adams's cross-examination of Wickham can be captured from extracts of the court proceedings:

> **Counsel**: When did you write this article?
> **Defendant**: Sometime during the week, probably on Thursday.
> **Counsel**: You remember a dinner given in honour of Mr Ward this week?
> **Defendant**: Yes, on the Friday night.

**Counsel:** Did you at that dinner say that you were going to bathe Bayley tonight?

**Defendant:** I did not.

**Counsel:** You wrote this article in a cool calculating manner?

**Defendant:** In the same manner in which I usually write my articles. I was not in a temper...

**Counsel:** You know that the sovereign duty of journalists is to be sure that their facts are correct before they write?

**Defendant:** Yes.

**Counsel:** You say you were thoroughly surprised. Were you thoroughly surprised the day after the election?

**Defendant:** I was thoroughly surprised at the whole transaction. I was surprised as soon as I found out how Mr Bayley acted.

**Chief Justice:** What were you surprised about?

**Defendant:** I was somewhat surprised at Mr Bayley's attitude in cancelling his advertisement and demanding payment on his account.

**Counsel:** When did you realize the full effect of Mr Bayley's action?

**Defendant:** I was thoroughly surprised when he refused to pay for the advertisement which was published.

**Counsel:** When you became fully surprised, did you think Mr Bayley up to that time intelligent.

**Defendant:** I still think him so.

**Counsel:** Do you still think him broadminded?

**Defendant:** No.

**Counsel:** Do you still think him honest?

**Defendant:** Do you want another libel case?[17]

Adams kept Wickham under rigorous cross-examination. The Special Jury, no doubt dominated by supporters and sympathizers of the planters, awarded the plaintiff (Bayley) damages in the sum of £1,450 and costs, a substantial award, which resulted in the end of the *Barbados Herald* as an organ for the ventilation of grievances of the working class. Governor Robertson, in a confidential dispatch to his superiors at the Colonial Office, claimed that he tried to convince Bayley that 'leniency in the matter might serve his own interest and that of the island' but he found the 'taste for vengeance and publicity too strong and so the *Herald* was sold.'[18] Aside from the personal squabble between Wickham, and Bayley and Adams, Robertson tacitly acknowledged that the end of the *Barbados Herald* brought to the surface of Barbadian society underlying racial and class tensions. His advice to Bayley was an attempt to defuse the situation and so maintain some social peace. This special episode was only one aspect of the black Barbadian struggle. In the local UNIA and the WMA, the contest for political power continued in a different form and fashion, quite unabated.

## Working-class Political Struggle and Activism: The Universal Negro Improvement Association (UNIA) and the Workingmen's Association (WMA)

The UNIA and the WMA, even though they functioned as separate organizations, shared similar aims and objectives. They were both influenced by the worldwide Garveyite black conscious movement. This was reflected in the social and political discourses they raised, and their style of organization. In fact, a close scrutiny of the existing police records on the surveillance of both organizations revealed a strikingly similar Pan Africanist ideology.[19] A flexibility of membership existed, whereby members of the UNIA and the WMA, such as Moses Small, Willie Brathwaite, George Belle, Walter Osbourne and Kenneth Turpin, moved between the two organizations with relative ease, and in some cases, were members of both associations at the same time.

On occasion, the two associations collaborated in joint efforts at political protest. For example, on August 7, 1933, the WMA and the UNIA staged a demonstration to commemorate the centenary of William Wilberforce. The joint procession left the WMA hall, Passage Road, St Michael, and travelled via Baxters Road, Tudor Street, Milk Market, Broad Street, Trafalgar Square and Belmont Road to Government House, where the British national anthem was played. They then proceeded via Welches, Hindsbury Road, Bank Hall, Eagle Hall, Barbarees Hill and back to the WMA hall on Passage Road.[20] At 7:00 p.m. the same day a well-attended meeting was held in the Workers' Hall to discuss the legacy of West Indian slavery. The speakers comprised working-class activists of the UNIA and the WMA, as well as C. A. Brathwaite, J. B. Grant and J. A. Martineau, three prominent members of the Democratic League.[21] A close collaboration between the UNIA and the WMA occurred regularly in support of candidates for the Democratic League during the annual elections.[22] In essence, this close working relationship could not have been possible if the two associations did not share a common ideology and were not, by extension, working towards the same objectives.

The UNIA and the WMA can, therefore, be conceptualized as socio-political protest movements, at a pre-party stage of development, which sought to make specific, concrete demands on the existing order.[23] They were political movements, in essence, which responded to what they perceived as gross exploitation of the Afro-Barbadian population. By a 'pre-party' organization, one means a rather loose and unsophisticated group which campaigns for change but fails to meet the criteria of a political party. A political party must have some continuity, should outlive its founding fathers, should have an organizational structure at the local and national levels, and have regular communication between these levels. It should also have the determination to capture political office at all levels, and a yearning to exercise power by obtaining popular support in some manner, especially by electoral contest.[24] The UNIA and the WMA, unfortunately, did not reach this level of organization and sophistication, and so cannot be considered as political parties in the modern sense.

In Barbados, the first branch of the UNIA was established in 1919. It was made up mainly of artisans and war veterans. Like the WMA, urban branches were established in Bridgetown, at Reed Street and Westbury Road, and in the rural districts of Crab Hill, St Lucy, and Indian Ground, St Peter.[25] By 1920, the UNIA was holding meetings regularly in Bridgetown and throughout the country districts, actively politicizing and mobilizing the black population. Around this time, the UNIA was boasting an active membership of over 1,800.[26]

The local UNIA placed much emphasis on 'the unity of the negro' and on a programme which encouraged its members to embrace the principles of self-help.[27] The active methods of political campaigning required to realize such noble objectives brought them into direct confrontation with the local white oligarchy. The UNIA organization was accused of being hostile to white interests and bent on creating racial unrest. For example, in 1923, Governor O'Brien wrote of 'hot-heads' in the UNIA who sent threatening letters to some planters, and were urging workers to strike.[28] Even though the potential for industrial unrest worried him, he stressed that Barbadians were generally a quiet, well-behaved people, who were very 'excitable and easily aroused.'[29]

He therefore considered the political activities of the UNIA very dangerous to the stability of Barbados.

## Official Hostility and Police Surveillance

The impending conflict which was apparently brewing between the UNIA and the white oligarchy was taken seriously by the latter. The local UNIA organization was perceived as a dangerous cell of the worldwide movement, which should be closely monitored. In a secret letter from the Secretary of State, A. L. S. Amery, to all Governors in the British West Indies, the original correspondence sent by Augustus Duncan, Executive Secretary of the West Indian Protective Society of America, described the UNIA as a 'trouble-making organization' which was 'radically anti-white and anti-British.' If its activities were not 'effectively checked by proper official action,' the correspondence stressed, 'strife will result between Whites and Blacks in the West Indies.'[30] In short, the UNIA as a black organization, was labelled as preaching racial hatred, and so should be treated with suspicion by Whites throughout the world, including those in the West Indies. Colonial administrators took Duncan's advice and the other negative references to the UNIA very seriously.

In Barbados, the authorities became more security conscious. A directive from the Secretary of State requested that legislation pertaining to the storage of arms should be adequate, relative to the fact that only 'fit persons' should be allowed to possess arms, and other stocks should be kept in places safe from 'pillage by a riotous mob.' He stressed the urgency of this legislation, due to the existence of 'unrest among the native population.' UNIA branches were closely watched, and those at Reed Street and Westbury Road infiltrated by police spies.[31] Melville Inniss, a UNIA activist, remarked on one occasion, '...the police are following us all about, but we would deceive them because we are not preaching sedition.' More importantly, the police in the various islands devised an elaborate system to monitor the movements of UNIA members and other so-called 'undesirable aliens.'[32] The Barbadian legislature passed the Expulsion of Undesirables Act 1927, as a necessary device to deal with 'agitators.'[33] In 1928, this legal measure was put in place to expel Marcus Garvey, during his tour of the West Indies. The Inspector General of Police wrote,

> No information has been gathered so far with regard to the arrival of Marcus Garvey, but I submit that it would not be advisable to allow

him to come here, and further that he should be now informed…
that should he come he will not be allowed to land. [34]

Again, in 1937, when Garvey embarked on another speaking tour, he
was closely monitored by the Barbadian police, who kept in close contact
with their colleagues in other parts of the British West Indies. It was decided
by the Executive Committee, acting on the advice of the Commissioner of
Police, that Garvey's reception in Barbados should be dependent on whether
'he behaved himself' in the other islands. His visit in October 1937 occurred
at a time when the July 1937 'disturbances' were still fresh in everyone's mind.
This made the local authorities very nervous about the effect his speeches could
have on the Afro-Barbadian population. Eventually, he was allowed to address
Barbadians, but only in an enclosed arena, where the security forces felt they
could control a crowd if any disturbance should occur.[35]

Local authorities made efforts to control the entry, and to monitor the
circulation of 'subversive literature,' especially the *Negro World* newspaper,
the New York-based publication of the UNIA. The Colonial Office suggested
that stricter control should be exercised over the press, by means of legislation
which give power to the authorities to suppress any publication considered as
'seditious or calculated to incite crime.' The Straits Settlements Ordinance XI
of 1915 was suggested as a guide, 'which will indicate the kind of legislation
which might be introduced.' The Ordinance gave sweeping powers to the
Executive and the security forces to seize any literature they deemed subversive.

Even the official church of the UNIA, the African Orthodox Church,
received its share of criticism. It was described as 'seditious against the
government of Great Britain' and by clever implication, a danger to the
preservation of the British Empire. Edwin Lewis, a former priest of the Church
and a bitter opponent of Marcus Garvey, wrote to the British Consul-General
in New York, informing him,

> This is not an institution that is in any shape to reform men and
> women, but rather doing the very best it can to demoralize a people
> under the guise of religion….[36]

This correspondence was passed on to all colonial officials in the British
Empire, with a warning to keep a close watch on the African Orthodox Church.
In Barbados, dossiers were kept on vocal members of the Church or any foreign
dignitary who was believed to have the slightest connection with the Church.

'Bishop Jack' of the Episcopal Orthodox Church was one individual subjected to such surveillance in his movement between St Vincent and Barbados. The Administrator of St Vincent and the Colonial Secretary of Barbados exchanged intelligence information on him. The former wrote, on one occasion,

> I understand that Jack intends returning shortly to Barbados. He is being watched by the police here and so far his lectures on Cuban conditions appear to have been harmless. [37]

The unwarranted hysteria of the colonial administrators concerning the UNIA was best demonstrated by a discussion about the organization, sparked off by incidents of maltreatment of migrant West Indian workers in Cuba during the 1920s. The issue first surfaced when Godfrey Haggard, of the British legation in Havana, complained, in November 1922, about unfair treatment of English-speaking West Indian labourers by the Cuban authorities. Since the West Indians could not speak or write Spanish competently, they were at a disadvantage in their dealings with the Cuban officials. Haggard thought that as 'British Subjects' they should be offered protection and advice. He suggested support for a fund to provide legal aid, but was unsure who should administer it. He thought the vibrant division of the UNIA in Havana 'could form the nucleus for collecting the fund.' Haggard, in essence, was seeking for the Havana division of the UNIA what he called 'semi-official recognition.'[38] The opinions of the colonial Governors of Jamaica, Trinidad and Barbados were sought on the issue by the Colonial Office. The gravity of the Cuban crisis and the sensitive nature of the plight of black West Indians did not appear to influence their decisions. Haggard's suggestion was intolerantly dismissed by them as a dangerous gesture to a racist organization. Governor O'Brien of Barbados, in particular, argued that any recognition of the Havana division of the UNIA would be seized upon by its headquarters in New York, and used by 'critics of the British Administration as charges of inconsistency.'[39] He appeared to be more interested in finding a way out of the dilemma for the British Government, than in assisting the distraught migrant West Indian workers in Cuba. The opinions of the Governors, in essence, amounted to an unjustified hostility and insensitivity to the aims of the UNIA. As a result of the negative rating given by the colonial administrators, recognition was denied to the UNIA. A. Grindle concluded,

In view of these dispatches the Marquis Gurzon will no doubt agree
that it would be undesirable for any recognition – even semiofficial
– to be given to the Association by the minister. [40]

The opposition to the UNIA, both at a local and at an international level,
by colonial officials, reflected a lack of appreciation for the aims and objectives
of the organization. A close scrutiny of the intelligence information gathered
by police spies would reveal that the UNIA and WMA were altruistic, and
indeed idealistic, organizations, seeking the upliftment of Afro-Barbadians
within the existing political and economic framework. They were not prone
to 'radicalism' and no evidence existed of any violent attempt to overthrow the
local oligarchy.[41] In fact, their methods of campaigning amounted to no more
than an appeal to the social conscience of the merchant-planter elite. Melville
Inniss echoed these sentiments on one occasion:

> I stand for compulsory education. Mr Austin was asked if he
> would vote for compulsory education and he replied no, that the
> Government could not afford it. I don't know what is his reason for
> saying no, but if the UNIA and the Workingmen's Association were
> properly organized we would be able to tell the Government we can
> put £2,000 to assist in compulsory education....[42]

Despite such noble gestures, the strong opposition to the UNIA continued.
The local press was in the forefront of the hostility to the UNIA, sometimes
portraying it in the most negative way and, at times, suggesting it was an
organization bent on the violent overthrow of the status quo. The *Barbados
Standard*, for example, wrote of the many West Indians who 'had their minds
poisoned by the organization which preaches sedition' and spreads 'Bolshevik
teaching in these colonies.' The *Standard* commented further,

> The time is sure to come when we also will be forced to seize and
> handle roughly those who would set race against race and reduce
> these colonies to the same condition that now exists in Russia. [43]

On another occasion the *Barbados Standard* called for the most brutal
suppression and isolation of the UNIA, by launching an attack on what it
considered as the wicked motives of its leaders:

An effort should be made to discover these hidden leaders who are doing a great deal of mischief. It should not be hard to pierce the veil, as we understand that meetings to incite workmen to continue the labour unrest are held weekly in various localities in the city. Those who are thus stirring devil's broth are, we may shrewdly guess, inspired by anything but altruism, and are as ready to rob and betray their dupes as to urge them on in a career of Bolshevism. These shy and untiring labour leaders, who are doing their dirty work in fancied seclusion and safety should, when unmasked and dragged into the limelight, be ostracized by employers of labour and shunned by all reputable members of the community....[44]

An examination of the local newspapers during the period under study would reveal many such attacks on the UNIA. In fact, added to the attacks on its leaders as seditious Bolsheviks, no opportunity was spared to use any weaknesses, apparent contradictions or internal squabbles of the organization against it. For example, in 1921, the *Barbados Advocate* highlighted Garvey's visit to Jamaica by reminding its readers that his marriage was recently annulled, the Black Star Line had only one completed trip to its credit, and its three vessels had been laid up for a long time. The *Advocate* rejoiced that he had not 'made much of a mark in Jamaica.'[45] Around the same time, the *Barbados Globe* wrote aptly of the rumor that immigration agents would not allow Garvey to enter the United States on account of his being an 'undesirable alien.' The *Globe* thought it was a most fitting tribute for 'Negro Moses.'[46]

When the Liberian Consul-General, in 1924, stated that no one leaving the United States under the auspices of the Garvey Movement would be allowed to land in the republic, the *Barbados Globe* again scorned the efforts of local Garveyites who talked of repatriation to Africa.[47] Again, when Amy Ashwood Garvey, former wife of Marcus Garvey, stated that the Negro was not ripe for political emancipation, the *Barbados Globe* cleverly employed her words as justification for the dismissal of requests by local black organizations for a liberalization of franchise qualifications in Barbados.[48] Probably the most stinging indictment against the UNIA came from an editorial of the *Barbados Globe* during Garvey's trial for mail fraud in the United States:

What is surprising in the Garvey case, and goes so far to prove the unfitness for self-control of the class he seeks to liberate, is the abundance of evidence, brimful of hostility and abuse, being supplied the Court by men who were once on the highest round of the ladder in the Garvey campaign, and as such must have drunk deep and oft of the advantages accruing if ever there were any. We are not favourable to the Garvey movement....Strong, however, as we are against the movement, we must confess to a deep sense of shame at the violent accusations being hurled at his head by men in whom he trusted and who must at some time have professed admiration for him. It is the hardest blow so far hit at the Garvey movement. Traitors from within wielding weapons.[49]

These criticisms of the UNIA forced the local organization onto the defensive. It therefore expended much of its energy and time reacting to charges, which did not make the task of the organization easy. In the process, much of its creditable work remained unrecognized and insignificant in the eyes of colonial administrators. At the Reed Street branch of the UNIA, however, pamphlets dealing with matters pertaining to African literature and history were periodically made available to its members, and discussions on the achievements of black civilization were held on a regular basis. Sometimes the visits of senior UNIA officials, such as Reverend R. B. Tobitt and Marcus Garvey, when they were allowed to speak, added some encouragement to these efforts. In addition, the energetic Alexandriana Gibbs and John Beckles ran a night school at Reed Street, which provided the only formal education for many underprivileged youth in Bridgetown.[50]

The task attempted by the local UNIA was made more difficult because of the lack of funds and the absence of encouragement by the local authorities. The organization kept few records, and so, vital information pertaining to its membership and activities is seriously lacking. However, around 1920 they boasted of a membership of over 1,800 and a 'representation' of agricultural workers throughout the island.[51] It is known that the Reed Street branch of the UNIA acted as the headquarters for the local organization and kept in contact with the New York-based organization. The Indian Ground branch of the UNIA was administered by two ardent Garveyites, H. I. Gill, the district shopkeeper, and Cyril Foster, a 'Speculator.' Meetings of the organization were held in Mr Gill's shop, but little is known about the other activities of the Indian Ground branch. The Crab Hill division of the UNIA, under the guidance of Gladstone Leacock, a migrant worker to Cuba during the 1920s, appears to have been a vibrant Organization.[52] By 1937, the UNIA was experiencing some difficulties with its membership, but Marcus Garvey's visit in the same year did much to revive the enthusiasm of its members.

## Formation of the Workingmen's Association (WMA)

The WMA was formed as an offshoot of the Democratic League in 1927, after O'Neal failed to gain recognition as the workers' bargaining agent during the dockworkers' strike. Much emphasis was placed on the principle of self-help among the working classes. WMA programmes revolved around the need for compulsory education, the demand to end child labour on the estates, workmen's compensation, franchise liberalization, slum clearance, and improved nutrition for the labouring classes. The method by which the WMA attempted to implement these plans – which irritated the ruling elite – mainly involved an active campaign of public meetings and demonstrations in the urban, and some rural districts. From the WMA headquarters at 'Workers Hall,' Passage Road, Bridgetown, other units of the organization were established at South District, St George; St David's Village, Christ Church; Venture, St John, Belleplaine and St Simon's Village, St Andrew; and Porey Spring, St Thomas.[53] In this way, the WMA tried to galvanize mass support in both rural and urban districts. Within 18 months the organization was boasting a membership of over 1,800, a reserve of $1,890, and $2,200 contributed by 'the people' to send O'Neal to England to protest against the dreaded Better Security Act.

The novel use of open-air meetings held by the WMA had the effect of changing the rather personalized style of political campaigning so evident in Barbados's political culture before the advent of Dr O'Neal on the political scene. His platform was shared by a band of working-class associates such as Frederick 'Moses' Small, Edwin Turpin, George Belle, William Marshall, Kenneth Wood, Walter Osbourne and Willie Brathwaite. These dedicated activists demonstrated a keen understanding of local social and economic conditions. The plight of the Afro-Barbadian was intellectualized as that of one exposed to the whims of a rapacious merchant-planter class. The Provision Dealers Limited (PDL), a conglomerate of importers, was always singled out for attack. Kenneth Wood referred to them as 'bloodsuckers of the working class, who organized themselves to get richer' while the masses got poorer.[54] O'Neal also spoke in a similar tone:

> The P. D. L. store is a few men who get together and import goods
> in large quantities and sell them in small quantity if they wish to
> do so. They also have the price fixed and you have to purchase, or
> go elsewhere where you will meet the same price; in days gone by
> things were not so. [55]

On another occasion, he commented,

> The merchants and others have organized themselves in one solid
> mass, but the time is coming when you shall purchase all of these
> estates....[56]

O'Neal was referring to the consolidation of the white corporate power
structure, which started in 1917. Its implications for the black working class
did not pass unnoticed, as concerns about profiteering and black economic
disenfranchisement were raised. Many activists felt that the merger of planter
and merchant capital was leading to unbearable living and working conditions
for the majority of the black population. Such fears had become part of the
arsenal of the WMA activists in their attacks on the oligarchy. They assailed the
sugar plantations, the largest employers of labour in Barbados, as institutions
hostile to the labouring classes. Constant references were made to the merciless
exploitation of child-labour gangs, bad working conditions, low wages and the
general insecurity of tenure of plantation workers. During a 1927 open-air
public meeting, Kenneth Wood echoed similar sentiments:

> The plantation owners have reported that their crop made them
> $40,000.00 but they will not say how much the poor labourers have
> made. Freedom is liberty, our enemies are the capitalists; we have
> made them rich but what is our reward? Glendairy and the almshouse.
> When we are sick we should be able to provide for six months but
> I am sorry to say we cannot.[57]

A deputation of WMA members, in evidence before the 1929 West Indian
Sugar Commission, related how the Master and Servant Act in particular made
the life of plantation labourers one of insecurity of tenure and uncertainty:

> **Mr Chairman**: I presume that is in accordance with the present
> laws of the island. Any located labourer who transfers his services
> to another estate is liable to be brought up in the Police Court and

punished with a fine or imprisonment. It is a Master and Servants' Law.

**Mr Sebro**: They (labourers) have an obligation to fulfil to the proprietors of the estate. They own the land, and if the labourers do not do as the estate owners would like them to do, they are turned off the estate. If the labourers seek any other working field, there is a chain or bond between the estate owners and managers which prevents them from getting work on another estate, so that the labourers have to remain where they are.

**Chairman** Do you mean that if a labourer is discharged from one estate he has very little chance of getting work elsewhere?

**Mr Sebro**: Yes, he must stand there and burn there.[58]

Under such deplorable working conditions, the WMA demanded the removal of the Master and Servant Act and the Better Security Act from the Statute Books, as a vital input into the reform of the plantation system.

The WMA, however, recognized the intensity of the struggle for political power which was in the firm grasp of a well-entrenched white oligarchy. The experiences of the 1927 dockworkers' strike had taught them their powerlessness without an economic base. The WMA therefore reasoned that the fight should be waged on the political, as well as the economic front. As a result, the WMA became the political arm of the organization while the Cooperative Supply Association, which started two groceries in Bridgetown and one in St Lucy, and the Loan and Friendly Society, were the economic arms.

## Scrutiny of a Colonial Governor

The economic ventures of the WMA, especially the Cooperative Supply Association, experienced financial difficulties as soon as they were established and, as a result, hampered the political agenda of the organization. The grocery in Bridgetown ran into financial difficulties, largely due to mismanagement, opposition from the mercantile community of Bridgetown to the venture, and a lack of regular customers. By August 1927, the Drug Store, also located in Bridgetown, was indebted to O'Neal to the tune of $720.00. A police report calculated the Druggist's salary at $80.00 per month, that of two other employees at $20.00 each, yet the store sold no more than $100.00 per month in drugs. The policeman thought it was 'only a show' doomed to failure in a short time.[59] Indeed, the attempt by the organization to sell goods to its members at lower prices than the established merchant houses was a well-meaning gesture but did not constitute sound business practice. Nevertheless, it was done. Governor Robertson's probing of O'Neal at the inception of these organizations is quite revealing:

> Accordingly I sent for Dr O'Neal, told him that I had read the programmes of the societies as published, and would like to have fuller information regarding them from him....I said that a cooperative supply association designed to supply necessaries to members at a cheaper price than the local market was a risky experiment, unless encouraged and even assisted by Government; that it would not be managed by experts, would have to face expert competition, and the danger of ignorance or even dishonesty in the management....[60]

Governor Robertson's observations were correct, but despite these conciliatory gestures, an underlying fear of, and opposition to, the attempts at business ventures by O'Neal and the WMA persisted. The Governor's inquiry about O'Neal's failure to seek Government help and sympathy, and about the secret meetings held by the Organization, bore this out. In fact, a lack of confidence in the judgment and maturity of O'Neal and the WMA was very evident. In the same dispatch, Robertson expressed his doubts:

> The impression left with me as a result of this interview was that information supplied to me by the Inspector-General was correct: that Dr O'Neal's intention was to promote strikes as the only means of improvement in wages; and that his objects are not entirely altruistic....[61]

The WMA no doubt had clear objectives in mind as to the means by which they should organize themselves to capture political power. However, in any polity, identifying the means to capture power, and seizing it, posed two completely different challenges. The WMA found it difficult to achieve the latter. They established strong links with Cipriani's Workingmen's Organization in Trinidad. In 1928, funds were raised to obtain a 'delegate' who, O'Neal claimed, 'is coming to get us amalgamated with the British Labour Party.' Many visiting trade unionists, from the West Indies and further afield, lectured WMA members on numerous occasions, on aspects of trade unionism, thereby raising their consciousness and improving their organizational skills. Frederick Roberts, a TUC delegate, and Arthur Cipriani, of the Trinidad Workingmen's Association, visited Barbados in 1927, and lectured at the WMA hall at Passage Road on trade union organization. Similar lectures were given by James Springer, an ex-soldier of the British West India Regiment during March 1932.[62] The WMA at this juncture emphasized solid organization, and the establishment of international links.

The WMA no doubt contemplated adopting an organizational structure along the lines of the British Labour Party. The underlying objective was to act as a bargaining agent for the local labouring classes. Failure to organize the waterfront workers in 1927 was countered by some success in the sugar industry. O'Neal boasted about the WMA's success in October 1927:

> The Association come on the scene to help you. We are going to stop this damn foolishness, but how are we going to stop it – by getting together. About six months ago wages were very low in the country; some were getting 8d. per day now getting 1/3 and upwards. This was changed by the Barbados Association. At the parish of St Andrew the canes were spoiling and the people won't work and now they are getting 1/8 per day and food. This is also taking place at St Lucy's parish. This is caused by combination of the Workingmen's Association....[63]

The seed of a vibrant labour union was being planted. Moses Small expressed the main objective of the WMA as a need to free the working class by putting Dr O'Neal in the House of Assembly 'to fight a multitude of wrongs in the House.'[64] Another activist, William Marshall, stressed what was expected from the workers:

> The Association (WMA) begs no apology of any man; we don't want you to beat anyone, nor set fire in the country, nor to castrate anybody, we want you to talk to your employers like men.[65]

O'Neal's election to the House of Assembly in 1932 was hailed as an important milestone in this struggle; a means by which the cause of the labouring classes could be advanced. Changes were expected to be achieved within the existing constitutional and parliamentary framework by a 'radical' transformation of the political order, rather than by violence and confrontation. Indeed, Seku Toure's maxim that oppressed people should seek first the political kingdom and all things will be added later was definitely embraced by the Barbadian working-class activists.

The attempts by the Democratic League, from 1924, to place its members in the House of Assembly were based on such a conviction. There was the widely held belief that the recruitment to political office, and the participation of Blacks in the legislative process, could place them in critical areas of decision-making. They could then use the colonial legislature to advance the cause of the labouring classes.

The WMA's bid to place O'Neal in the House of Assembly met with many difficulties. One of the most disheartening setbacks was that it did not meet with the full approval of some black middle-class members of the Democratic League, many of whom disassociated themselves from his activities with the organization. O'Neal's abrasive methods of political agitation, as well as his close association and identification with working-class activists, were never perceived as respectable conduct for a medical practitioner. In essence, the black middle class could accept the Democratic League's strategy of seeking political office by electoral contest, but the raucous political speeches at open air meetings, the protest against social inequality, the marches, and the threats to organize strikes, by the WMA, were too prone to open race and class conflict to be sanctioned by respectable middle-class aspirants. O'Neal, in short, was perceived as a traitor to his class and scoffed at by the black middle class.

Even some black working-class activists in the WMA were aware of the black middle class's perceptions of Dr O'Neal. George Belle was forthright in his condemnation of them:

> Why Dr Sealy and others of the leading class of the Negroes could not do as Dr O'Neal has done, and let the other fellows [whites] see that the professional class of the Negroes are uplifting the lower ones, then they themselves will come along with us? How long are you going to allow yourselves to be always fooled? [66]

On another occasion Edwin Turpin spoke in a similar tone:

Comrades, we are here in connection with the labour question; the Doctor O'Neal is a man of Education, he has come to us to teach us the way that we may be able to better condition and educate our children; therefore, it is our duty to hold on to him and support this course; you will not find another man of his ability to come among us to teach us about life whether political or social or take part with us in anything else; therefore it is our duty to clamour for that which is right.[67]

William Marshall was very direct in his assessment of the black middle class, 'Where are those black Harrisonians, why don't they come here and assist their poor colour up, the only one that you will see is the great Dr O'Neal?'[68] A distinct lack of confidence was definitely expressed in the attitude of the black middle class, especially the professionals, by these working-class activists.

## Succumbing to the Pressure of Victimization

For reasons not easy to explain, neither the WMA nor the UNIA developed into full-fledged political parties. Probably this was due to the intimidation and victimization of the leadership and membership of these organizations. Indeed, the leaders of both organizations were actively persecuted because of their activities. James Chase, a UNIA member, spoke of being told by his employer that he heard he was a member of both the WMA and the UNIA.[69] Fitzgerald Haynes, President of the UNIA, in 1928, unexpectedly submitted his resignation to the Secretary, claiming 'I am a servant of the Government…I see a lot of funny things happening.' When scolded as a coward by his colleagues, he insisted that being a government employee influenced his decision to relinquish ties with the UNIA.[70] William Marshall, a WMA activist, and an employee of the Cigarette Factory at Roebuck Street, was told he could not continue his employment there much longer because of his affiliation with Dr O'Neal's association. Marshall claimed that he rebuked his employers for involving themselves in the 'Negro business.'[71] However, a minute in a police file has shown that he succumbed to the repeated pressure of victimization:

William Marshall, prominent member of the above Association, also one of the leading speakers, who used to work at the Cigarette Factory Roebuck Street but was dismissed many months ago, he wrote and begged the managers of the above factory to take him back. They said yes, but at a reduced pay to that which he used to get. Marshall said that he repented much of having joined the Association.[72]

Joseph Garner, an ex-soldier who served in the British West India Regiment, became actively involved with the political activities of the WMA and the UNIA on his return to Barbados. He received no help from the Returned Soldiers Committee and no 'further chance on inquest as a juror' because of these activities. In addition, a thorough review of his citizenship was made in contemplation of expelling him as an undesirable citizen.[73] A similar fate awaited John Catwell, ex-serviceman of the British West India Regiment in Sierra Leone, West Africa, who became an active member of the WMA and the UNIA. A police dossier kept details of his personal history and employment which they used to victimize him:

John Catwell
Born 3.1.1873 at St Philip, Barbados
Educated: Ebenezer
lst Employment: Servant
lst Government employment: Soldier W.I. Regiment
lst employment as Auxiliary Postman: 1.3.1929
Promoted 3rd Grade Postman: 9.7.28
Promoted 2nd Grade Postman: 1.4.1931
He is a man of strong character and individuality inclined to be truculent but he is a good worker. I will keep an eye on him.
He is on City Route No. 6 Public Buildings, Pier Head, Bay Street, Dunlow Lane to foot of Garrison Hill.[74]

Catwell was dismissed on a Civil Service regulation and forced to resign on reaching age 65, even though his good health, good work ethic and his willingness to continue were acknowledged as admirable qualities. These, however, were overlooked because of his political activities.

Similar details were kept on other UNIA and WMA members with the sole purpose of discovering any means by which they could be pressured into discontinuing their political activities. Those who found themselves without an independent livelihood were particularly vulnerable. A minute by the Police again exposed this intention clearly:

Leach Worrell, Westbury Road. Shopkeeper.

Annie Hooper, Westbury Road, St Michael. Looks after domestic work.

Doris Bennett (Demerarian)

Melville Inniss, St Hills Road, Carrington Village. Employed as a Porter of Government Railway Bridgetown.

George Belle, Bank Hall, St Michael, Used to keep a provision shop, but now clean...

Chase Gap, Halls Road. Sells wood and coal at home.

Edwin Miller, New Orleans, a ship labourer.

William Yard, Church Village, Bridgetown and a vendor of aerated drinks.[75]

Melville Inniss, Annie Hooper and Edwin Miller, in particular, were constantly harassed on their jobs by their employers and by the Police. This type of psychological pressure reminded them that their radical activities coupled with their dependence upon a job for personal survival were incompatible. The strategy of persecuting the political activists of the UNIA and the WMA no doubt played a part in hindering the progress of these organizations.

The plan to direct the full force of persecution at the leading political activists of the UNIA and WMA is the *modus operandi* observed in all attempts to destabilize or suppress any organization. The most obvious targets are the leaders, the source of all ideas, tactics and inspiration for the members, and so it is logical to believe that if this group is removed, or neutralized, the main body of the membership should become a harmless group of disoriented and demoralized people. In addition, leaders who are preoccupied with their own personal safety can hardly find the time to work for the advancement of the organization, or to provide the motivation for the regular members which will ensure the continuity of the organization. This destabilization appears to have been one of the main factors that inhibited the progress of the UNIA and the WMA.

The colonial authorities were also quite clever in extending the strategy of intimidation and victimization to the regular members of the UNIA and WMA, and any other potential members. A general fear pervaded the society. Afro-Barbadians were afraid of associating with members of these organizations. The surveillance of the UNIA and WMA meetings by the police resulted in a subtle form of intimidation which kept away all but the brave few. In the rural districts, drivers of estate gangs attended meetings to discover who attended, in order to report them to estate owners. A deputation of the WMA before the West Indian Sugar Commission ventilated this policy of intimidation fully in October 1929:

> **The Chairman**: Doesn't the Working Men's Association exist for the purpose of informing that class of persons as to what are his rights? Have you no organization for keeping your people informed of their rights?
>
> **Mr Sebro**: Yes, Sir, we have, but what happens is that intimidation prevents them from getting information from the Association. If anyone is seen coming for information he is victimized, and after victimization you know what happens. The labourer has his bread and butter to work for. All the Association has to give them is knowledge, and that doesn't help. The poor fellow sees hard. After so many years of intimidation, it is very hard for the labourers to understand what is told them...
>
> **The Chairman**: Are you quite sure that they are afraid to come to your Association because they would be victimized?
>
> **Mr Sebro**: We have understood all of that from them. We have often asked them to come to us for information and they say they cannot come, because they are afraid to do so.
>
> **The Chairman**: Are your meetings conducted in an orderly manner?
>
> **Mr Sebro**: Our meetings are conducted in an orderly manner. They are attended by Police whose very presence causes a scare among the members....
>
> **Mr Moses Small**: Another point is this. Very often you will find the driver of an estate present at our meetings in the country to see if any of them are there. He writes down their names and takes them to the manager of the estates, who calls them up, questions them, and cautions them not to attend the meetings of the Association...

**The Chairman:** The Police have attended your meetings, but they have never taken action against you.

**Mr Sebro**: No, Sir.

**Mr Small:** What we are trying to show is that the people, owing to the fact that they are victimized, are scared at the presence of the policeman. The people are afraid that they might be carried before the Police Magistrate, if they visit the Association, and be treated badly, if they become members.

**The Chairman**: In your memorandum you go on to say that you have received a considerable number of letters from labourers setting out their grievances. They have begged hard not to mention their names, but some of them are from Mount Gay, Oxford, Cane Garden, Spring Hall, Bromefield, Bourbon and other plantations in the leeward parishes. As I say, we cannot go into the grievances of labourer against their employers, because this is not part of our commission.[76]

The security apparatus used against the WMA and the UNIA extended to covertly opening mail from the WMA to the Labour Party and from the local UNIA to its parent organization in New York. On occasion, mail was seized. In addition, licenses to hold fund-raising dances and concerts at their Passage Road and Westbury halls, were denied. Israel Lovell, President of the Westbury branch of the UNIA, was prosecuted for 'keeping a place of public entertainment' without first holding a licence.[77] The suppression of the UNIA and the WMA focused strongly on the priority list of the security forces, and no stone was left unturned in achieving this.

By the late 1930s, the UNIA and the WMA appeared to be going through a phase of stagnation. Members of both organizations became the leading members and organizers of other groups such as the Barbados Progressive League in the late 1930s. O'Neal died in November 1936 and the Barbados Political Association was formed by an old Garveyite, Louis Sebro, out of the remnants of both the WMA and the UNIA. However, it appeared as though, from November 1936 until the arrival of Clement Payne in March 1937, a political lull occurred in Barbados.[78] The paucity of police reports on the period attest to the low level of political activity. The Barbados Political

Association itself was in a state of stagnation and only came to life when the Letters Patent issue surfaced in March 1937.[79] Political activity, however, did not cease entirely. It was carried on in a different form, and at a different level, in the many social and cultural clubs such as Dan Blackett's Social Physical Cultural Club, the Bank Hall Cultural Club and Arlington Newton's Universal Ulotrichian Society. These organizations did not engage in the same manner of political campaigning as the UNIA and the WMA, but it is known that, apart from their social activities, they also provided the platform for political discussions of issues.[80] In this way, they served as outlets for grievances and, in the process, helped to politicize their largely Afro-Barbadian membership.

The Universal Ulotrichian Union was the most politically-oriented of these low-keyed social groups. Its leader, Arlington Newton, started his political activities in the form of trade union organization during the First World War, in St Kitts. He was accused of stirring up industrial unrest in Antigua, in March 1918, and was deported in the process. On arrival in Barbados, he continued his activities. There is no evidence of any active political recruitment in Barbados, even though he wrote numerous petitions to the Secretary of State on behalf of the working classes. His following was arrogantly described as 'small' and his position in Barbados as one of a 'prophet with little honour.'[81]

Newton's campaign focused upon the formation of a West Indian Federation, the liberalization of the franchise, and the improvement of living conditions for the labouring classes. He made a most pertinent observation on Barbadian society when he stated, 'a fundamental readjustment must be instituted and talent in official circles must take the place of class and caste distinction.'[82] The argument is advanced here that the activities of individuals like Arlington Newton and Fitzherbert King – a graduate of the College of Preceptors, London, who was described as possessing an 'inordinate love for writing'[83] – cannot be easily dismissed. The petitions did indeed capture the attention of some colonial administrators, and so, in a way, pressured the political establishment into recognizing the need for change. However, it is very difficult to measure the precise impact such forms of political agitation made on the consciousness of the black working class.

## The Arrival of Clement Payne in March 1937

Clement Payne's arrival in Barbados on March 26, 1937 injected some vigour into the political climate of Barbados. Payne was the son of Barbadian parents, and had spent most of his adult life actively involved in political and trade union activity in Trinidad. According to his memoirs, he was an organizer of the Trinidad and Tobago National Union Centre at Crystal Hall, Henry Street, Port of Spain, and a member of the African National Congress, an affiliate to a similar body in West Africa. He was also involved in the West Indian Youth League, the Eastern Literary and Dramatic Club and the Thespian Debating Club. As a member of the Eastern section of the Trinidad Workingmen's Association, which was later transformed into the Trinidad Labour Party, he organized the first political debating club in the island. The last public duties he performed before leaving for Barbados were 'to assist in re-organizing some of the defunct divisions of the Universal Negro Improvement Association.'[84] In essence, Payne arrived in Barbados as an experienced political campaigner eager to continue his political activity.

He aptly wrote,

> I arrived at one definite conclusion and that was to organize the working people of Barbados; this I went about with my best zeal and interest and I got the help and support of a good many eager workers who were only too willing to see that the masses received proper political education and from amongst them I selected the most capable speakers with the required ability and began my big Campaign of ORGANIZING. I started a series of MASS MEETINGS with the one objective afore stated, and here began the romance of my political career in Barbados.[85]

His effort was an instant success, if the enthusiasm of his following and the alarm of the merchant-planter oligarchy are employed as criteria for measuring his success. With his grassroots political activists, Menzies Chase, Ulric Grant, Darnley Alleyne, Mortimer Skeete and Israel Lovell, all able campaigners from the UNIA and the WMA, Payne created a political storm with his attacks on the white oligarchy and the black middle class, the latter of whom he labelled 'bluffers.'[86] He stressed the need for the workers to be organized if they were to make any progress against the capitalists. Payne called for the establishment of old age pensions, workmen's compensation, and compulsory education. He condemned, in the most vehement way, Italy's invasion of Ethiopia. His quick success alarmed the local white oligarchy and exposed the lethargy of the black middle class.

The key to understanding Payne's influence on Barbados resided in his identification with the working class of Barbados. Whereas other organizations appeared to work on behalf of the workers, Payne advocated working *with* the workers and using their power and solidarity as a political force. It was probably the first time in modern Barbadian political history that anyone placed so much confidence in the organizing potential of the labouring classes. As an experienced and astute campaigner, Payne was able to touch the political nerve of the working classes by exploiting contemporary events to educate the masses. For example, when in June 1937 news of Trinidad's industrial unrest and rebellion reached Barbados, Payne held special public meetings, which were well publicized, to bring the workers up to date. The meetings were well attended, and Payne's first-hand knowledge of the industrial climate in Trinidad was an asset to the process. At the same time as the Trinidadian crisis, a strike broke out at the Central Foundry in Barbados and, when the newspapers failed to report it, Payne went on the attack. He accused the *Barbados Advocate* of assuming a 'hush-hush policy,' and the other newspapers of deceiving the public.[87] He seized the opportunity to demonstrate how the interests of the workers were neglected by a planter-dominated press. By this time, he thought the 'people were serious about organizing themselves,' and so the search was on for a Hall to start the Barbados Progressive Workingmen's Association to fulfil this purpose. This organization was never formed, as Payne was arrested by two detectives on July 22, after attending a Committee Meeting.

Within the relatively short period of four months, Payne had taken over the leadership of the working class from the Barbados Political Association. Why was he able to displace the Association so easily? The answer resides in the lethargic attitudes of its members, their preoccupation with respectability, and the fear of victimization on the part of its leaders and the black middle class who patronized it. According to Louis Sebro, one of its early leaders, the Association's aim was 'to advance the condition of the working men,' not through the medium of violence, but in a 'constitutional way.' Payne's methods, he insisted, were 'different.'[88] He did not elaborate on what he meant by 'different' except to admit that he never heard Payne advocating violence, even though he understood that he told the people that their employers were robbing them. Political canvasser, H. A. Bourne, in his evidence before the Deane Commission, spoke of attending Payne's meetings with the sole purpose of trying 'to break them up,' but he was always rebuked by the crowd; who accused him of not 'telling them what Payne told them.'[89] During Payne's trial, some people were overheard to mutter, 'because he opening we eyes they are trying to lock him up.'[90]

It should not be implied that the consciousness of the labouring classes was sharpened to the extent of making them a class in the Marxist scheme of class struggle – that is, that their deprived state of existence raised their consciousness to the extent of uniting them in a violent overthrow of the merchant-planter oligarchy. Nevertheless, the depressed living conditions of the urban folk and the work of the UNIA and the WMA made them receptive to Payne's message. It was his presence which focused, and eventually triggered, the underlying class conflict. The black professional class failed to recognize the key role which Payne played in the months leading up to the July 1937 rebellion. This ignorance was reflected in their perceptions, as they gave evidence before the Deane Commission. H. A. Bourne thought Payne had a 'bad style' of inciting 'the ignorant class' with his rhetoric – 'educate and agitate but do not violate.' Such speeches were, according to him, of a 'drastic kind.' Dan Blackett, on the other hand, said Payne was not a politician but a mere labour organizer.[91] H. A. Vaughan admitted that he never attended any of Payne's meetings, but he considered his political thoughts as 'vapid.' He expressed surprise at the size and the enthusiasm of the crowd in the courtyard during Payne's trial.[92] E. D. Mottley said he heard Payne on several occasions, and at some of his meetings he adopted the wrong 'principle' of preaching 'black against white.' He thought he was a 'Communist.'[93] Governor Mark Young referred to Payne simply as an 'agitator' – in short, a trouble-maker.

All the above assessments of Payne, except in the case of Dan Blackett, failed to explain his sensational popularity with the labouring classes. They all had an element of hostility towards him, and moreover, failed to recognize that he had come to grips with underlying tensions and conflicts in Barbados in a way that the black professional class, excepting O'Neal, had never recognized. Payne had exposed the class antagonisms and institutional racism in a forthright way. He had to be silenced in order to curb his influence over the labouring classes.

The police kept a close watch on Payne during his sojourn in Barbados and, in the last days of his campaign, even the printers refused to print advertisements and hand bills for his public meetings. However, it is the Revd W. A. Beckles, AME Church minister and editor of the *Advocate Weekly*, who provides the clue to this attempt to isolate and suppress Payne:

Your Excellency will remember too that it was I who, in the interests of peace and order, sent you a pamphlet of Payne's first public meeting, suggesting to you to take steps to nip the trouble in the bud. My fears were by no means exaggerated or unfounded as subsequent events [riots] only too clearly revealed....[94]

Beckles played a personal role in trying to suppress Payne's influence. There is no reference to his political meetings in the *Advocate Weekly* or in the sister paper, the *Advocate Daily*, the newspaper with the largest circulation in 1937. Beckles also played a personal role in Payne's conviction at his trial:

In connection with the riots which are still fresh in the public memory, it was I who told you, Sir, of Payne's knowledge of his birthplace. I was summoned by the Police to give evidence. I told you, the rioters were asking everywhere for me.[95]

From the available evidence, it seems as though there was a concerted effort to undermine Payne. When that method failed, deportation was employed as a last resort, on July 25, 1937. It is common knowledge that this action by the Barbadian authorities acted as a detonator for the social pressures, which had been building up for a long time and which burst asunder in the form of 'rioting' in Bridgetown and some rural districts. Payne's deportation acted as the trigger factor that led to the eventual outbreak of the rebellion of July 1937. However, it is erroneous to simply dismiss the events as riots and disturbances for, as a subsequent examination in another chapter will reveal, there was more political protest exhibited by the crowds than previously thought.

# 5

# REACTION IN BARBADOS TO THE ITALO-ETHIOPIAN CONFLICT, 1935

O ctober 1935 was a distressing time for the people of the African state of Ethiopia. A highly disciplined army sent by Benito Mussolini, Italy's fascist leader, invaded the Horn of Africa like the fury of a tropical storm. His well-equipped army with its 'modern' technology, including an Air Force, rained down bombs and deadly poisonous gas on helpless Ethiopians, many of whom were mere herdsmen wielding primitive weapons. Their spears, clubs and clumsy rifles proved no match for a modern, ruthless army determined to crush with impunity any local resistance. To many contemporaries, a most unfair contest ensued, as the blood-thirsty military tiger of Italy pounced upon the meek, helpless lamb of Ethiopia. Mussolini had once again fulfilled the boast he once made to his mother, that one day he would 'astonish the world.'[1]

Mussolini had secretly sanctioned the invasion of Ethiopia since January 3, 1933. This decision followed closely on his subjugation of Northern Somalia in 1928, and the conquest of Cyrenaica in 1932. Basking in the glory of these two successes, his craving for further success waxed strong. As a result of a combination of a bitter racial dislike for people of African descent and a need to revenge Italy's defeat at the battle of Adowa, 1896, military aggression against Ethiopia proceeded in utmost earnestness.[2]

## Reaction in the African Diaspora

Italy's unprovoked attack on Ethiopia met considerable condemnation throughout the African diaspora. Richard B. Moore, the Barbadian-born Pan-African activist residing in Harlem, New York, captured the mood of Afro-Americans there: 'A new wave of consciousness spread through Harlem as the people reacted strongly against Italy in October 1935. Organizations were set up to mobilize support.'[3]

There was a similar response to the news in the British-colonized West Indies. In St Lucia, a meeting at Clarke's Theatre, Castries, passed a resolution expressing 'deep sympathy towards Ethiopia in her present struggle' with Italy.[4] At a mass meeting in the Town Hall, Port-of-Spain, Trinidad, three resolutions condemned the aims of Mussolini and appealed to Britain to 'intercede to ensure the independence in the ancient Empire of Ethiopia.' A mass meeting held at the Queen's Park Pavilion, St Georges, Grenada, ended with a resolution which denounced Italy's wanton and lawless aggression against Abyssinia. Hundreds of ex-servicemen in Jamaica 'pledged immediate service, should Britain be drawn into the war' on the side of Ethiopia.[5]

In Barbados, Italy's aggression was met with vehement protests. Clennel Wickham, a prominent journalist writing in the local newspaper, the *Barbados Advocate Weekly*, captured the spirit of Barbadian solidarity, and West Indian shock. He wrote:

> The interest shown by West Indian Communities in the Italo-Abyssinian quarrel is significant. In every colony, big and small, there have been public meetings and demonstrations, and strongly worded Resolutions have been dispatched to His Majesty's Government.[6]

Wickham kept the conflict alive in the minds of the Barbadian public through his column, 'People and Things.' Moreover, the *Barbados Advocate Weekly*, the *Barbados Weekly Observer* and the *Barbados Weekly Herald*, perhaps recognizing the striking impact that the Italo-Ethiopian conflict had made on a large portion of their readers, carried front-page captions on the war, almost uninterrupted from October 1935 until March 1939. The news items relayed by foreign correspondents were usually accompanied by photographs graphically exposing the awesome war machinery of Italy, and the excesses committed against the people of Ethiopia. In this way, the horrors of the war were kept in the local public's focus through blow-by-blow accounts. An incredible imprint therefore had been made on the minds of Afro-Barbadians.

In another section of the print media, Wynter Crawford, writing in the *Barbados Weekly Observer*, rebuked Italy's aggression in a forthright way:

Italy's imperialism has momentarily cast its gaze to the independent African State of Abyssinia, and is intent upon its absorption. Mussolini, after recapitulation in its vaguest terms of a list of grievances, which even if they had been well founded, were of the most trivial, indeed, puerile character, calmly announced the Italian Government's intention of establishing a complete protectorate over the African State by military force if necessary. There is hardly a more revolting instance of the predatory imperialism of modern Europe. In order to satisfy the nationalistic and imperial ambitions entertained by Italian statesmen and by a relatively minute section of the community, masses of innocent men, women and children will be slaughtered. There can surely be few parallels in history to the indifference towards the opinion and conscience of civilized States which the aggressor has shown in entering on this quarrel.[7]

On another occasion, Crawford expressed the intense condemnation of Italy's aggression:

There is no checking this intense spirit of anti-Italian feeling which is gradually permeating the entire West Indies. The West Indian negro with any kind of blood flowing in his veins is man enough to realize that this quarrel is his own, and so fearlessly to express his sympathy with his Ethiopian brother, regardless of whatever may be the British attitude.[8]

An editorial in another local newspaper, the *Barbados Weekly Herald*, was no less terse:

What a gruesome sensation fills our minds as we conjure up the picture that must be presenting itself in Ethiopia. Think of what the telegrams tell us and what reaches us by induction: Women, children and other peaceful people going about their business in the villages, seeing aeroplanes possibly for the first time in their lives, being bombed while they held white flags. Red Cross Hospital bombed and nurses killed. The terror-stricken villagers as defenceless as they are numerous, having bombs from aeroplanes dropped among them promiscuously and without mercy.[9]

Every means was employed by the print media in Barbados to ventilate the aggression of fascist Italy. In the 'Poem of the Week' in a local newspaper, the writer condemned Mussolini's lust for power in a cogent way. The poem is entitled 'The Duce's Hour':

> Put back the clock and then – put back the clock;
> Progress is but a word for idle mention.
> Geneva deals in clocks, but this shall shock
> The forward sweep of any such invention.
> Put back the clock to lust of blood and power!
> Strew havoc – but remember in your strewing
> The desert sands may well record the hour
> Of yet another tyrant's last undoing.[10]

Newspapers also resorted to political satire in cartoons, to influence their readers about the Italo-Ethiopian conflict. Two popular characters, John and Susie, sit over a drink to discuss the Italo-Ethiopian war in Barbadian dialect:

> Uh see oh million bodies Sue,
> Lay rottin in the Sun.
> Well I was in de war zone gal
> But uh din have muh gun...
>
> Uh was in Abyssinia Sue
> En all dese tings uh see
> Uh see aeroplanes fly
> Straight from Italy
>
> Uh human in uh lion skin
> Was givin ordahs Sue
> E name was Mussilini, he
> Wus saying wuh fuh do.
>
> 'Exterminate the nigguh boys
> 'And occupy duh land
> 'Italians need expansion lands,
> 'So wipe out every man.'[11]

The use of graphic pictures and cartoons in the local vernacular proved to be very effective. In a series entitled 'Talk of the Town,' the writer seized the opportunity to use the local dialect to deliver biting political commentary in a satirical way. On occasion, not only was Italy's aggression rebuked, but calls for action such as economic sanctions were mooted. The view was expressed that Ethiopia was suffering at the hands of Italy, largely because it was a black nation. Furthermore, the apparent reluctance of the League of Nations to side with Ethiopia, and indeed, of the white nations of Europe to forcefully condemn Italy or to impose economic sanctions, smacked of shameful hypocrisy. Even the local Established Church, still a bastion of racial prejudice in the early twentieth century, was accused of hypocrisy because of its silence on the matter:

Uh wondah why de Church suh mute
Bout this impendin war
Duh en ask from de pulpit yet
Wah dis dispute for

De nineteen fourteen-eighteen war
Find parsons pun the knees
Duh se to pray dat war should cease
Three times pun a Sundee

But den dat was ah righteous war
En Germany was wrong
Democracy was threatenrd, Sue
The first was sharpened strong…

No pulpit was en gwine wage
Selassie skin is black.
De Allies en gwine pull duh sword
Fuh turn Italians back.[12]

During personal contact with Sam Gibbs, a Barbadian who lived through the Italo-Ethiopian conflict, he spoke passionately of his eagerness to obtain local newspapers to keep abreast of the situation in Ethiopia.[13] Gibbs, it must be stated, was socialized in an environment of anti-colonial activity and Pan-African struggle. His mother, Alexandriana Gibbs, was an ardent Garveyite of both the Reed Street and Westbury branches of the Universal

Negro Improvement Association (UNIA) in Bridgetown, Barbados. She spoke regularly at the UNIA meetings at their Hall, and at public meetings held in Bridgetown and the rural districts throughout the island. Apart from her reputation as a fiery public speaker, Alexandriana Gibbs also acted as the local agent for the *Negro World* newspaper, the New York based publication of the UNIA. In addition, she operated a night school at the Reed Street branch of the UNIA which provided the only source of formal instruction for many black underprivileged children.[14] In short, Sam Gibbs's socialization in the local Pan-African tradition provided the consciousness for his empathy toward black Ethiopians in their time of peril. Other Afro-Barbadians were also stimulated by the diet of Pan-African ideology relentlessly espoused by the local UNIA and Charles Duncan O'Neal's Working Men's Association (WMA). The horrors of the Italo-Ethiopian conflict, in essence, occurred at a time that assisted in cementing a growing racial consciousness in the island.

### The Early Activities of the WMA and Ethiopianism

Anti-colonial organizations with a Pan-African persuasion emerged in Barbados during the 1920s. Charles Duncan O'Neal's WMA, founded in 1926, was one such organization. In much the same distinctive character as the UNIA, its pro-Garveyite working-class leaders such as George Belle, Edwin Turpin, John Catwell, Leach Worrell, Anne Hooper and William Yard placed much emphasis on 'the unity of the Negro' and black self-help. They made constant references to the slavery experiences of black West Indians and viewed the period as one largely responsible for the legacy of economic and political disfranchisement of black West Indians. These activists always argued that the major task necessary for a cultural and political recovery of black people was the recapture of Ethiopia as the 'Mecca' of the continent. These sentiments were expressed during the 1920s, long before the outbreak of the war between Italy and Ethiopia. This nostalgic emphasis on the glories of Ethiopia has been identified by scholars as 'Ethiopianism,' and it played a big part in raising the consciousness of West Indians of African descent. So it did not take much for the local population to identify with the plight of Ethiopia in 1935, in that the name of the country was well known because of political activists. Frederick 'Moses' Small, a WMA activist and an ardent convert to Garveyism, said on one occasion, in the heat of a public meeting,

> We [the black race] will not be satisfy until we walk on the continent
> of Africa, then we will be able to sing more lusty. We are clamoring
> for better conditions for our people. We are scattered all over the world
> and not represented. The time will come when God said He will rebuild
> the temple.[15]

He reminded his audience to reject the teachings of the local religious leaders who 'eat the flesh of their flock and drink their milk.' Instead, he urged the local labouring classes to think about providing for the 'future generation.'[16]

The theology of the African Orthodox Church, embraced at the prayer meetings held by local activists of the WMA, identified with the glories of Africa's past. They espoused Garvey's insistence that the Christian scriptures should be interpreted from the experience of Africans. At the same time, the teachings of the Christian churches in Barbados, especially the Anglican Church, were seen as hostile to the interest of the black population. These churches were denounced as 'deceivers' and 'sky pirates' who pointed the masses 'towards the sky while they were living like dogs on earth.'[17] At times, Ethiopia was cited in relation to the Biblical people of Axum, and Afro-Barbadians were exhorted to exhibit pride in their African ancestry, and to embrace the tenets of Christianity which portrayed the black race in a positive light.[18]

Some political activists went a step further. For example, Melville Inniss, an active member of the Westbury branch of the UNIA, made an effort to recruit black Barbadians for repatriation to Liberia in order to escape the horrors of Barbadian life.[19] There is no evidence that any Afro-Barbadians accepted his offer. Nevertheless, the motives for the recruitment drive suggest the degree of socio-economic pressure which Barbadians of African descent were forced to endure. Italy's aggression towards Ethiopia could not have come along at a better time – just as the ideological consciousness of the black population was aroused by political agitation, spearheaded by local black Pan-Africanists, which emphasized racial pride.

During a UNIA meeting, Chrissie A. Braithwaite, a black Assemblyman and a member of the Democratic League, lamented the plight of Afro-Barbadians during the early twentieth century:

> You [black Barbadians] are a downtrodden race. For many years
> you were heavers of wood and drawers of water. You are denied an

education; the environment in which you are placed, you are unable to help yourselves.[20]

The WMA, it must be stressed, played a significant role in galvanizing racial awareness in Barbados. The horrors of Italy's actions in Ethiopia and the apparent hypocrisy of members of the League of Nations, therefore, were good political fodder for a conscious population steeped in the Pan-African philosophy of Marcus Garvey.

## Response of the Colonial Office

The acute nature of the protests by the local branches of the UNIA and the WMA made it difficult for the Colonial authorities to ignore the feelings of the black population on any racial or political issue. Governor Mark Young, acting on the suggestions of his superiors at the Colonial Office, ordered an investigation in Barbados, to ascertain if there were any Italian missionaries on the island, who, if found, were to be deported immediately.[21] This directive was no more than a feeble gesture to appease local tempers as well as to seek revenge for similar action taken by the Italian authorities against British missionaries in Ethiopia. The search was futile, in that the majority of local Christian missionaries were expatriates of English or North American birth. It was, nevertheless, a reaction to the growing consciousness of the black section of the population.

Specific directives were also issued by the Colonial Office, urging West Indian colonial governments to boycott any Italian ships which ventured into the region. These ships were to be given the minimum of fuel and no handling of their cargo was to be encouraged.[22] Again the instructions were meaningless as far as Barbados was concerned, in that, Italy was no major trading partner of Barbados during the 1930s. Such a privileged trading status belonged to the United Kingdom and, to a lesser extent, Canada and the United States. For example, in 1935, 40.9 per cent of Barbados's imports came from the United Kingdom, 14.1 per cent from Canada, 11.7 per cent from the United States, 18.9 per cent from 'other parts of the British Empire' and 14.4 per cent arrived from 'other foreign countries,' in which Italy was not included. On the other hand, Barbados's exports – 97 per cent being sugar and its by-products, molasses and rum – were destined for the United Kingdom.[23]

## Response of Local Business Houses

The intense feeling of racial consciousness generated by the Italian-Ethiopian conflict reached such a pitch in Barbados that some enterprising local business houses, in their quest to attract customers, exploited it. In the *Barbados Advocate Weekly* an advertisement ran,

> The Ethiopians lack of modern war equipment has been a handicap to them. Why be handicapped by old fashioned cooking appliances? See the Modern Gas Appliances at the Gas Showroom.[24]

Another sales pitch for a local radio station went, 'WAR Radio Distribution Barbados Ltd $2.00 per month. Brings you up-to-the-minute news direct from British, French (relayed in English) and American stations.'[25] Still another advertisement played on the feelings of Afro-Barbadians towards the Italo-Ethiopian war: 'Rumours of War are RIFE – BUT – Business go on as usual....'[26] A. E. Taylor, who considered himself 'the poor people friend,' advertised:

> Nations at War for themselves
> Taylor at WAR FOR YOU
> During Next Week we will be offering
> SPECIAL AFTER-STOCK BARGAINS.[27]

The Barbadian mercantile community, dominated by the white sector of the population, recognized the impact of Garvey's Pan Africanist ideas upon the black population. They therefore sought to exploit black Barbadians' resentment of Italy's aggression in Ethiopia to their advantage.

## Fund-raising Efforts

Some local organizations were formed with the intention of providing financial support to Ethiopia in its time of distress. When members of the Abyssinian Welfare Fund held a fund-raising concert at the Beulah School in the eastern parish of St Phillip, it was described as 'a brilliant and unqualified success, with Bridgetown and other neighboring parishes well represented.'[28] At their prayer meetings held in the rural districts of the island, the UNIA solicited special collections for the Ethiopian cause.

A prayer service held by the Bethany Christian Mission in the heart of Bridgetown received a 'healthy contribution from the audience, for the

Ethiopian Red Cross Fund.'[29] A similar response was seen at the Abel Eversley's Mission Hall in Britton's Hill. At the Empire Theatre, some of the island's leading artistes held a well patronized concert in aid of the Abyssinian Red Cross Fund. Other prayer meetings and fund-raising efforts were conducted at the AME Church, the First West Indian Spiritualist Church, the Zion Pilgrim Baptist Church and the Evangelical Church of God.[30]

These meetings were generously supported by the working-class Afro-Barbadian audiences, who were themselves wilting under the pressure of a prolonged economic recession, and were in need of cash themselves. Their generosity was therefore seen as admirable in the circumstances, and clearly demonstrated their sympathy for the nation of Ethiopia.

The Italo-Abyssinian war, in short, served to exasperate the state of race relations between the white and black populations in the West Indies. Murchison Fletcher, the colonial Governor of Trinidad, cited 'racial feeling endangered by the Ethiopian War' as one reason for the social upheavals there in 1937.[31] In Barbados, a similar observation was made by some members of a black middle-class delegation who called on Governor Mark Young at the peak of the July 1937 rebellion. They readily admitted that racial feeling played a part in precipitating the unrest. Walter W. Reece, a prominent lawyer, remarked *inter alia*, 'The question now is not an economic one but a racial one....The wealthy section [whites] are not giving the other section [blacks] a square deal.'[32] Another member of the delegation, Grantley H. Adams, a lawyer-politician who later played a prominent role in the ill-fated West Indian Federation of 1958–62, expressed similar sentiments at the meeting.[27] Adams remarked that undoubtedly the Abyssinia war had a great deal to do with the matter, and it was the first time he really saw the 'beginning of the people talking about white against black.' Ernest D. Mottley testified before the Deane Commission that Clement Payne and his cohorts preached the colour question and took advantage of the Italo-Ethiopian war to stir up the ill will of the people. Clement Payne and his supporters, at their meetings leading up to the July 1937 rebellion, made reference to the invasion of Ethiopia in 1935. On one occasion Payne declarted,

> England and France sold out Ethiopia to the Italians. It is the intention of the other race to annihilate us. It is an advantage that has been taken of the Ethiopians and you should tell your children about these things.[34]

Wynter Crawford and Hylton Vaughan, in their evidence before the Moyne Commission in 1938, sensed a connection between the outbreak of the local upheavals and the Italo-Ethiopia conflict. Dan Blackett and Roland Edwards alluded to the heightened racial feelings during the 1937 rebellion in Barbados in their testimony to the Deane Commission.[35]

The resentment of Afro-Barbadians at Italy's invasion of Ethiopia, it must be stated, never subsided, even after the local rebellion of 1937. In fact, two years later, in 1939, their racial consciousness was stirred again, with the outbreak of the Second World War in Europe. British Colonial Officials, anticipating the outbreak of war, tried to recruit the Pan-Africanist ideology of the black West Indian population for their struggle against Italy in Europe. In Barbados, for example, a broadcast station was hurriedly set up with a programme 'designed specially to appeal to the poorer coloured sections of the community.'[36] D. E. Chase, the local Information Officer, was quite clear about its intentions:

> It is considered that under the conditions existing in Barbados, and perhaps in some other West Indian Colonies, the most valuable medium of propaganda is wireless broadcasting. It must, however, be remembered always that the section of the population at which such propaganda is to be chiefly aimed is the poor and less responsible labouring class, rather than the more educated.[37]

Chase continued, in his analysis, to perceive the Afro-Barbadian population as imbued with a 'naturally peaceful and happy disposition' as well as 'emotionally unstable, credulous and irresponsible to the last degree.' These intrinsic character traits, he argued, made the black Barbadian an easy prey for enemies of the British government.[38] Therefore, everything was to be done to target Afro-Barbadians for the British war effort. Chase immediately identified the Italo-Ethiopian war as the most effective propaganda subject to be championed by the British in order to recruit Afro-Barbadians against Italy.

This strategy was employed not only by local expatriate colonial administrators in the West Indies, but also at the Colonial Office itself. A comprehensive propaganda scheme was worked out for the region. A report from the Ministry of Information in the United Kingdom, which was circulated to all colonial governors in the British West Indies, cited the racial feelings exacerbated as a result of Italy's conquest of Abyssinia to be important propaganda fodder to be used against Italy. Mention was made of the Trinidad newspaper, the *People*, which maintained a correspondent at Djibouti who kept the region informed of events in Ethiopia. The report alluded to the *Union Messenger* of St Kitts which identified Haile Selassie of Ethiopia as 'our emperor.' Indeed, the colonial authorities were alarmed at the 'highly sympathetic references to the fate of Abyssinia in the West Indian press.' Furthermore, some disquiet was expressed at the 'Ras Tafari' and the 'King of Kings Salvation Mission' who had allowed their opposition to Italy to develop into a 'general anti-white feeling.'[39] Even though the British Colonial Officials felt uncomfortable at the heightened racial consciousness of Blacks in the West Indies, they were quite emphatic that such anti-Italian sentiments should be harnessed for the British war effort.

John Waddington, Barbados's Governor at the outbreak of the Second World War, wrote to his superiors at the Colonial Office complaining about a general feeling among Afro-Barbadians that the war was a white man's conflict which did not concern them. As a result, unlike the First World War, when over 2,000 men volunteered for active duty in the British West India Regiment, only 500 were interested in serving during the Second World War, mainly in the Royal Air Force. Hundreds were attracted by the high wages being offered in British ammunition factories and on US naval bases, but as to the giving of their lives for 'King and country,' such enthusiasm was apparently lacking. The colonial Governor opined that there was a generally held opinion by black Barbadians 'that during the Abyssinian war when Negroes were bombed, Britain did nothing' but was now willing to help the Poles 'because the latter are white.'[40]

Afro-Barbadians, like other black people of the African diaspora, reacted with shock and disgust at the invasion and conquest of Ethiopia by Italy in 1935. Protests were widespread, and remarkable bonds of solidarity were demonstrated with the people of Ethiopia. This solidarity was cemented largely by a local anti-colonial movement spearheaded by four branches of the UNIA, and later by Charles Duncan O'Neal's WMA, all adherents of a Pan-African ideology. These organizations succeeded in placing the struggle against colonialism and imperialism in Africa and the Caribbean on the agenda of Afro-Barbadian awareness since the 1920s. In short, the horrors of the Italo-Ethiopian war occurred at a time when the consciousness of the black population was aroused by intense political activity. It was therefore easy to use the conflict to further sharpen the political consciousness of the masses as the Pan-African activists did, or to divert it to the cause of the British war effort as the British colonial officials attempted to do. The evidence has shown, however, that black West Indians, and Afro-Barbadians in particular, were suspicious of the colonial officials' intentions.

The Italo-Ethiopian war, in essence, helped to crystallize Garvey's teachings of the 1920s and the 1930s, especially in relation to the need for unity among descendants of Africa in the black diaspora. During her hour of need, Ethiopia received much moral, and some financial support, from black West Indians. Afro-Barbadians, perceived as backward, conservative and uninterested in the affairs of African nations by local and expatriate Whites, were as vibrant in their protests against the atrocities of Italy as any other West Indians. Ethiopia was never perceived as another African nation with a battle of its own, but rather as a black nation persecuted by an international tyrant. Afro-West Indians let their opposition be known and they were very loud in their protests. In Barbados, when the rebellion started in July 1937, many social commentators and political activists were adamant that there was a racial element that was precipitated by the 1935 conflict between Ethiopia and Italy.

# 6

# RACE, CLASS AND THE JULY 1937 SOCIAL REBELLION

Immediately after the First World War, and as late as 1934, the Barbadian authorities had put in place an elaborate scheme against any impending social upheaval. Highly secretive plans were put into operation for the mobilization of the security forces, including the Volunteer Force, in case there was any kind of disorder.[1] This reinforcement of the island's security preparedness commenced in the 1920s in direct response to what was perceived as increasing 'restlessness' and the political mobilization of the Afro-Barbadian population by 'agitators' in the UNIA and the WMA. Yet, despite this vigilant preparation, the rebellion of July 1937 took the local authorities by surprise – surprise that it came at a time and with a fury which betrayed the long-held belief that black Barbadians were happy, docile and contented.[2]

This chapter will focus on the causes of the rebellion, as well as the nature of the 'unrest,' with the express purpose of understanding the intentions of the 'crowds' during the rebellion. Since few written records have survived, an attempt will be made to reconstruct the events through oral evidence and a critical analysis of the actions of the rebels, in order to reach some tentative conclusions concerning their intentions. The use of such a methodology has been pioneered elsewhere by E. P. Thompson, George Rudé, Charles Tilly, James Davies, Eric Hobsbawm and others.[3] To a large extent, they have argued that rioting crowds possessed a 'collective mentality,' that is, they are highly structured and, their behaviour and goals follow established political and moral traditions. In essence, rioting crowds are not basically lawless elements, but highly politicized people. All of these features of rioting crowds in Europe cannot be rigidly applied to the Barbadian situation because of the striking disparities between the two societies. Nevertheless, some aspects of the same methodology, where applicable and relevant, will be employed as a tool in order to gain a better understanding of the rebellion of July 1937.

Moreover, I view the 'unrest' of the 1930s in the British Caribbean, and indeed in Barbados, as more akin to rebellions than to riots. A rebellion is a violent uprising with the intention of effecting some change, with stated objectives by the rebels, who may be armed, or may confront the armed apparatus of the state during their actions. 'Disturbances' and 'riots' suggests haphazard interruption of tranquility by a mindless mass of people with no highly developed political consciousness. Inasmuch as there appeared to be 'trigger factors,' that is, specific incidents or events that stimulated the crowds to 'riot' during the 1930s, a close examination of their actions and behaviour would reveal more method in their madness. This aspect of the Barbadian rebellion will receive much attention here.

## Rebellion in the City of Bridgetown

The first evidence of 'disturbances' in Barbados occurred on the night of July 26, when a crowd, expecting to see Clement Payne before his deportation, went on the rampage. They vented their anger by smashing street lights in Nelson Street, Bay Street, Beckwith Street, Probyn Street and Jordan's Lane in the city. Cars outside the Empire Theatre were smashed and a bus belonging to the General Motor Company was damaged. This early activity appeared to be spontaneous and disorganized, except for a clash with the police at Golden Square which resulted in a sort of pitched battle between the two forces. The rebels, fighting with sticks and stones, kept up a constant bombardment. After a few minutes of missile throwing, the greatly outnumbered police were forced to make a hasty retreat amidst a hail of missiles.[4]

The next day, July 27, violence flared up again when a huge gang of rebels gathered on the wharf. They collected sticks and stones and, turning in the direction of Broad Street, smashed almost every store window, including Whitfield's, the City Pharmacy, the Ideal Store, Hope Ross Ltd, Emptage Electrical Co., Collins Ltd, Johnson's Stationery, Hutchinson & Co., and C. P. Harrison. Bridgetown was in chaos, especially Broad Street, the hub of the merchant-planter class business activity.[5] There appeared to be some purposive acts of destruction in these activities on Broad Street, for in three days of smashing and looting, Fogarty's Store remained untouched.[6] An eyewitness account testified that on July 27, when a rebel attempted to smash the show window, a crowd was overheard to exclaim, 'Leave Fogarty. He does give we a break.'[7] Why did the rebels behave in such a way?

William Fogarty's store on Broad Street was well known to the general public as a bargain centre, especially for cheap cloth, thereby affording many working-class Barbadians the opportunity at least to own a 'Sunday best.' In addition, it was one of the first stores, if not the only one in Bridgetown, to extend credit to the labouring classes. Perhaps by sparing Fogarty the wrath of looting, the rebels were expressing notions of fair play. In essence, they were perhaps exercising self-conscious precepts of justice through their behaviour and actions. In short, there was method in their apparent madness, on that fateful July 27 morning.

One can also detect vengeful acts on other white-owned business houses, not only on Broad Street, but in Baxters Road, Tudor Street and Lower Broad Street, which appeared to have been motivated by different feelings.[8] Eckstein Garage and Service Station on Lower Bay Street was looted and the window smashed. Cole's Garage was also smashed, the gasoline service tank destroyed and new cars pushed into the sea near the Victoria Bridge. The staff was also attacked.[9] The Vauxhall-Bedford Service Station of Robert Thom Ltd was next attacked, the gasoline tanks damaged, the day's cash stolen and two lorries pushed into the sea.[10] A parcel delivery van from Johnson and Redman was commandeered and set on fire in Westbury Road. Four cars parked in the Lower Green, opposite the Barbados Mutual Assurance Society, were overturned and two of them set on fire. Attention was then turned on the Barbados Mutual building itself where the white employees hid themselves amidst shouts encouraging others to kill 'the blasted sons of white bitches' inside. An attempt to burn the building was thwarted by armed police and the fire brigade.[11] Around 2:30 p.m. on July 27, a piece of cloth was set alight under the door of V. H. C. Hinds's business place at the corner of Nelson Street. This was put out by the Fire Brigade. E. B. Skeete, Chairman of Trustees of Goodridge House, Spry Street, reported the presence of a smoldering rag under the garage door.[12]

A gang of rebels also made an attempt to set fire to the exclusive Bridgetown Club, a bastion of vulgar racial discrimination. Two cars were set on fire, as well, at the nearby Cable Office. The *Barbados Advocate* described the fracas between the crowd and the police in front of the Bridgetown Club:

> Every window was attacked and those within the building were in
> desperate dread of their lives. A charge by Policemen with batons
> was easily repelled by an angry mob and the situation looked more

dangerous than ever. An armed party replaced the batons and the Police Magistrate read the Riot Act. Efforts were made to plead with the crowd but they turned a deaf ear. Suddenly the air was darkened with stones, bottles and other missiles dropped in the ranks of the Police and the order was given to fire.[13]

Some fell dead and a few were wounded, but the majority of the rebels scattered in haste amidst a hail of rifle fire.

The defiance of the crowds in their confrontation with the police was a very noticeable feature of their behaviour during the affair at the Mutual Building and the Bridgetown Club. Such behaviour was certainly out of character with the general notion of the passive Barbadian, espoused by colonial authorities. The police at the Brittons Hill post were 'marooned' by a large group of rebels, until reinforcements arrived. During the clash, a policeman was severely beaten, and another policeman, E. O. Plunkett, was almost torn to pieces in Trafalgar Square and in Probyn Street.[14] The blow-by-blow account of the rebellion in Bridgetown seems to suggest that it was more than aimless, senseless destruction of property – as described by the *Barbados Advocate* and the Report of Deane Commission at the time. The references to the rebels as 'unruly,' 'violent,' and 'lawless' conjure up, no doubt, images of anarchy, probably because of the spontaneity of the upheavals, and the subsequent violence, destruction and looting. However, an assessment of the behaviour and the actions of the rebels, beyond the outward appearances, would reveal an element of control and direction in these outbursts. The participants clearly attacked select white-owned businesses, and property, the living expression of their oppression. Similar types of behaviour can also be clearly identified in other upheavals in other societies.[15]

The attempts at arson during the rebellion of July 1937 are indeed a most revealing aspect of the participants' behaviour. The use of fire during other widely-research upheavals has highlighted its use as a symbol of ultimate defiance of, and a total obliteration of, the oppressors.[16] The chemical action of fire completely destroys or transforms any physical matter it comes in contact with, and so, during rebellions the use of fire as a weapon symbolizes the destruction of the oppressor in a total way, which could not be used before. The July 1937 rebellion in Barbados saw some attempts at arson by the participants. Perhaps the Barbadians, like other rebels, were expressing a long-suppressed subconscious desire to erase the oppressor, through the use of fire. In short, they were employing a 'weapon of the weak' to get even with their oppressors.

## Upheavals in the Rural Districts of the Island

From July 29, there was a significant shift in the rebellion, from Bridgetown to the rural districts. It took on some features which were more conspicuous here than in the urban area. For example, the presence of large, organized groups, moving around in gangs, was very evident. A crowd of 400 raided potatoes at Golden Grove estate. Mr Browne, the manager of Claremont estate, fired a shot at a 'crowd' stealing potatoes from his estate. On the evening of July 28, Sergeant M. and four men arrived at Clifton Hill plantation, St John, to find a 'threatening crowd' of about 200 raiding a potato field. Nine rounds of ammunition were fired over their heads and they ran into a nearby canefield.[17] A gang of rebels at Hannay's plantation dug a field of potatoes. A rebel group which assembled at Walker's plantation proceeded to cut the cattle loose. On July 28, Douglas Pile, planter and assemblyman, reported the presence of a 'roving crowd' of about 200 who arrived from 'above,' raided the potato fields at Brighton plantation and then went 'to Carmichael and stopped people working there' by threatening them with violence if they should continue to work. J. A. Haynes of Newcastle plantation, St John, reported to the police, on the morning of July 29, that a 'crowd' was threatening his cattle.[18]

Even when the size of a 'crowd' could not be determined, their purposeful acts and the extent of the damage inflocted usually conveyed some impression of their motives. For example, on the night of July 30, two acres of sweet potatoes at Vaucluse plantation, St Thomas, were dug.[19] This large acreage (approximately 3,000 holes) could not have been dug by a small group in such a short space of time. At Battaley's plantation, St Peter, about 1,500 yams were also dug in a night. The managers of Four Hill and the Rock plantation reported having received letters informing them that their yams would be dug up on the night of August 2.[20] These yam and potato raids, and the attacks on the plantation livestock, appeared to be purposeful acts perpetrated with some degree of revenge. Perhaps one can also speculate that the participants seized the opportunity to attack the plantation, which, through its oppression of the Afro-Barbadian, was perceived as a hostile institution.

The tendency of some rebels in the rural districts to confront armed police, and in some cases to discharge firearms, was also quite noticeable. At

Greens, St George, a group of about 50 rebels were so 'provoking' that the security forces were compelled to read the Riot Act.[21] Attacks on Kingsland and Searles factories by large 'crowds' were repelled by the Volunteer Force. Marines from the HMS *Apollo* were dispatched to 'scenes of disorders' after firearms were discharged in Lower Broad Street, Lukes Alley and Swan Street. The Commandant of the Local Forces wrote, on one occasion,

> ...11.00 a.m. Capt. F. B. Armstrong reports that while proceeding with two sections past Wilson Hill s/w of St John's church, he came upon Sgt. Grant in charge of Police Patrol being threatened by a mob. Capt. Armstrong persuaded Police to wait and then addressed the mob. Mob refused to be pacified and Volunteers and Police tried to arrest ringleader by encircling him together with portion of the mob....[22]

A confrontation at Walker's plantation, St George, on July 29, was even more dramatic:

> 1.40 p.m. L/cpl. Watts reports that at approximately 1.20 p.m. when passing Walkers plantation, St George, there was a crowd of about 200 digging potatoes. He and two men proceeded to the scene. As he approached, the men came towards him and threatened him. He ordered them to stop and warned them that he would have to fire if they continued to threaten him. They still came on at him and he fired two shots to scare them, the crowd dispersed through the canes.[23]

These confrontations between the rebels and the police, it must be stated, were not in the form of well-organized, prolonged clashes as occurred elsewhere.[24] However, one can see some evidence of mass behaviour and collective action in these social upheavals. Moreover, it appeared as though the participants in the rebellion were, in a way, making a political point through their actions of defiance when confronted by the forces of the state. For a time, it seems as though some rebels were prepared to tackle armed policemen, even though they were aware of the shoot-to-kill powers given to the police by the Riot Act.

It must be stated, however, that the failure of any clear leader to emerge out of the upheavals is an indication that the unrest did not get beyond the stage of being just a rebellion. There were no 'Dottin brothers' or General Green, as in the 1876 Confederation riots. During the Confederation disturbances, there was ample evidence of the coordination of some looting by a defined leadership. No such leadership was observed during the 1937 rebellion in Barbados. Some mention was made by Herbert Sealy of Paragon about cyclists from Bridgetown 'touring the district for the past two days [August 2–3] instructing certain people in the district to hold their hands for the time, and wait.'[25] This report seems to suggest that there was a link between the rural incidents and the urban ones, and that there was elaborate planning and organization. No link can be identified, for there is no supporting evidence.

The deliberate sabotage of communication lines, a fear Governor O'Brien had expressed in 1920, cannot go unmentioned. On July 29, there was a report from Sunbury plantation, St Philip, about the raiding of potato fields and the destruction of telephone lines between Sunbury, Crane, Bentley, Edgecombe, Brighton and Windsor.[26] Corporal Bancroft reported the destruction of the line to District C.[27] Shortly after, the lines to District D, St Thomas and District F, St Joseph, were also cut. The police got around this inconvenience by hurriedly setting up a transmitter station. The line to Constant plantation, St George, was out. At Porters, St James, three strands of barbed wire were placed across the road. In addition, there was widespread stoning of police vehicles as they made their patrols around the island.[28] It seems reasonable to suggest that a concerted effort was made to harass the security forces and to isolate them by deliberately impeding communication links.

## Figure 6.1
## List of Some Participants in the City

| Name | Age | Occupation |
|---|---|---|
| Irvin Broody | 42 | Cooper |
| Joseph Rollock | 33 | Labourer |
| Clarice Brooks | 26 | Washer |
| Alexander Collymore | 26 | Labourer |
| John Bailey | 14 | Labourer |
| Dudley White | 28 | Labourer |
| Seymour Walker | 27 | Labourer |
| Leroy Cumberbatch | 22 | Cooper |
| Mortimer Skeete | 43 | Hawker |

| | | |
|---|---|---|
| Henry Goodman | 30 | Shopkeeper |
| Clyde Griffith | 17 | Apprentice |
| Ivy Thompson | 25 | Domestic Servant |
| Olliver Phillips | 25 | Labourer |
| Irene Agard | 26 | Domestic Servant |
| Charles Downes | 23 | Boatman |
| Israel Lovell | 54 | Carpenter |
| James Barrow | 26 | Porter |
| George Alleyne | 36 | Labourer |
| Joseph Reece | 34 | Barber |
| Fitz Weekes | 40 | Wood Seller |

Source: Advocate Weekly, August 7, 1937. See also 1937, November Sessions Grand Indictment for Sedition, Barbados Archives.

## Figure 6.2
## List of Dead and Wounded on August 5, 1937 as a Result of the Disturbances

| Parish | Dead | Wounded |
|---|---|---|
| St Michael | 3 | 22 |
| Christ Church | 1 | 1 |
| St Philip | 1 | 1 |
| St John | 1 | 3 |
| St George | 1 | 4 |
| St Joseph | nil | nil |
| St Thomas | nil | nil |
| St Andrew | nil | nil |
| St Peter | 2 | 2 |
| St Lucy | nil | 3 |
| St James | 1 | 1 |
| District not stated | 1 | nil |
| Total | 11 | 37 |

Source: 'Plans for Dealing with the Disturbances July/August 1937.' GHY/113, Barbados Archives.

## Strikes and Rumours of Strikes

An uneasy state of industrial relations developed during, and immediately after, the rebellion. On July 7, 1937, the industrial climate was upset by a strike at the Central Foundry. This followed a strike of the Lightermen and Stevedores on July 30, four days after the outbreak of violence.[29] Haphazard work stoppages, less organized and coordinated, also mushroomed on many sugar estates between July 26 and August 9. On August 2, the labourers of Dunscombe and Farmers estates in St Thomas went on strike, demanding 40 cents per day, an increase of ten cents, as a wage.[30] The manager of Sandford estate, St Philip, reported how discontented workers, who had gone on strike earlier, returned to work on August 3, 'influenced to go to work at present wages.'[31] On August 9, labourers of Four Hill plantation, St Peter, turned up, but refused to work. On the same day, cane hole labourers at Walkes Spring plantation, St Thomas, went on strike for increased wages.[32] On August 5, a labourer, Jacob Deane, was reported to be 'encouraging the labourers at Gibbes plantation, St Peter, to strike' and threatening a Mrs. Hutchinson, with an agricultural fork.[33] It was known that a 'crowd' raiding a potato field at Carmichael plantation, St George, was encouraging labourers there to quit.[34] J. A. Haynes of Park House reported on July 29, that 'all of his labourers left at 10:30 a.m., saying that if they work they would be attacked by rioters.'[35]

This sudden upsurge in strikes and rumours of strikes was probably directly related to the general feeling of protest sparked off by the rebellion. Moreover, it must be noted that the strikes could have been a continuation of a familiar form of political protest employed by the labouring classes during the early twentieth century, so it would have been a natural reaction of the masses during the rebellion. The uneasy industrial climate of July–August 1937 cannot be separated from the social upheavals of the time or from previous forms of protest. Instead, the strikes and the rebellious activities of July 1937 must be seen as closely connected forms of political protest, manifesting themselves at different levels of intensity. In short, the rebellion of July–August 1937 represented the highest manifestation of political protest, while the strikes and rumors of strikes were milder levels of protests. The common strand in both cases was the central fact that they were making the same political point, namely, the need to redress the economic, social and political injustices experienced by the Afro-Barbadian population.

At the end of the July 1937 rebellion, more than 16 people had been killed, 21 injured, and hundreds were awaiting trial on various charges, ranging from stone throwing to arson and treason. Indeed, the labouring classes had protested with a fury that stunned the local authorities. There is no evidence that any members of the black middle class were active participants in the rebellion. Instead, they were busy distancing themselves from the 'rioters' and even condemning their actions.[36] Moreover, like Governor Mark Young, they were trying to understand what really happened during the latter days of July 1937.

This confusion was highlighted when, on July 29, a delegation comprising C. A. Braithwaite, Grantley Adams, H. A. Vaughan, J. E. T. Brancker and W. W. Reece called on Governor Young. They spoke in unison about the deplorable standard of living of the labouring classes. The group offered no innovative proposals to improve conditions, but instead suggested the setting up of a commission to investigate social and economic conditions in the island.[37] Governor Young embraced this proposal with much enthusiasm, no doubt because it had the potential to vindicate his administration of any charges of neglect. It also provided the breathing space needed by him to analyse the crisis in detail.

The deputation also went a step further, hinting at the possible racial aspects of the rebellion. Walter Reece spoke of a feeling in the society of one class against another; that 'the wealthy section (whites) not giving the other section (blacks) a square deal.' He concluded,

> The question now is not an economic one but a racial one, although since the advance in prices of foodstuff the wage question has been pronounced.[38]

Adams spoke of the 'colour feeling' being high, and how 'at the Freshwater Club the police were always summoned to keep people away.'[39]

The representatives of the black middle class had revealed the race and class issues which featured in the 1937 rebellion. In private communication with the Governor they ventilated these issues, but publicly they suppressed them and, in the true spirit of multi-racial harmony, avoided even any mention of race and class issues. They embraced the notion that Afro-Barbadians were illiterate, impulsive people who were led astray by dangerous agitators. These views were strikingly similar to those expressed by the merchant-planter class.

## Labouring Classes' Perceptions of the Rebellion

So much has been written on the perceptions of the merchant-planter class and the black middle class about the 1937 rebellion that it is necessary to consider the perceptions of the labouring classes, so as to bring some balance to the picture.[40] Jonathan Mullins, a labourer of Colleton plantation, St John, made a direct link between the economic hardship of the black population and the rebellion of July 1937. He wrote to the Colonial Secretary:

> I have being a labour of Colleton plantation, from my youth and never feel such hardship as what going on now, on the account of wages, of the Agricultural L.br. [sic] are destitute in a kind of a starving position. their need help which cause the Rioting. 3.0rr [sic] shillings per week cannot feed their family, some weeks the weekly rent is taken out of that amount. The small children sometimes about the road crying for hunger and feeling of the children which cause they parents to steal.[41]

Jonathan Mullins, in a humble way, exposed the severe material deprivation which the majority of the labouring classes encountered in Barbados. The situation he portrayed seemed a hopeless and desperate one for the labouring classes, as far as he was concerned. However, his plea to the 'Governor, judges and lawyers to see if it is any good can be done for the imprisoned rioters'[42] hinted at a deep-seated conservatism which dominated the thoughts of the labouring classes. These thoughts were devoid of any spirit of revolutionary change. In essence, even though the labouring classes were collectively feeling the economic pinch, and could perceive their situation on a class basis, they never contemplated a violent overthrow of the local oligarchy.

An anonymous agricultural labourer of St Philip wrote in a similar tone:

> To you Sir this is a brief cause of the raiding which has occurred in the countryside area of St Philip. I hope your Excellency will look into the state seriously. I am a man with a family of (6) six unable to work and I am Agricultural labourer digging cane holes at ten cents per hundred. Some days I can dig three hundred. But owing to the drought the earth is so hard some days I possibly can't dig two hundred. On this cause my wages can only at the highest point amount to 1$ 44cts....Now Sir consider for me the state of my

condition. Some mornings I can scarcely supply them with sweetened hot water furthermore with coffee. On the twenty-ninth when this raiding commenced in Foul Bay, Saint Martins, Four Roads and the Rices district, the shopkeepers had closed their shops since the 27th day of the month and would not deliver goods causing the people to starve....It was merely hungryness which cause the people to break the shops and potato fields.[43]

This labourer, like Mullins, revealed a struggle to survive, on the part of agricultural labourers. His explanation of raiding in the rural parish of St Philip is simplistic, in that he tried to draw a direct connection between the short period of closure by the shops and the raiding. These potato raids were not new to the working classes but were indeed a typical response of workers to oppression. However, one detects a strong desire to seek sympathy for the raiders and to denounce the 'deadly act' of the shopkeepers, rather than to give a true picture of the rebellion. The fact that the writer beseeched the Governor 'to look up our representation' also reveals, as with Mullins, an inherent faith in the existing colonial polity.[44]

From St John, an agricultural labourer, writing under the pseudonym 'Grievous Citizen,' brought the most vivid understanding of local race and class issues of all the working-class views which can be traced:

...The planters and owners who claim to be representatives of the people lies in the House of Assembly and say they pays a large amount of wages to each individual. For instance, Sir, labour is 16 cents and a hole of potatoes is sold for 16 cents, what is left if I buy a hole... Mr Taylor at Wakefield has a dog, it gets Beef steak 3 times a week, ovaltine and other things and we the working men don't even get good salt fish. The owners say they are not able to pay any more, but the trick, is they all form a syndicate in the factories and sells the crop and buys the poor man canes at a little price the plantation Books show nothing of a clearance but blend the factory with the plantation....[45]

A feeling of low self-worth permeates the discourse of 'Grievous Citizen,' especially in relation to the white elite. A complete distrust of the merchant-planter elite is ever present in his analysis. It is difficult, however, to determine if the consolidation of the corporate economy played any part in shaping the writer's ideas. He was suspicious of the close collaboration between the sugar estates and the factories. In fact, his suspicions in relation to the small peasant, and the price for their canes, were thoroughly investigated by the Deane Commission. Similar sentiments were expressed by other working-class people. The underlying feature of these perspectives suggests limited opportunities for employment of blacks, a feeling of neglect perpetrated by the whites, and a fear of victimization.

## Assessment of the Rebellion

Previous attempts to explain the causes of the 1937 rebellion in Barbados have associated them almost exclusively with the distressing economic conditions brought on by the Great Depression of the 1930s.[46] This depression created havoc throughout the entire capitalist world. However, this explanation, valid as it would appear on the surface, ignored the peculiar social, political and racial problems which precipitated the rebellion. For example, some witnesses who testified before the Deane Commission, mainly Dan Blackett and Roland Edwards, mentioned 'race' in relation to the July rebellion.[47] But they were all harassed and harangued very harshly whenever the issue of race was even mentioned. In fact, the report of the Deane Commission itself went to great lengths to stress that the fact 'that shops of coloured citizens, irrespective of their political leanings, were attacked and looted is in our opinion conclusive proof that the disorderly crowds were not acting under the stimulus of racial hatred.'[48] It was politically expedient for the local white oligarchy to stress the economic conditions which could have started the rebellion. To address the racial issues would have been embarrassing, or even threatening, to them as a class. In essence, the discussion of racial issues in connection with the rebellion could have shaken the ideological foundations on which their rule was grounded. I have alluded to the theory of multiracial harmony before. There was, therefore, an uneasy avoidance of racial, and to a lesser extent, political issues, by the Deane Commission.

The Deane Commission's evasion of the racial factors during the 1930s, therefore, should be viewed as an illogical, simplistic and unscientific sociological investigation of the most important political protest in the history of modern Barbados. The Commission never attempted to understand the behaviour and the actions of the 'crowds' beyond the biased perception that they were unlawful, unruly mobs. In short, the response of the local oligarchy was typical of a ruling class reacting to threats to its dominance. Moreover, there is no evidence to suggest that the Commission examined in detail the pattern of the behaviour exhibited by the rebels, to determine the extent to which the property, or the person, of all racial groups was affected. If this mode of investigation was never adopted by the Deane Commission, there is no basis for dismissing the racial factors in the 1937 rebellion. The overwhelming evidence suggests that there was a marked imbalance of attacks on the property of Whites by Blacks – much more so than on other racial groups.

In a society where the overt expressions of racial prejudice and racial discrimination were suppressed and/or denied, there is no simple explanation for the violent actions of rebels, who had been stereotyped as passive. It seems reasonable to suggest, as already stated, that the Afro-Barbadian population was demonstrating their sense of a moral economy. Moreover, the practice of raiding estate provision grounds, a mode of protest dating back to the nineteenth and the early twentieth century, did not die a sudden death. For the majority of Afro-Barbadians, the plantation was a hostile institution, and whenever the opportunity presented itself, the labouring classes attacked their perceived enemy. July 1937 was no different, hence the raids on plantation fields during the unfolding of the rebellion.

During a personal exchange with some senior citizens, who lived through the 1930s, they all spoke in unison of the difficult conditions which faced the black population in Barbados.[49] The agricultural workers, in particular, attributed their miserable living conditions to white oppression and the drudgery of plantation life. Constant references were made to the low wages, harsh working conditions and the general insecurity of tenure that marked plantation life. The plantation, without a doubt, invaded every facet of Barbadian life, subjecting the black population to a hostile, exploitative environment. The behaviour of Afro-Barbadians during the 1937 rebellion reflected protests in relation to their perceived life of hopelessness. To suggest, therefore, as the Deane Commission has intimated, that the Afro-Barbadian population of 1930s was unaware, or devoid of, a racial consciousness, is to deny them even an elementary understanding of the very environment in which they struggled daily to survive.

The observations of many contemporaries point to racial elements during the 1937 rebellion, or at least to the conclusion that some rebels were motivated by racial concerns. Reverend E. S. Pilgrim of the Bethel Methodist Church spoke of people who 'appeared to have had some vague sense of injustice,' and the general feeling that the masses 'were being kept down by people at the top.' He stressed that Payne and his associates told the people that, and they seemed to have agreed with them.[50] Roland Edwards testified before the Deane Commission that the 'rioting' in Barbados had been caused by 'racial prejudice which existed throughout the whole universe and oppress the poorer class of people.'[51] Dan Blackett of the Barbados Physical Culture Club was most forthright in linking the rebellion of 1937 to racial concerns:

> ...As we go along, however much we may try to fool ourselves that there is no racial feeling, we are bound to realize, unless we close our eyes, that this racial feeling is the chief cause of the recent disturbances.[52]

Apart from the local and regional conditions which served to raise the political and racial consciousness of black Barbadians, the Italo-Ethiopian conflict also played a part. At the outbreak of the conflict in 1935, the news took the West Indies by storm. The horrors of the overpowering aggressive fascist state of Italy were graphically exposed. The apparent 'hypocrisy' of the League of Nations was perceived as a blatant betrayal of an African nation. The conflict, in short, crystallized Marcus Garvey's doctrine of the need for black people to organize themselves in the face of white aggression. The extent to which the Italo-Ethiopian conflict influenced the behaviour of the 'crowds' during the 1937 rebellion cannot be measured with much accuracy. However, there is enough evidence to suggest that it did precipitate some racial feeling among the black population. This phenomenon has been emphasized before.

To identify the racial factors in the 1937 rebellion can be a very complicated matter. In fact, to view the rebellion as simply a 'race war,' as has occurred in other countries, would be an exaggeration. The covert nature of Barbadian race relations did not permit such extremes in behaviour. It can be suggested, however, that the July 1937 rebellion was a racial conflict, in that the numerically dominant Afro-Barbadian population rebelled in reaction to, and against, a set of policies carried out by a white minority. These policies, as already mentioned, were conceived in sentiments of racial bigotry. The Afro-Barbadian population, in short, was aware of how the institutionalized racism of the white oligarchy oppressed them. The key, therefore, to unlocking the complex door of race and class factors during the 1937 rebellion can be found in a penetrating analysis of the motives, actions and behaviour of the white and black population alike. The economic factors which surfaced during and after the rebellion must not be seen in isolation, but as part of a fundamental race and class struggle for control of economic resources and political power.

## The End of an Era

The rebellion of July 1937 signalled the beginning of the end of an era. There was no doubt in anyone's mind, especially among the local oligarchy, that something was fundamentally wrong, and things could not continue in the old way. The moment for the empowerment of the masses had arrived. There is ample evidence to indicate that Governor Mark Young and the deputation representing the black middle class were just as bewildered as the plantocracy. The setting up of the Deane Commission was a desperate attempt, not only to provide an opportunity to reassess the situation, but to provide some guidelines to proceed toward inevitable change. The 1937 rebellion was the turning point in modern Barbadian political history.

I have argued that the 1937 rebellion in Barbados was the ultimate expression of mass discontent by the black labouring classes. But the precursors to the rebellion were to be found during an earlier period, especially immediately after the First World War. All the signs of a festering sore of mass social and political discontent had manifested themselves in the form of industrial unrest, potato raids, praedial larceny and crime. But the unsympathetic colonial officials and the merchant-planter elite did not read the true meaning of the escalation of these activities in the society. A few benevolent Whites were able to bring an objective analysis to bear on this situation, but even this small group was not devoid of a feeling of white supremacy. The majority of Euro-Barbadians, especially the ruling elite who dominated the political, financial and social institutions, viewed the signs of discontent, in their customary stereotypical way, as simply vicious crime and lawlessness perpetrated by a lazy, barbaric black population. Instead of embarking on a path to social, economic and political reform to assist the healing of the festering sores of discontent, the merchant-planter elite resorted to bandages of harsh, punitive laws, long prison terms, brutal corporal punishment and increased police surveillance of the Afro-Barbadian population.

One must not forget the Malthusian policy of deliberate neglect of the black population. I have suggested that if these earlier hints of discontent, most visible between 1918 and 1925, had been tackled, perhaps the rebellion of 1937 could have been avoided, or would never have exploded with the ferocity with which it did. In short, the social gangrene which was building up from the early twentieth century – and, one can argue, even from the nineteenth century – could not be contained indefinitely in the oppressive bandages of the merchant-planter elite. It had to give way to the pressure of discontent and the need for empowerment by the black labouring classes at some time in the future. That time was July 1937.

It is important, however, to avoid the suggestion that the rebellion of July 1937 was largely a revolt of the stomach rather than of the mind. As already stated, the harsh economic conditions facing the West Indies during the 1930s cannot be denied. However, it is also a fact that West Indians had always faced dreadful times, and so, if one attempts to draw a direct correlation between harsh economic conditions and rebellion, one might be disappointed to discover that there is no evidence of endemic social upheavals despite the economic conditions. In essence, the occurrence of 'social unrest,' including the Barbadian experience, is much more complex than previously thought. This book exposes the complexity of social discontent – and ultimately rebellion – in Barbados, by addressing the race and class factors in the July 1937 rebellion.

The racial attitudes and practices of the local merchant-planter elite must carry a large portion of the blame for the rebellion. One cannot over-emphasize how racial attitudes pervaded the various institutions of the society, to the extent of deliberately excluding and disfranchising the majority of the black population. Moreover, the entrenched system of institutionalized racism denied the Afro-Barbadian even a remote opportunity to lift himself out of the miserable state of poverty in which he found himself. This book has shown this state of affairs to be deeply ingrained in the racial attitudes, beliefs and practices of the white elite.

The racial ideology which stereotyped the black population as inferior provided the justification for treating these people with disrespect. All endeavours, or even suggestions, which could have relieved the poverty facing the labouring classes, were opposed at all levels of government, especially in the Legislature and Vestries. Eugenic ideas embraced by many influential members of the white community dictated that it would be prudent to neglect the black population by allowing them to wallow in their poverty. Nature did not provide for anything else, not even empowerment. The merchant-planter elite, as a result, was a racist, parasitic, unenlightened class, blinded by its own selfish pursuits. As a result, they were bankrupt of the essential innovative ideas necessary to launch Barbados on a path of social and economic progress.

The black middle class, except for Charles Duncan O'Neal, Clennel Wickham and Wynter Crawford, was largely a class imbued with the English value system and committed to continuing the political tradition of non-confrontational political tactics. As an educated group, they possessed the organizational skills and leadership ability to take over from the merchant-planter elite whenever the opportunity presented itself. They played this role well. The majority of them refused to identify in any meaningful way with the UNIA or with, O'Neal and the WMA. Instead, they stuck to 'respectable' methods of recruitment to political office by contesting annual elections under the banner of the Democratic League, petitioning the Colonial Office, and seeking meetings with the Governor. It is the opinion given in this book, nevertheless, that they played a critical role in the political transformation of Barbados and so cannot be ignored. However, they remained a conservative and opportunistic group who benefited from the bitter struggle of the working classes, and from their ability to convince the local oligarchy and the Colonial Office that they were 'responsible' leaders.

The driving force for change in Barbados, therefore, was achieved by the activities of working-class activists in the UNIA and the WMA, and by other methods of political protest such as strikes, rumours of strikes, potato raids, and finally, the July 1937 rebellion. The real actors on this stage of change were Moses Small, Willie Braithwaite, George Belle, Clement Payne, Edwin Turpin, Menzies Chase, Ulric Grant and other activists of humble working-class backgrounds. In their own humble way, the various socio-political movements at their disposal were used as fronts for their onslaught on the local white oligarchy. The fact that the merchant-planter elite made such a desperate effort to suppress these organizations, and to keep their leaders under close surveillance, is testimony of their importance. This book has shown that it was the pressure applied by the black working classes, rather than any paternal benevolence by the ruling elite, which brought about socio-political change in Barbados.

Indeed, the local oligarchy resisted change with all their might. It took the rebellion of July 1937 to bring them to their senses, and even then they did not give up without a fight. Any further discussion of the 'fight' during the

1940s and the 1950s would be outside the scope of this book and is, indeed, another study in itself.

# APPENDICES

## APPENDIX I

**Revenue and Expenditure in Barbados: 1918–39**

| Year | Revenue (£) | Expenditure (£) |
|---|---|---|
| 1918–19 | 347,497 | 347,817 |
| 1919–20 | 420,136 | 351,851 |
| 1920–21 | 454,286 | 508,391 |
| 1921–22 | 340,814 | 409,055 |
| 1922–23 | 519,213 | 402,524 |
| 1923–24 | 444,646 | 420,461 |
| 1924–25 | 504,696 | 364,530 |
| 1925–26 | 404,132 | 394,249 |
| 1926–27 | 387,462 | 418,711 |
| 1927–28 | 414,884 | 481,252 |
| 1928–29 | 441,732 | 459,626 |
| 1929–30 | 453,802 | 450,696 |
| 1930–31 | 404,555 | 429,143 |
| 1931–32 | 415,645 | 424,088 |
| 1932–33 | 457,843 | 425,875 |
| 1933–34 | 510,270 | 490,909 |
| 1934–35 | 479,960 | 414,109 |
| 1935–36 | 530,644 | 463,147 |
| 1936–37 | 483,142 | 460,869 |
| 1937–38 | 528,278 | 546,274 |
| 1938–39 | 559,484 | 560,038 |

Source: Annual Colonial Reports 1918–40 (H.M. Stationery Office)

# APPENDIX I I

**Parochial Revenue from All Sources for the Year 1920–21 to 1929–30**

| Year | Revenue (£) | Expenditure (£) |
|------|-------------|-----------------|
| 1920–21 | 125,758 | 173,013 |
| 1921–22 | 127,855 | 120,248 |
| 1922–23 | 127,337 | 114,661 |
| 1923–24 | 106,346 | 106,076 |
| 1924–25 | 132,788 | 127,486 |
| 1925–26 | 128,535 | 126,554 |
| 1926–27 | 124,478 | 118,852 |
| 1927–28 | 129,289 | 130,164 |
| 1928–29 | 142,222 | 132,646 |
| 1929–30 | 134,995 | 130,918 |
| Total | 1,279,603 | 1,280,621 |

Source: CO28/310/9. Secret. Robertson to Passfield. February 11, 1931.

# APPENDIX III

**Direction of Trade Imports into Barbados 1921–40**

| YEAR | UK % | Canada% | Other parts of the British Empire % | USA % | Other foreign countries % |
|------|------|---------|------------|-------|------------|
| 1921 | 35.9 | 22.5 | 12.7 | 22.2 | 6.7 |
| 1922 | 31.6 | 22.1 | 16.1 | 24.1 | 6.1 |
| 1923 | 32.9 | 24.1 | 16.6 | 19.6 | 6.8 |
| 1924 | 33.0 | 22.4 | 15.1 | 21.4 | 5.1 |
| 1925 | 36.3 | 20.9 | 15.2 | 18.7 | 8.9 |
| 1926 | 30.9 | 26.5 | 18.5 | 21.6 | 8.5 |
| 1927 | 33.5 | 19.3 | 18.5 | 19.9 | 8.8 |
| 1928 | 35.4 | 20.7 | 17.2 | 17.3 | 9.4 |
| 1929 | 33.9 | 18.7 | 17.6 | 19.6 | 16.2 |
| 1930 | 33.8 | 15.5 | 19.3 | 19.7 | 11.7 |
| 1931 | 34.7 | 17.5 | 18.2 | 18.8 | 10.6 |
| 1932 | 45.6 | 15.1 | 18.1 | 10.2 | 11.0 |
| 1933 | 48.0 | 11.8 | 17.5 | 10.4 | 12.3 |
| 1934 | 42.3 | 14.4 | 18.0 | 12.9 | 12.4 |
| 1935 | 40.9 | 14.1 | 18.9 | 11.7 | 14.4 |
| 1936 | 42.7 | 14.1 | 18.5 | 10.4 | 14.3 |
| 1937 | 41.2 | 14.5 | 17.4 | 11.3 | 15.6 |
| 1938 | 40.7 | 13.1 | 17.6 | 11.8 | 16.8 |
| 1939 | 35.4 | 17.6 | 17.0 | 15.9 | 14.1 |
| 1940 | 35.6 | 25.4 | 19.1 | 10.9 | 9.0 |

Sources: Reports of the Barbados Chamber of Commerce for the years 1925–40 Barbados Chamber of Commerce Minute Book 9 Barbados Public Library, Serial No. BS 28–29.

# APPENDIX IV

## Total Estimated Value of the Imports and Exports of Barbados 1921–40

| YEAR | IMPORTS | EXPORTS |
|------|---------|---------|
| 1921 | 2,642,273 | 1,467,903 |
| 1922 | 2,480,320 | 1,259,794 |
| 1923 | 2521,882 | 2,189,740 |
| 1924 | 2,556,297 | 1,858,301 |
| 1925 | 2,293,777 | 1,421,035 |
| 1926 | 2,155,167 | 1,287,161 |
| 1927 | 2,300,168 | 1,603,551 |
| 1928 | 2,349,159 | 1,531,265 |
| 1929 | 2,039,601 | 1,287,300 |
| 1930 | 1,731,786 | 1,062,916 |
| 1931 | 1,491,644 | 1,064,051 |
| 1932 | 1,656,876 | 1,379,066 |
| 1933 | 1,740,161 | 1,378,765 |
| 1934 | 1,914,554 | 1,479,277 |
| 1935 | 1,840,783 | 1,135,136 |
| 1936 | 2,004,484 | 1,493,335 |
| 1937 | 2,220,650 | 1,646,709 |
| 1938 | 1,353,955 | 2,086,901 |
| 1939 | 2,028,991 | 2,445,753 |
| 1940 | 1,683,030 | 2,302,777 |

N.B. These figures do not include the value of goods imported into the island and afterwards exported, nor do they include the value of intransit goods. They represent only the value of goods duty paid for home consumption.

Source: Report of the Barbados Chamber of Commerce for the Years 1925–41 in Barbados Chamber of Commerce Minute Book and General Meeting and Committee of Management and Letter book 1905–44, Barbados Public library.

# NOTES

## Introduction

1. Jerome Reich, *Colonial America* (Englewood Cliffs, N.J.: Prentice Hall Inc., 1984), 25–33.
2. Hilary Beckles, 'Carib Resistance to European Colonization in the Caribbean. The Seventeenth Century,' Seminar Paper, Journal 7 (1992): 6.
3. Peter Hulme, *Colonial Encounter: Europe and the Native Caribbean, 1797–1992* (London: Methuen, 1986), 225–26.
4. Ronald Parris, 'Race Inequality and Underdevelopment in Barbados, 1627–1973' (Unpublished dissertation, Yale University, 1974), 92.
5. Ibid., 92.
6. Ibid., 90.
7. Richard Sheridan, *Sugar and Slavery – An Economic History of the British West Indies 1623–1775* (Baltimore: Johns Hopkins University Press, 1973), 13; see also Vincent Harlow, *A History of Barbados, 1627–1685* (New York: Negro University Press, 1969), 324.
8. Richard Ligon, *A True and Exact History of the Island of Barbados* (London: Frank Cass & Co. Ltd, 1970), 46.
9. Hilary Beckles, *Black Rebellion in Barbados – The Struggle against Slavery, 1627–1838* (Bridgetown, Barbados: Antilles Publication, 1984), 22.
10. William Sewell, *The Ordeal of Free Labour in the British West Indies* (London: Frank Cass & Co. Ltd, 1968), 67–72.
11. Ibid., 66.
12. '[John Poyer] A letter addressed to Lord Seaford by a Barbadian (Bridgetown 1801)' in Hilary Beckles, 'On the Back of Slaves: The Barbados Free Coloured Pursuit of Civil Rights and in the 1816 Slave Rebellion' in *Immigrants and Minorities* 3 no. 2 (July 1984): 167–87.
13. Claude Levy, *Emancipation, Sugar, and Federalism: Barbados and the West Indies, 1833–1876* (University of Florida Press, Gainesville, 1980), 60.
14. Beckles, 77.
15. Levy, 7.
16. Parris, 250.
17. Beckles, 52–120.
18. See *Report of the West India Royal Commission 1897,* Appendix C, Vol. 'Minutes of Proceedings, Reports of Evidence, and Copies of Certain Documents received in London,' 79.

19. Cecilia A. Karch, 'The Transformation and Consolidation of the Corporate Plantation Economy in Barbados, 1860–1977' (Unpublished dissertation: Rutgers University, 1974), 44.
20. Ibid., 60.
21. Otis Starkey, *The Economic Geography of Barbados – A Study of the Relationships between Environmental Variation and Economic Development* (New York: Columbia University Press, 1939), 130.
22. Bonham Richardson, *Panama Money in Barbados, 1900–1920* (Knoxville: University of Tennessee, 1985), 223.

# Chapter 1

1. For a further discussion of the race issue, see Nancy Forxney, 'The Anthropological Concept of Race,' *Journal of Black Studies* 8 no.1 (September 1987): 35–53. See also St Clair Drake, *Black Folk Here and There – An Essay in History and Anthropology* 1 (Los Angeles: Center for Afro-American Studies, University of California, 1987), 13–32.
2. John Lewis, *Anthropology* (London: W. H. Allen & Co. Ltd, 1969), 56.
3. Lolita Prasard Vidyashi 'On Race and Racism; A New look at the Old Question,' in *Racism, Science and Pseudo-Science* (UNESCO, 1983), 52–54.
4. Ibid., 53; see also Oliver Cox, *Race Relations: Elements and Social Dynamics* (Detroit: Wayne State University Press, 1976), 210.
5. Dante Puzzo, 'Racism and the Western Tradition' *Journal of the History of Ideas* 24 no.4. (October–December 1964): 579–80; see also Pierre Van Den Berghe, *Race and Racism: A Comparative Perspective* (New York: John Wiley & Sons Inc., 1967), 21–34.
6. Van Den Berghe, 7, 20; see also E. Ellis Cashmere and Barry Troyne, *Introduction to Race Relations* (London: Routledge and Kenan Paul, 1983), 7.
7. Michael Banton, *Race Relations* (London: Tavistock Publications, 1969), 7.
8. Ibid., 8; see also Van Den Berghe, 20.
9. St Clair Drake. 14–16.
10. Ibid., 34.
11. Cashmere and Troyne, 60.
12. Ibid., 12.
13. See *Barbados Blue Books 1881–1946.*
14. Ronald Glenfield Parris, 349
15. BS81, Pongas Mission Documents, Reference Department, Barbados Public Library.
16. W. F. Robertson, *Memorandum on the Educational System of Barbados*; see also 'Annual Report of Education Board 1930–31' in *Minutes of Council and Assembly 1930–1931*, UWI Library, Cave Hill.
17. Ibid.

18. Kenneth Wood, 'W.M.A. meeting, Grazettes Village, St Michael' in *Report on Cerain Meetings.*

19. Stokely Carmichael and Charles Hamilton, *Black Power – The Politics of Liberation in America* (London: Johnathan Cape, 1967), 4.

20. Ibid., 4.

21. Ibid., 4; see also George Bernard *Wayside Sketches – Pen Pictures of Barbadian Life* (Barbados: n.p., 1985), 13.

22. George Bernard, 3.

23. Vera Rubin, 'Culture, Politics and Race Relations' *Social and Economic Studies* 11 no. 4 (December 1962): 434–36.

24. George Bernard, op. cit., 3.

25. 'The Report from a Select Committee appointed to enquire into the Origin, Causes and Progress of the late insurrection,' (H. Walter, Mercury and Grazettes Office, 1816), 12.

26. Ibid., 34–36.

27. Ibid., 22.

28. Ibid., 23.

29. *Minutes of the Proceedings of the Assembly, 1875–1876*, Department of Archives, Barbados.

30. Sir Harold Austin's Address to the Royal Commission 1939, First Day.

31. Reports of the Commission appointed to enquire into the Disturbances which took place in Barbados on the 27th of July and subsequent Days, *The Barbados Disturbances* compiled by W.A. Beckles.

32. Joseph Semia, *Gramsci's Political Thought* (Oxford: Clarendon Press, 1981), 23–43.

33. Ibid., 26.

34. Richard L. Mumford *An American History Primer* (San Diego: Harcourt Brace Jovanovich, 1990), 16.

35. Christine Bolt, *Victorian Attitudes to Race* (London: Routledge and Kenan Paul, 1971), 75–107.

36. Ibid., 27

37. V. E. Chancellor, *History for their Masters*, (London, 1910), 118–22 quoted in James Walvin, 'Recurring Theme: White Images of Black Life During and after Slavery' in *Slavery and Abolition* 5 no. 2, (September 1984); see also Douglas Lorimar, *Colour, Class and the Victorians – English Attitudes to the Negro in the Mid-nineteenth Century* (London: Leicester University Press, 1978), 12–17; and L. T. Ragatz, *Fall of the Planter Class in the British Caribbean 1768–1833* (New York: Octagon Books Inc., 1971), 27.

38. Thomas Carlyle, 'Occasional Discourse on the Nigger Question' in *English and Other Critical Essays* (New York: Everyman's Library, Dutton, 1967), 305–307.

39. Anthony Trollope, *The West Indies and the Spanish Main* (London: Frank Cass & Co. Ltd, 1968), 222.

40. James Froude, *The English in the West Indies* (New York: Negro Universities Press, 1969), 50.

41. Daniel Kevles, *In the Name of Eugenics – Genetics and the Uses of the Human Heredity* (Berkeley: University of California Press, 1986), Chapters 1, 4, 9; see

also Allan Chase, *The Legacy of Malthus – The Social Costs of the New Scientific Racism* (New York: Alfred A. Knopf, 1977), 3–7; and R.C. Lawonthin, et al., *Not in Our Genes* (New York: Pantheon Books, 1984), 7.

42. Allan Chase, op. cit., 28.
43. The *Agricultural Reporter* (September 22, 1916): 3.
44. The *Barbados Standard* (November 19, 1921): 5.
45. See the *Barbados Observer*, December 19, 1942, a clipping enclosed in secret dispatch Grattan Bushe to Oliver Stanley, January 12, 1943. CO 281327114.
46. Thomas Malthus, *An Essay on Population Vol. 2* (London: J. M. Bent and Sons Ltd, 1961), 179.
47. Ibid., 150.
48. See Clennel Wickham, 'Men and Matters,' *Barbados Advocate* 1933–1938. Wickham used the Column to comment on social and political issues.
49. CO 28/306/10: Minority Report 'B,' January 21, 1927. See also J. H. Hawkins, Fourth Public Session, Tuesday October 22, 1929, in *Proceedings of West Indian Sugar Commission* (Advocate Co. Ltd. 1929).
50. CO 28/306/10: Secret dispatch, Robertson to Amery, April 13, 1927.
51. The *Barbados Standard* (October 21, 1916); see also the *Barbados Standard* (July 21, 1917): 5.
52. The *Barbados Standard* (April 8, 1916), 5.
53. The *Barbados Standard* (October 14, 1916), 5.
54. For a discussion of the Sambo personality, see Stanley Elkins, *Slavery a Problem in American Institutional and Intellectual Life* 2nd edn (Chicago: University of Chicago Press, 1974), 82–86; and Orlando Patterson, *The Sociology of Slavery – An Analysis of the Origins, Development and Structure of Negro Slave Society in Jamaica* (London: Fairleigh Dickinson University Press, 1969), 174–81.
55. The *Barbados Weekly Herald* (Saturday, March 6, 1921), 4.
56. The *Barbados Weekly Herald* (Saturday May 21, 1921), 5.
57. The *Barbados Weekly Herald* (Saturday, February 12, 1921), 4.
58. See Ronald Parris, *Race, Inequality and Underdevelopment in Barbados*; see also Cecilia A. Karch, 'The Transformation and Consolidation of the Corporate Plantation Economy in Barbados.'
59. Karl Marx and Frederick Engels, *The Communist Manifesto* (New York: International Publishers, 1948); see also David Mclellan, *The Thought of Karl Marx* (New York: Harper and Row, 1971), 151–65.
60. David Mclellan, 170.
61. Anthony Giddens, *The Class structure of the Advanced Societies* (London: Hutchinson and Co. Ltd, 1981), 42.
62. Max Weber, *The Theory of Social and Economic Organization* (New York: The Free Press, 1968), 424–29.
63. Ibid., 440.
64. Petition of Fitzherbert King, in Acting Governor to Walker Long, July 1, 1918, CO 28/293: Jenkins to Long, July 1, 1918.
65. See *Report on Certain Meetings* GH4/37/38. Department of Archives, Barbados.

66. The *Agricultural Reporter* (September 29, 1919), 31; The *Agricultural Reporter* (October 13, 1919), 3; *The Barbados Globe* (February 3, 1919), 4.
67. See *Report on Certain Meetings*.
68. Secret General Remarks on Affairs in Barbados, August 20, 1931 GH3/6/10. Department of Archives, Barbados.
69. Ibid.
70. Arthur Lewis, *Labour in the West Indies – The Birth of a Workers' Movement* (London: New Beacon Books, 1971), 63.
71. *Annual Colonial Report 1937*; see also C. C. Skeete, *The Condition of Peasant Agriculture in Barbados* (Advocate Ltd., 1930), 21.
72. Enclosure 'Memorandum on the Agricultural Problems of Barbados' S. J. Saint (October 16, 1940), 7; see also Christine Barrow, *The Plantation Heritage in Barbados: Implications for Food Security, Nutrition and Employment,* (Kingston: ISER, Mona, 1995), 3–4.
73. *Annual Colonial Report 1936*, 7.
74. Ibid.
75. *Report of the Commission appointed to enquire into the Disturbance*, 241.
76. Francis Mark, *History of the Barbados Workers' Union* (Bridgetown: Advocate Commercial Printing, n.d.), 22–32.
77. *Report of the Commission Appointed to Enquire into the Disturbance*, 256.
78. Ibid., 250.
79. Ibid., 252.
80. Ibid., 260.
81. Ibid., 260.
82. Ibid., 256.
83. Ibid., 256.
84. Ibid., 257.
85. Ibid., 257.
86. *Proceedings of West Indian Sugar Commission*, (Bridgetown: Advocate Co. Ltd, 1929), 58–59.
87. Ibid., 60.
88. The *Barbados Weekly Observer*, Saturday, May 14, 1936, 10.
89. The *Barbados Weekly Observer*, Saturday, March 29, 1936, 4.
90. CO 28/298: Charles O'Brien to Secretary of State, October 21, 1920.
91. Ibid., 134.
92. Ibid., 135.
93. Ibid., 136
94. WMA Meeting, July 21, 1937, in *Report on Certain Meetings*.
95. Willie Brathwaite, 'WMA Meeting, Fairchild Street, July 22, 1927' in *Report on Certain Meetings*.
96. Edwin Turpin, 'WMA Meetings, Fairchild Street, July 21, 1927' in *Report on Certain Meetings*.
97. Petition of Workers of the Waterworks Department, November 30, 1933, in *Minutes of Council and Assembly 1933–34*.
98. Cecilia A. Karch, 231.

99. *Report on a Housing Survey of 8 Slum Tenantries in Bridgetown, June 1944–April 1945* (Housing Board Office, Parochial Buildings, Bridgetown), 7.
100. Ibid., 10–11.
101. Ibid., 36–37.
102. *Report of a Committee Appointed by His Excellency for the General Improvement of Housing and Domestic Sanitation in Barbados* (Advocate Company Ltd., August 1943), 4.
103. Interviews with Tony Hinds, Bank Hall, August 6, 1992.
104. The *Barbados Weekly Herald*, Saturday, April 20, 1926.
105. *Annual General Report, 1924*, 6.
106. CO 28/314/10: Confidential. Mark Young to Cunliffe-Lister, May 7, 1933.
107. *Annual General Report, 1924*, 10.
108. Ibid., 12.
109. Young to Cunliffe-Lister.
110. Young to Cunliffe-Lister; see also the *Barbados Weekly Herald*, September 1, 1929, 4.
111. Young to Cunliffe-Lister.
112. CO 28/318/4: Minutes by M. Ponynton. May 6, 1937; see also Minutes by M. Ponynton, June 11, 1937.
113. Legislative Council Debates June 1, 1937, and the House of Assembly Debates, June 8, 1937 – bound Volumes, UWI Main Library, Cave Hill.
114. 'Petitions of the Voters Association' in Documents laid at Meeting of May 11, 1937, in *Minutes of Council and Assembly 1937–1938*, UWI Main Library, Cave Hill.
115. Ibid.
116. 'Petitions of Chamber of Commerce' in Documents laid at Meeting of May 11, 1937.
117. 'Petitions of the Agricultural Society' in Documents laid at Meeting of Assembly, May 11, 1937.
118. W. Ormsby-Gore to Mark Young, dispatch No.236, September 13, 1937 in Documents laid at Meeting of Assembly, May 11, 1937.
119. CO 28/306/5: W. C. F. Robertson to L. C. M. S. Amery, December 20, 1926.
120. Ibid.
121. *Annual Colonial Report 1936–1937*, 6.
122. CO 28/306/7: *Annual Report of the Public Health Inspector (Acting) 1927*; see also 'Memorandum by a committee appointed by the General Board of Health to move recommendations for the Reorganization of the Public Health Administration of the Island' in *Minutes of the Council and Assembly 1939–1940*.
123. *Barbados Annual Blue Books 1918–1930; Annual General Reports 1924–1938*; see also CO 28/311/10: Young to Cunliffe-Lister, May 7, 1933.
124. CO 28/311/10: Young to Cunliffe-Lister, May 7, 1933.

# Chapter 2

1. G. Martel, et al., *The Origins of the First World War* (London: Longman, 1991), 12.
2. Ibid., 16.
3. R. Albrecht-Carrie, *The Meaning of the First World War* (New Jersey: Prentice Hall, Inc., 1968), 67.
4. No.207: L. Probyn to Lewis Harcourt, (Department of Archives, Barbados).
5. Pamphlet A 105: 'A few Notes on the History of the British West Indies Regiment,' (Department of Archives, Barbados), 13.
6. T. E. Fell and A. Somer-Cocks, 'The Great War,' 55; see also the *Agricultural Reporter*, May 6, 1920, 4.
7. *Colonial Report: Barbados (1922–23)*, 6; see also CO 28/301: *Annual Report for 1922*, 23, J. B. Howell, Acting Colonial Secretary, August 25, 1918.
8. CO 28296: Vote of the House of Assembly, July 30, 1918; see also T. E. Fell and A Somer-Cocks, 'The Great War, 1914–1918,' 158. CO 28/129.
9. T. E. Fell to Walter Long, September 25, 1918. No.157 in Col. 2/1/5: Dispatches from Governors to Secretary of State (Department of Archives, Barbados).
10. Fell to Long 'The Great War,' 19.
11. The *Barbados Globe*, May 3, 1918; O'Brien to Milner, February 17, 1919. No. 304 in Dispatches from Governors to Secretary of State.
12. Probyn to Long, July 12 1917; see also Probyn to Long dispatch No. 4, January 16, 1918 in Dispatches from Governors, 170–71.
13. Probyn to Long, dispatch No. 182, September 13, 1917. 132, in Dispatch from Governors, 140.
14. The *Agricultural Reporter*, July 8, 1916, 6.
15. The *Agricultural Reporter*, 4.
16. The *Barbados Standard*, February 20, 1916, 4.
17. The *Barbados Globe*, May 3, 1918, 3.
18. L. Probyn to Bonar Law, August 19, 1915, (Department of Archives, Barbados).
19. Fell to Somer-Cocks, 'The Great War.'155; CO 28/293: J. Challenor Lynch to T E Fell, October 9, 1918 enclosed in dispatch No.173, October 14, 1918.
20. Lynch to Fell, October 9, 1918. CO 28/293.
21. Lynch to Fell, October 9, 1918. CO 28/293.
22. CO 28/296: Wood-Hill to O'Brien in O'Brien to Milner, October 16, 1919.
23. *The Barbados Standard*, July 9, 1921, 5.
24. W. F. Elkins, 'A Source of Black Nationalism in the Caribbean: The Revolt of the British West Indies Regiment at Taranto Italy' in *Science and Society* (Spring 1970): 98.
25. CO 318/348: enclosure in dispatch No. 27, February 13, 1919, in Elkins 'A Source of Black Nationalism,' 100.
26. 'Petition of J. C. Hope and eleven soldiers of the British West India Regiment in Egypt to J. Challenor Lynch'; see also M. Murphy to Secretary of State, December 6, 1918. CO 28/293.

27. The *Weekly Herald*, Saturday, June 21, 1919, 4.
28. C. L. Joseph, 'The British West Indian Regiment 1914–1918' in *Journal of Caribbean History* 2, (May 1971); see also Major Maxwell Smith to Major General Thinillier, December 27, 1918. Department of Archives.
29. C. L. Joseph, The British West Indian Regiment, 60.
30. Maxwell Smith to Thinillier, December 27, 1918.
31. Maxwell Smith to Thinillier, December 27, 1918.
32. Secret: Milner to O'Brien, September 30, 1919, in 'Labour Troubles and Unrest,' G H 2/5/1 (Department of Archives, Barbados).
33. Elkins, A Source of Black Nationalism, 103.
34. The *Barbados Weekly Herald*, May 1, 1920.
35. Probyn to Long, December 7, 1917 in Dispatches from Governors to Secretary of State Col. 2/1/52.
36. The *Barbados Globe*, July 16, 1919, 3.
37. Ibid.
38. The *Agricultural Reporter*, July 21 1919, 3.
39. Louis Sebro, open air meeting, Fairchild Street, May 27, 1932, in the *Report on Certain Meetings*.
40. Confidential: O'Brien to Milner, October 13, 1919. (Department of Archives, Barbados).
41. O'Brien to Milner, October 13, 1919 CO28/296; Secret: Milner to O'Brien, September 30, 1919. (Department of Archives, Barbados) CO28/296.
42. Milner to O'Brien. September 30, 1919, CO28/296.
43. O'Brien to Milner, October 13, 1919, CO28/296.
44. W. F. Elkins, 'Marcus Garvey, The Negro World, and the British West Indies: 1919–1920' *Science and Society* 36 (1972): 64–65.
45. The *Barbados Globe*, August 20, 1919, 3.
46. The *Barbados Globe*, August 20, 1919; see also Robert Mullen, *Blacks in America's Wars* (New York: Pathfinder, 1973), 50.
47. Ibid.
48. Selwyn Ryan, *Race and Nationalism in Trinidad and Tobago: A Study of Decolonization in Multiracial Society* (Kingston: ISER, UWI, 1972), 29.

## Chapter 3

1. The *Agricultural Reporter* (May 21, 1919), 3.
2. Clennel Wickham, *Colour Question – Some Reflections of Barbados*, (n.p., 1934), 3.
3. Ibid., 4.
4. W. F. Wilkins, 'A Source of Black Nationalism in the Caribbean: The Revolt of the British West Indies Regiment at Taranto Italy' in *Science and Society*, (Spring 1970); see also the *Mirror*, May 15, 1916, quotation from a letter by Private G. Gopaul in 'Trinidad Disturbances of 1917–1920: Precursors to 1937' in

*Trinidad Labour Riots of 1937: Perspectives 50 years Later*, edited by Roy Thomas (St Augustine, Trinidad: Extra-Mural Studies Unit, UWI, June 1987).

5. GH3/5/1/ Very Secret: 'Address to Representative Planters' July 30, 1919, in *Labour Troubles and Unrest in the West Indies 1919–1920*, (Department of Archives, Barbados).

6. Probyn to Long, December 7, 1917. Dispatch No. 233 in Dispatches from Governors to Secretary of State (Department of Archives, Barbados).

7. 'Report of the Returned Soldiers Committee' in *Minutes of Council and Assembly 1922–1927* (Bound Volumes, UWI Main Library, Cave Hill), 13.

8. The *Barbados Globe*, January 7, 1920, 4; The *Agricultural Reporter*, April 14, 1919, 3.

9. 'Debates of the House of Assembly, November 11, 1919,' (Bound Volumes, UWI Main Library, Cave Hill), 27.

10. The *Agricultural Reporter*, August 8, 1919, 3.

11. CO 28/293: 'Minutes by the Inspector of Health' enclosed in Dispatch No. 43, April 4, 1918.

12. The *Barbados Standard*, May 6, 1916, 3.

13. The *Agricultural Reporter*, September 18, 1916, 3; see also 61B Colonial Report: Barbados (1917–18), 10.

14. Fell and Somers-Cocks, 'The Great War,' 55; see also the *Agricultural Reporter*, May 6, 1920, 4.

15. 'Report of Proceedings, Imperial Sugar Cane Research Conference' (London 1931). 26–27.

16. The *Agricultural Reporter* (January 18, 1922); see also Fell and Somers-Cocks 'The Great War,' 161.

17. The *Agricultural Reporter* (June 24, 1921), 3; see also 'Colonial Reports: Barbados' (1916–17), 11.

18. W. E. Jackson, Acting Governor's Address to Legislative Council. April 7, 1925, in *Minutes of Council and Assembly 1925–1926*, (UWI Main Library, Cave Hill).

19. 'F. J. Clarke, Speaker of the House of Assembly to His Excellency the Governor's Reply' in *Minutes of Council and Assembly 1925–26*, (UWI Main Library, Cave Hill).

20. 'The Governor's Address at the Opening of the Legislative Session 1935–1936' in *Minutes of Council and Assembly 1935–36*, (UWI Main Library, Cave Hill).

21. UNIA Meeting, Westbury Road, June 12, 1932; see also WMA meeting. Passage Road, October 10, 1927 in *Report on Meetings*.

22. Extract from the 'Report of the West Indian Sugar Commission for the Year 1929–30,' (Government Printing Office, Barbados), 66.

23. 'Confidential Note to Memorandum of Financial Position of the Sugar Industry' in GH/7/5 Sugar Industry, December 1921, (Department of Archives), 2.

24. Colonial Report: Barbados (1922–23), 5.

25. Ibid., 6.

26. The *Barbados Advocate*, January 16, 1922, 3.

27. The *Agricultural Reporter*, January 18, 1922, 3.

28. 'Report of the Joint Select Committee appointed to consider and report on the present condition of the sugar industry and its future prospects' in *Minutes of the Council and Assembly 1935–1936* (UWI Main Library, Cave Hill).
29. 'The Governor's Address at the Opening of the Legislative Session 1935–1936,' Documents laid at the Meeting of the Assembly of the 10th December, 1935.
30. The *Barbados Advocate Weekly*, December 19, 1935, 4.
31. The *Barbados Globe*, June 20, 1921, 4.
32. The *Agricultural Reporter*, January 17, 1922, 5.
33. The *Agricultural Reporter*, May 6, 1920, 4; Ibid., May 12, 1920, 3; Ibid., May 29, 1920, 4.
34. CO 28/299: 'Comment on Annual General Report' in O'Brien to Winston Churchill, (July 27, 1921), 525.
35. House of Assembly Debate 1919–1920, July 27, 1920; see also the *Barbados Globe*, July 28, 1920, 4.
36. The *Barbados Herald*, July 31, 1920, in O'Brien to Milner, September 30, 1920. CO28/295.
37. House of Assembly Debates, July 27, 1920 (Main Library, UWI, Cave Hill).
38. CO 28/298: The *Barbados Herald*, July 31, 1920 clippings enclosed in dispatch O'Brien to Milner, September 30, 1920.
39. House of Assembly Debates, July 27, 1920 (Main Library, UWI, Cave Hill).
40. The *Barbados Standard*, March 2, 1918, 5.
41. The *Agricultural Reporter*, April 14, 1919, 3.
42. The *Barbados Globe*, July 28, 1920, 3.
43. The *Barbados Globe*, October 6, 1921, 3.
44. CO28/929: O'Brien to Milner, September 30, 1920.
45. The *Agricultural Reporter*, August 4, 1919), 3.
46. The *Agricultural Reporter*, October 28, 1919, 3.
47. Ibid., 4.
48. Ibid., 6.
49. The *Barbados Globe*, January 2, 1918, 3.
50. The *Barbados Standard*, February 10, 1917; see also the *Barbados Standard*, February 24, 1917, 3.
51. The *Agricultural Reporter* (August 21, 1919), 3.
52. 'Monthly Meeting of the Council of Chamber of Commerce August 1, 1918' *Council of the Chamber of Commerce Minute Book 1929–1944*, Barbados Public Library.
53. Minutes by C P Clarke, Attorney General, May 28, 1919, CO 28/296. UWI Main Library, Cave Hill.
54. CO 28/296: O'Brien to Milner, October 19, 1919.
55. The *Barbados Standard*, February 24, 1917, 3.
56. Ibid., 4.
57. The *Barbados Globe*, January 2, 1918, 3.
58. The *Agricultural Reporter*, October 13, 1919, 3; see also the issue of April 14, 1919, 3.
59. The *Barbados Herald*, December 13, 1919, 4.

60. Ibid.

61. The *Barbados Weekly Standard*, March 8, 1919, 5.

62. The *Official Gazette* LIV no. 22, March 17, 1919; see also the *Barbados Standard*, March 8, 1919, 5.

63. The *Official Gazette* LIV no. 22, March 17, 1919.

64. The *Barbados Standard*, March 8, 1919, 6.

65. Ibid.

66. Report of the Inspector General of Police 1918–1919, 5; see also the *Barbados Standard*, January 11, 1919, 3.

67. O'Brien to Milner, June 27, 1919, No. 172 in Dispatches from Governors op.cit., 376–378.

68. 'Annual report of the Organization and Administration of the Barbados Police Force for the Year 1933–1934' in *Minutes of the Council and Assembly 1933–1934* (UWI Main Library, Cave Hill).

69. 'Address to Representative Planters' July 30, 1919, in *Labour Troubles and Unrest in the West Indies 1919–1920,* GH3/5/1 (Department of Archives, Barbados).

70. Ibid.

71. Ibid.

72. 'Meeting in the Council Chamber on 23rd December' in *Labour Troubles and Unrest* (Department of Archives, Barbados); see also J. E. Greene and Christine Barrow, *Small Business – A Case of Survival* (Barbados: ISER, UWI, Cave Hill, 1979), 32–33.

73. 'Meeting in the Council Chambers on 23rd December' in *Labour Troubles and Unrest* (Department of Archives, Barbados), 4.

74. Ibid., 6.

75. The *Barbados Globe*, June 22, 1920, 3.

76. The *Barbados Standard*, February 8, 1919, 4.

77. The *Agricultural Reporter*, February 8, 1919, 5.

78. The *Barbados Globe*, February 10, 1919, 4.

79. 'Debates of the House of Assembly, November 13, 1917,' (Bound Volumes, Main Library, UWI, Cave Hill), 90.

80. Ibid., 90.

81. *The Barbados Standard*, March 2, 1918, 5.

82. Ibid., November 12, 1921, 5.

83. 'Debates of the House of Assembly, July 19, 1921,' (Bound Volumes, Main Library, UWI, Cave Hill), 380–82.

84. The *Barbados Globe*, June 22, 1921, 3.

85. 'Meeting in the Council Chambers on 23rd December' in *Labour Troubles and Unrest* (Department of Archives, Barbados).

86. House of Assembly Debates, April 27, 1920 (Main Library, UWI, Cave Hill), 234.

87. The *Agricultural Reporter*, July 26, 1921, 3.

88. The *Barbados Standard*, March 2, 1918, 5.

89. The *Barbados Globe* (February 3, 1919), 3.

90. 'Meeting in the Council Chambers on 23rd December.'

91. Ibid., 5
92. Ibid., 7
93. Ibid., 8; the *Agricultural Reporter*, February 22, 1919, 3; see also the *Barbados Standard*, January 4, 1919, 2.
94. 'Report of the Unemployment Committee 1934' in *Minutes of Council and Assembly 1933–34* (Bound Volumes in UWI Main Library, Cave Hill).
95. CO 28/299: Francis Jenkins 'Food Prices and Profiteering' in *Labour Troubles and Unrest* (Department of Archives, Barbados), 3.
96. Ibid., 6.
97. Ibid., 7; the *Agricultural Reporter*, July 6, 1920, 3; the *Barbados Globe*, March 13, 1922, 4; see also the *Barbados Globe*, April 16, 1924, 3.
98. 'Food Prices and Profiteering,' in *Labour Troubles and Unrest* (Department of Archives, Barbados), 9.
99. Ibid.
100. Meeting in the Council Chambers on 23rd December' in *Labour Troubles and Unrest* (Department of Archives, Barbados), 7.
101. 'Food Prices and Profiteering.'
102. Ibid.
103. 'Meeting in the Council Chambers on 23rd December.'
104. Ibid.
105. 'The Twelfth Annual Report of the Public Health Inspector 1924,' in *Minutes of Council and Assembly 1925–26* (UWI Main Library, Cave Hill).
106. 'Ten Years of Sanitary Progress' *Official Gazette* (April 24, 1924): 12–14.
107. CO 28/302: Dr A. P. Wright and Dr L. Fairfield. Extract from a Confidential Report.
108. Duke of Devonshire to O'Brien, September 14, 1923 (UWI Library, Cave Hill).
109. Ibid.
110. See *Barbados Blue Book for the Year 1923–1924*; see also The House of Assembly Debates 1923–1924 (Main Library, UWI, Cave Hill).
111. The *Barbados Globe* (April 7, 1924), 3.
112. Ibid., 3.
113. O'Brien to the Duke of Devonshire, January 17, 1922.
114. *The Barbados Globe* (April 7, 1924), 3.
115. 'Governor's speech at the Opening of the Legislative Session 1928–1929,' *Minutes of the Council and Assembly 1928–1929* (Bound Volumes in the Main Library, UWI, Cave Hill).
116. Ibid.
117. Ibid.
118. 'Draft Legislative Reply of the Legislative Council to His Excellency, the Governor of 1928' in *Minutes of Council and Assembly 1928–1929* (UWI Main Library, Cave Hill).
119. CO 28/306: J. W. Hawkins and A. J. Hanschell, Ministry Report 'B' (January 21, 1927), 2.
120. Ian Albery *Complete Psychology* (London: Hodder & Stoughton, 2004), 12.

121. Ibid., 14; see also Malwyn Jones, *The Limits of Liberty* (Oxford: Oxford University Press, 1985)..

122. Hawkins, et.al., Minority Report, 3.

123. 'Proceedings of the West Indian Sugar Commission, October 1929' (Advocate Co. Ltd.), 54.

124. Ibid., 56.

125. UNIA meeting, Westbury Road, October 29, 1929 in *Report on Certain Meetings*.

126. 'The Half-Yearly Report of the Poor Law Inspector, January–June 1913' (Department of Archives, Barbados), 14.

127. Ibid., 16.

128. The *Agricultural Reporter*, September 11, 1916, 4.

129. 'The Eighth Annual Report of the Public Health Inspector 1920' *Minutes of the Council and Assembly 1920–1921* (UWI Main Library, Cave Hill); see also CO28/302 Extract from Confidential Report of West Indies Commission to the National Council for Combating Disease.

130. Ibid., 10.

131. Ibid., 12.

132. Dr C. A. Seagar 'Report on Medical and Sanitary Administration in Barbados, April 22, 1932' in *Minutes of Council and Assembly 1932–1933* (UWI Main Library, Cave Hill).

133. 'Report of the Chief Medical Officer, March 31, 1933' in *Minutes of Council and Assembly 1933–34* (UWI Main Library, Cave Hill).

134. Ibid.

135. Seagar, 'Report on Medical and Sanitary Administration in Barbados,' (UWI Library, Cave Hill).

136. Acting Governor to Legislative Council, May 6, 1939, Message No. 22, in *Minutes of Council and Assembly* 1939–40 (UWI Main Library, Cave Hill).

137. CO 28/306/10: Secret. Robertson to Amery, April 13, 1927 (UWI Main Library, Cave Hill).

138. Clennel Wickham, *The Advocate Weekly* (July 27, 1937), 3.

139. Legislative Council to W. F. Flinn, April 22, 1939, *Minutes of Council and Assembly*; see also Message No. 32./1937, Young to Legislative Council, August 3, 1937, in *Minutes of Council and Assembly 1937–38* (UWI Main Library, Cave Hill).

140. *Official Gazette*, June 16, 1932, 18–20.

141. 'Report of the Employment Agency for the Quarter ending 30th September 1929' *Minutes of Council and Assembly 1940–1941* (UWI Main Library, Cave Hill).

142. Clennel Wickham, *Advocate Weekly*, August 29, 1936, 3; see also Louis Sebro's evidence, third day, Deane Commission, 1937.

143. CO 28/297: O'Brien to Viscount Milner (March 11, 1920), 126.

144. T. Grannum, 'Representative Government in Barbados: A Failure,' *Barbados Advocate*, January 4, 1922.

145. Charles O'Brien to Winston Churchill, January 31, 1922, CO 28/301.

## Chapter 4

1.  Melville Inniss, UNIA meeting, Westbury Road, St Michael, October 14, 1932; Report on Meetings 1932 Department of Archives, Barbados.
2.  Kenneth Wood, WMA Public Meeting, Grazettes Village, St Michael, August 5, 1927.
3.  Ralph Miliband, *Marxism and Politics* (Oxford: Oxford University Press, 1978), 157–58; see also Norman Barry, *An Introduction to Modern Political Theory* (London: Macmillan, 1981), 73–77.
4.  'Publications addressed to the Working Class 1932–33' GH3/6/4, (Department of Archives, Barbados).
5.  Clennel Wickham, *Barbados Advocate Weekly*, August 17, 1935; see also *Barbados Advocate Weekly*, November 28, 1936, 3.
6.  F. A. Hoyos, *Grantley Adams and the Social Revolution*, (London: Macmillan, 1974); see also pamphlet by G. Herbert Adams (January 18, 1937) 217/6/7 Box 11, (Department of Archives, Barbados).
7.  The *Barbados Weekly Herald* started in 1919. It ceased its connection with Wickham as editor after 1930. Wickham wrote a column in the *Barbados Advocate Weekly* until his death in 1938.
8.  Hoyos, *Grantley Adams and the Social Revolution*; see also the debate between Adams and Wickham in the *Barbados Weekly Herald* and the *Barbados Agricultural Reporter* between 1926 and 1930.
9.  Hoyos, *Grantley Adams and the Social Revolution*, 123–25; see also Ronald Parris, 'Racial Inequality and Underdevelopment in Barbados 1627–1974,' (unpublished PhD diss., Yale University, 1974), 480–1.
10. Keith Hunte 'Charles Duncan O'Neal: Apostle of Freedom,' *New World Quarterly* l nos. 1 and 2, (Barbados Independence Issue).
11. Political Meeting, High Street, January 5, 1929, *Report on Certain Meetings*. GH4/370, (Department of Archives, Barbados).
12. *The Barbados Agricultural Reporter* for the years 1927–28.
13. 'Minutes of Chamber of Commerce, 1927' BS26, (Barbados Public Library); see also *Barbados Weekly Herald*, April 16, 1927, 4.
14. Samuel Hall, WMA Meeting, Passage Road, November 9, 1927, *Report on Certain Meetings*, (Department of Archives, Barbados).
15. Charles Duncan O'Neal, WMA Meeting, Passage Road, November 9, 1927, *Report on Certain Meetings*.
16. F. A. Hoyos, *The Rise of West Indian Democracy: The Life and Times of Grantley Adams*, (Bridgetown: Advocate Press, 1963), 30–1.
17. Ibid., 63.
18. CO 28/310/86: Secret. Robertson to Thomas 'General Comments on Barbados,' August 20, 1931.
19. Abstract of Intelligence No. 31 for week ending 10th August, 1933 (Department of Archives, Barbados).
20. Ibid.

21. Ibid.
22. WMA Meeting, August 9, 1933 in *Report on Certain Meetings.*
23. Neville Duncan, *Movements as Subculture – A Preliminary Examination of Social and Political Protest in the Anglophone Caribbean* (n.p., November, 1983), 1.
24. Maurice Dwerger, *Political Parties* (London: Methuen and Co. Ltd., 1964), 283–96.
25. I have been informed by oral sources of the possibility of other branches of the UNIA existing at Harrington, St Phillip, and Horse Hill, St Joseph.
26. UNIA meeting, April 19, 1920, in *Report on Certain Meetings.*
27. Ibid.
28. O'Brien to Duke of Devonshire, January 6, 1923, in *Labour Troubles and Unrest* (Department of Archives, Barbados).
29. Ibid.
30. Secret: Amery to O'Brien, February 5, 1920, in *Labour Troubles and UnreSt*
31. Milner to O'Brien, September 30, 1920 CO281.
32. Melville Innis, UNIA meeting, Westbury Road, April 28, in *Report on Certain Meetings.*
33. 'Coordination of Police Work in British West Indies in Respect of Undesirable Alien,' GH3/7/31, (Department of Archives, Barbados).
34. Secret. Inspector General of Police to Colonial Secretary, March 24, 1928, in *Report on Certain Meetings.*
35. 'Plan for dealing with the Disturbances July–August' GH/113. (Department of Archives, Barbados).
36. Edwin Lewis to British Consul-General, September 24, 1927, in *Labour Troubles and Unrest* (Department of Archives, Barbados).
37. Bishop Jack of the Episcopal Orthodox Church, GH3/6/3, (Department of Archives, Barbados).
38. Godfrey Haggard to Marquis of Kedleston, November 9, 1922, in 'Expediency of Recognizing Local Branch of UNIA Association in Cuba for Assisting West Indian Labourers' (Department of Archives, Barbados).
39. O'Brien to Duke of Devonshire, January 16, 1923, in 'Expediency of Recognizing Local Branch of UNIA.'
40. Secret: Grindle to Curzon, May 26, 1923, in 'Expediency of Recognizing Local Branch of UNIA.'
41. See *Report on Certain Meetings.*
42. Melville Inniss, joint WMA–UNIA meeting, Westbury Road, May 12, 1932, in *Report on Certain Meetings.*
43. The *Barbados Standard*, June 21, 1920, 4.
44. The *Barbados Standard*, February 22, 1919, 5.
45. The *Barbados Advocate*, May 11, 1921, 3.
46. The *Barbados Globe*, August 8, 1924, 3.
47. The *Barbados Globe*, August 9, 1924, 3.
48. The *Barbados Globe* (June 27, 1923), 5.
49. Ibid., 5.

50. Personal interview with John 'Gold Bead' Francis, Reed Street, Bridgetown, January 12, 1987; Sam Gibbs, Literary Row, Bridgetown, January 13, 1987.
51. UNIA meeting, Westbury Road, March 10, 1920, in *Report on Certain Meetings*; personal interview with Catherine Leacock, Crab Hill, St Lucy, October 16, 1987.
52. Personal interview with Tony Hinds, Advocate Co. Ltd., Barbados, November 11, 1987.
53. WMA meeting, Fairchild Street, January 13, 1928; see also WMA meeting, Passage Road, May 16, 1928.
54. Kenneth Wood, Public Meeting, Fairchild Street, November 2, 1927, in *Report on Certain Meetings*.
55. O'Neal, WMA meeting, October 27, 1927 in *Report on Certain Meetings*.
56. O'Neal, WMA Meeting, Passage Road, November 6, 1927.
57. Kenneth Wood, WMA Public Meeting, Grazettes, St Michael., August 5, 1927, in *Report on Certain Meetings*.
58. Fourth Public Session, Tuesday October 22, 1929, in *Proceedings of West Indian Sugar Commission* (October 1929, Advocate Co. Ltd.).
59. Corporal R. Hurley to Inspector of Police, September 18, 1927, in *Report on Certain Meetings*.
60. CO 28/306/10: Robertson to Amery, April 13, 1927.
61. Ibid.
62. O'Neal, WMA meeting, Beckwith Street, Bridgetown, February 11, 1928, in *Report on Certain Meetings*.
63. WMA meeting, July 27, 1927, Passage Road, October 13, 1927; UNIA meeting, Westbury Road, September 10, 1929, in *Report on Certain Meetings*; WMA meeting, Passage Road, October 12, 1927, in *Report on Certain Meetings*.
64. Moses Small, Meeting at UNIA Hall, October 12, 1927, in *Report on Certain Meetings*.
65. William Marshall, Passage Road, Stephenson Road, Delaware Village, August 19, 1927
66. George Belle, WMA meeting, Fairchild Street, November 3, 1927, in *Report on Certain Meetings*.
67. Edwin Turpin, WMA open-air meeting, Gills Gap, Eagle Hall, St Michael, November 10, 1927, in *Report on Certain Meetings*.
68. Ibid.
69. James Chase, UNIA open-air meeting, Stephenson Lane, August 19, 1927, in *Report on Certain Meetings*.
70. Fitzgerald Haynes, UNIA meeting, Westbury Road, May 22, 1928, in *Report on Certain Meetings*.
71. Minutes by Police Officer, June 2, 1932, in *Report on Certain Meetings*.
72. Minutes by Police Officer, August 18, 1933, in *Report on Certain Meetings*.
73. Minutes by Police Officer, June 2, 1932, in *Report on Certain Meetings*.
74. Minutes by Police Officer, April 21, 1932, in *Report on Certain Meetings*.
75. Ibid.
76. Fourth Public Session, October 22, 1929, *Proceedings of the West India Sugar Commission*, 58–9.

77. Minutes by Police Officer, June 2, 1932 (Department of Archives, Barbados).
78. There was a fall-off in the meetings until Payne arrived on the scene.
79. Secret. 'Abstract of Intelligence for the week ending 27th May 1937,' GH6/107. (Department of Archives, Barbados).
80. CO 28/293: O'Brien to Long, October 10, 1918 (Department of Archives, Barbados).
81. Ibid.
82. Secret. Acting Governor to Long, July 1, 1919.
83. Ibid.
84. Clement Payne, *My Political Memoirs of Barbados* (n.p.), 3
85. Ibid., 6
86. Ibid., 8; see also Louis Sebro, Day 18, Deane Commission, in W.A. Beckles
87. Clement Payne, op. cit., 10
88. Louis Sebro, Day 18, Deane Commission.
89. H.A. Bourne, Day 2, Deane Commission, The Barbados Disturbances.
90. Ibid.
91. Dan Blackett, Day 10, Deanr Commission.
92. H. A. Vaughan, Day 2, Deane Commission.
93. E. D. Mottley, Day 5, Deane Commission; 'Disturbances, Draft Despatches and Rough Notes, July–August, 1937,' GH/109, (Department of Archives, Barbados).
94. W. A. Beckles, 'Application for Official Recognition of His Services, 22nd February, 1938,' GH6/91, (Department of Archives, Barbados).
95. Ibid.

# Chapter 5

1. Derek Heater, *Our World this Century* (Oxford: Oxford University Press, 1985), 43.
2. E. M. Robertson, 'Race as a factor in Mussolini's Policy in Africa and Europe,' *Journal of Contemporary History* 23 no. 1 (January 1988): 40.
3. Richard B. Moore, 'Harlem and Pan African Politics' in *Richard B. Moore, Caribbean Militant in Harlem; Collected Writings 1920–1972* edited by W. Burghardt Turner & Joyce Moore-Turner (Indianapolis: Indiana University Press), 1973.
4. The *Barbados Weekly Observer*, August 3, 1935, 6.
5. Ibid., August 30, 1935, 6.
6. Clennel Wickham, 'The Italio-Ethiopia Quarrel – West Indian Stand Admirable,' *Barbados Advocate Weekly*, December 7, 1935, 3.
7. The *Barbados Weekly Observer*, August 10, 1935, 3.
8. Ibid., August 17, 1935, 7.
9. The *Barbados Weekly Herald*, November 4, 1935, 4.
10. The *Barbados Weekly Observer*, August 3, 1935, 1.
11. Ibid., August 31, 1935, 7.

12. Ibid., October 5, 1935, 7.
13. Sam Gibbs, Personal Interview, October 27, 1987.
14. Ibid.
15. *Report on Certain Meetings*, (Department of Archives, Barbados).
16. Moses Small, 'WMA meeting, Passage Road, February 12, 1928' in *Report on Certain Meetings* (Department of Archives, Barbados) GH4/37/38.
17. Moses Small, op. cit.
18. George Belle, 'WMA meeting, Grazettes Village, St Michael, May 5, 1927'; see also Moses Small, 'WMA meeting, Dunlow Lane, Bridgetown' in *Report on Certain Meetings*.
19. Melville Innis, 'UNIA meeting, Westbury Road, St Michael, May 5, 1932' in *Report on Certain Meetings*.
20. Chrissie Brathwaite, 'UNIA Meeting, May 12, 1932' in *Report on Certain Meetings*.
21. CO 28/306/6: Duke of Devonshire to O'Brien (September 14, 1923).
22. Ibid.
23. Financial Situation 1922, GH3/7/6 (Department of Archives, Barbados).
24. The *Barbados Advocate Weekly*, November 8, 1935, 15.
25. Ibid., November 12, 1935, 12.
26. Ibid., November 8, 1935, 9.
27. The *Barbados Weekly Observer*, November 8, 1938, 5.
28. Ibid., 4.
29. The *Barbados Weekly Observer*, November 30, 1935, 6.
30. Ibid., 7.
31. The *Barbados Advocate*, July 10, 1937, 8.
32. 'Complaints and Grievances in Connection with the Recent Disorders, 6 August 1937' GH/111 (Department of Archives, Barbados).
33. Ibid.
34. 'A Criminal Investigation Department Special Branch Report' quoted in G. Addington Forde, *The 1937 Disturbances of Barbados – A Summary of the Report of the Deane Commission of Enquiry* (n.p, 1999), 42.
35. W. A. Beckles, *The Barbados Disturbance 1937 – Review Reproduction of the Evidence and Report of the Commission* (Bridgetown, Advocate Co. Ltd. 1937).
36. 'Memorandum by the Government Information Officer' enclosure in secret dispatch of April 1940, in E. J. Waddington to Malcolm MacDonald (April 26, 1940), 107.
37. 'Extract from a Statement made by the Information Officer D. D. Chase, 11 November 1939' enclosure in secret dispatch of 17 November 1935, W. W. Flinn to Malcolm MacDonald (1939), GH3/10/5, 87.
38. D. D. Chase to Colonial Secretary, 'Outbreak of War' (August 24, 1939), GH3/10/5.
39. Secret. 'Report on the West Indies (Including British Guiana and British Honduras) 4 July 1939,' Ministry of Information, Publicity Division, GH3/10/5 (Department of Archives, Barbados).

40. No. 114. Telegram to Secretary of State, 15 September 1939, GH3/10/5, (Department of Archives, Barbados), 43.

## Chapter 6

1. 'Scheme of Organization against Civil Disturbances 1934' GH3/4/3, (Department of Archives, Barbados).
2. The *Barbados Advocate* (July 28, 1937), 1.
3. E. P. Thompson, 'The Moral Economy of the English Crowd in the Eighteenth Century' *Past and Present* No. 3, 1971; George Rude, *The Crowd in History, 1730–1848: A Study of Popular Disturbance in France and England* (New York: John Wiley and Sons, Inc., 1964), 237–68; Eric Hobsbawm, *On History* (London: Weidenfeld & Nicolson, 1997); Robert Ted Gurr, *Why Men Rebel* (Princeton: Princeton University Press, 1971).
4. 'Disturbances, Draft Despatches and Rough Notes, July–August 1937' GH4/109, (Department of Archives, Barbados).
5. The *Barbados Advocate*, July 28, 1937, 3.
6. Ibid., 5; see also 'Reports on Progress of Disturbances 1937' GH4/110, (Department of Archives, Barbados).
7. Leon 'Uncle' Clarke, Personal Interview, Hall Road, St Michael, October 11, 1988; also Don Shepherd, South District, St George, October 15, 1987.
8. The *Barbados Advocate*, July 28, 1937, 6.
9. Ibid., 6.
10. The *Barbados Advocate*, July 29, 1937, 8.
11. The *Barbados Advocate*, July 28, 1937, 8; see also Edward Stoute 'Flashbreak to 1937 Riots' *Barbados Advocate News*, (September 20, 1981), in Bonham Richardson, *Panama Money in Barbados, 1900–1920* (Knoxville: University of Tennessee Press, 1985), 241.
12. The *Barbados Advocate*, July 28, 1937, 7.
13. Ibid., 7.
14. Ibid., 8.
15. Andrew Gordon, 'The Crowd and Politics in Imperial Japan: Tokyo 1905–1918,' *Past and Present* no. 121 (November 1988): 144–70; Robert Woods, 'Individuals in the Rioting Crowd; A New Approach,' *Journal of Interdisciplinary History* XIV no.1 (Summer 1983): 1–24; Colin Lucas, 'The Crowd and Politics between Ancien Regime and Revolution in France,' *Journal of Modern History* 60 no. 3 (September 1968).
16. Paul Hanson, 'The "Vie Chere" Riots of 1911: Traditional Protest in Modern Garb' *Social History* (Spring 1988): 467–69; Juan Cole, 'Of Crowds and Empire: Afro-Asian Riots and European Expansion, 1857–1888,' *Comparative Studies in Society and History* 31 no. 4 (January 1980); Andrew Gordon, 'The Crowd and Politics in Imperial Japan: Tokyo 1905–1918,' *Past and Present* no. 121 (November 1988): 141–70.

17. 'Report Commandant Local Forces to Mark Young' in *Situation Reports 1937*, GH4/110, (Department of Archives, Barbados).
18. Ibid.
19. Urgent. Staff Officer Local Forces to Private Secretary 31.3.37, (Department of Archives, Barbados).
20. *Situation Report* for period 2.8.37. (Department of Archives, Barbados).
21. Ibid.
22. 'Report Commandant Local Forces to Mark Young' in *Situation Reports*.
23. Commandant Local Forces to Young (July 29, 1937) in *Situation Reports*.
24. George Rudé, *The Crowd in History*, 150; Colin Lucas, 'The Crowd and Politics between Ancient Regime and Revolution in France,' *Journal of Moodern History* 60 no. 3 (September 1998): 421–57.
25. Confidential. 'Report by Captain Lamb and Mr Stevenson to Mark Young' August 1, 1937, in *Situation Reports*.
26. Commandant Local Forces to Young, July 31, 1937, in *Situation Reports*.
27. Ibid.
28. The *Barbados Advocate*, July 31, 1837, 9.
29. 'Report of the Commission appointed to enquire into the Disturbances,' 240.
30. Staff Officer to Private Secretary, August 2, 1937, in *Situation Reports*
31. 'Situation Reports for Period 6.00 a.m. 9.8.37 to 6.00 a.m. 10.8.37' (Department of Archives, Barbados).
32. Ibid.
33. 'Reports for Period 5.8.37 to 6.8.37' in *Situation Reports*.
34. 'Reports by Captain Lamb, July 29, 1937' in *Situation Reports*.
35. Ibid.
36. 'Disturbances, complaints and grievances, including Governor's interview,' (Department of Archives, Barbados).
37. Ibid.
38. Ibid.
39. Ibid.
40. F. A. Hoyos, *Grantley Adams and the Social Revolution*, 70; see also Francis Mark, *The History of Barbados Workers Union*, Ch. 3.
41. Letter of Johnathan Mullins, St John, August 3, 1937, in 'Complaints, Grievances in Connection with the Disturbances' GH4/111.
42. Ibid.
43. Anonymous Letter from St Phillip in 'Complaints, Grievances in Connection with the Disturbances.'
44. Ibid.
45. Letter of Grievous Citizen in Complaints, Grievances in Connection with the Disturbances.'
46. F.A. Hoyos, op. cit.
47. See evidence of Grantley Adams, Dan Blackett, in 'The Barbados Disturbances Reproduction of Evidence and Report of Commission' compiled by W. A. Beckles.
48. Ibid., 240.

49. Personal Interview, Chelston Jones, Eastlyn, St George, November 16, 1988; Personal Interview, Wynter Crawford, Atlantic Shores, Christ Church, December 17,1988; Personal Interview, Gibbons Miller, Venture, St John, December 17, 1988.
50. 'The Barbados Disturbances Reproduction of Evidence and Report of Commission.'
51. Ibid.
52. Ibid.

# BIBLIOGRAPHY

## Primary Sources: Archival Material

*Barbados Blue Books*, 1916–39.

Barbados Chamber of Commerce, Produce Book – General.

Barbados General Agricultural Society – Minute Books 1910 BS.40

Barbados House of Assembly Records – Select Committee Minute Book 1916–1948, No. BS.25

Complaints and Grievances in Connection with the Recent Disturbances, GH4/111.

Condition of Sugar Industry Especially re Small-holding GH4/58.

Coordination of Police Work in the British West Indies in Respect of Undesirable Aliens 1936–3?, GH3/7/31.

Council Minute Book 1927–1943, Serial No. BS.28

Debates of the Council and Assembly, 1918–40.

Department of Science and Agriculture: Annual Reports

Detective Reports on Meeting 15 July 1927, 14 October 1932, GH4/37/38.

Dispatches from Governors to Secretary of State December 1916 to December 1920. C02/1/52

Disturbances – Governor's rough drafts, dispatches and notes 1937, GH4/109.

Educational System of Barbados, GH4/49.

Emancipation Centenary – Proposed Message from the King 1933, GH3/739.

Extract from the Report of the West Indian Sugar Commission for the Year 1929–30.

Financial Situation 1922. GH3/7/6.

International Labour Conventions 1932, GH3/7/22.

Italian-Abyssinian War – Instructions on dealing with ships of War 1935–36, GH3/7/27.

Italian Missionaries in British territories 1937, GH3/7/32.

Labour from the British West Indies for Improvements to the Panama Canal 1939–40, GH3/7/46/1.

Lightermen-Stevedores Strike 30 July–8 August, 1937, GH4/112.

Meeting Minute Book, Serial No.BS 28and 29.

Official Gazette, 1918–40,

Position of Sugar Industry 1936. GH4/96.

Proposed Visit to 'Barbados and Jamaica by Hilde Riquadias to Investigate Conditions of Negro Workers 1938 GH3/7/40.

References to 'Big Six' Comptroller of Customs re 1937, GH4/107.

Refusal of Certificates of Naturalization to Members of Foreign Political Organization. GH3/7/30.

Reports on Political meetings held re 'Constitutional Crisis,' GH4/107.

Reports on Progress of Disturbances 1937 – Situation Reports July 29–August 12, GH4/110.

Scheme of Organization against Civil Disturbances GH/3/4/3.

Sugar Industry 1921–22 GH3/7/5.

Unrest in the West Indies 1919–20 GH315/1.

## Newspapers

*Advocate Daily*, 1937–45.
*Barbados Advocate Weekly*, 1933–38.
*Barbados Agricultural Reporter*, 1916–22.
*Barbados Globe*, 1918–25.
*Barbados Observer*, 1934–40.
*Barbados Standard*, 1916–21.
*Barbados Weekly Herald*, 1919–30 and 1930–40.

## Secret and Confidential Despatches, Microfilm in UWI Library, Cave Hill

CO28/293 Lionel Probyn to Colonial Office.
CO28/294 Charles O'Brien to Colonial Office.
CO28/295 Charles O'Brien to Colonial Office.
CO28/296 Charles O'Brien to Colonial Office.
CO28/297 Charles O'Brien to Colonial Office.
CO28/298 Charles O'Brien to Colonial Office.
CO28/299 Charles O'Brien to Colonial Office.
CO28/300 Charles O'Brien to Colonial Office.
CO28/301 Charles O'Brien to Colonial Office.
CO/28302 Charles O'Brien to Colonial Office.
CO28/303 Charles O'Brien to Colonial Office.
CO28/304 W. C. F. Robertson to Colonial Office.
CO28/305 W. C. F. Robertson to Colonial Office.
CO28/306 W. C. F. Robertson to Colonial Office.
CO28/307 W. C. F. Robertson to Colonial Office.
CO28/308 W. C. F. Robertson to Colonial Office.
CO28/309 W. C. F. Robertson to Colonial Office.
CO28/310 W. C. F. Robertson to Colonial Office.
CO28/311 W. C. F. Robertson to Colonial Office.
CO28/312 Mark Young to Colonial Office.

CO28/313 Mark Young to Colonial Office.
CO28/314 Mark Young to Colonial Office.
CO28/315 Mark Young to Colonial Office.
CO28/316 Mark Young to Colonial Office.
CO28/317 Mark Young to Colonial Office.
CO28/318 Mark Young to Colonial Office.
CO28/319 W. C. F. Robinson and J. D. Owen to Colonial Office.
CO28/320 J. D. Owen to Colonial Office.
CO28/321 John Waddington to Colonial Office.
CO28/322 John Waddington to Colonial Office.
CO28/323 John Waddington to Colonial Office.
CO28/324 John Waddington to Colonial Office.

## Official Documents

Beckles, W. A., compiler. *The Barbados Disturbances 1937, Reproduction of the Evidence and Report of the Deane Commission*. Barbados: Advocate Co. Ltd, 1937.
Browne, G. St Orde. *Labour Conditions in the West Indies*. Cmd.6070 (1939).
West India Royal Commission, Report, London, 1897.
West India Royal Commission, Report, Cmd.6607 1945.
West Indian Sugar Commission, Report, Cmd.3517, 1930.

## Personal Interviews

Best, Seon, Indian Ground, St Peter, January 7, 1987.
Blackman, Federick, Crab Hill, St Lucy January 7, 1987.
Broomes, Hal, Crab Hill, St Lucy, January 1, 1981.
Clarke, Seon, Hall Road, St Michael, October 11, 1986.
Francis, John, Reed Street, Bridgetown, January 12, 1987.
Gibbs, Sam, Litery Row, Bridgetown, January 13, 1987.
Green, Elridge, Crab Hill, St Lucy, January 7, 1987.
Jones, Chelston, Eastlyn St George, November 5, 1986.
Leacock, Catherine, Crab Hill, St Lucy, January 6, 1986.
Sealy, Eric Passage Road, St Michael, January 25, 1987.
Shepherd, Dan, South District, St George, October 2, 1986.
Wickham, John, Literary Editor, Nation, November 6, 1987.

## Secondary Sources: Books, Articles, Unpublished Theses

Allen, Michael. 'Sugar and Survival: The Retention of Economic Power by White Elites in Barbados and Martinique.' *Peasants, Plantations and Rural Committees in the Caribbean*, edited by Malcolm Cross and Arnaud Marks Guilford. England: University of Surrey.

Banton, Michael. 'The Internal and External Conditions of Racial Thought.' *Ethnic and Racial Studies* 6 no. 2 (April 1983).

Banton, Michael. *Race Relations*. London: Tavistock Publications, 1969.

Barrow, Christine, and J. E. Green. *Small Business in Barbados – A Case of Survival*. Cave Hill, Barbados: ISER, 1979.

Barrow-Makiesky, Susan. 'Class, Culture and Politics in a Barbadian Community.' Unpublished PhD diss., Brandeis University, 1976.

Beckford, George. *Persistent Poverty; Underdevelopment in Plantation Economies of the Third World*. London: Oxford University Press, 1972.

Bell, Wendell and Walter Freeman. *Ethnicity and Nation Building: Comparative International and Historical Perspective*. Los Angeles: Sage Publications, 1974.

Belle, George. 'The Politics of Development: A Study in the Political Economy of Barbados.' PhD thesis, Manchester University, 1977.

———. 'Political Economy of Barbados 1937–1947: 1966: 1972.' MPhil, University of the West Indies, 1970.

Benn, Denis. *The Growth and Development of Political Ideas in the Caribbean 1774– 1983*. Mona, Kingston: ISER, UWI, 1987.

Berghe, Pierre Van Den. *Race and Racism – A Comparative Perspective*. New York: John Wiley and Sons Inc, 1967.

Bernard, George. *Wayside Sketches – Pen Pictures of Barbadian Life 1985*. n.p.

Bolt, Christine. *Victorian Attitudes to Race*. Routledge and Kegan Paul: London, 1971.

Bottomore, T. B. *Classes in Modern Society*. London: Allen and Unwin Ltd, 1965.

Carlyle, Thomas. *'The Nigger Question,' English and Other Critical Essays*. New York: Everyman Library, 1967.

Cashmore, E. Ellis, and Barry Troyne. *Introduction to Race Relations*. London: Routledge and Kegan Paul, 1983.

Castles, Francis. *Politics and Social Insight*. London: Routledge and Kegan Paul, 1971.

Casseres, Benjamin Gomes. 'Economic Development, Social Class and Politics in the Caribbean – An Historical Comparison of Curacao and Barbados, 1870–1958.' PhD thesis, Brandeis University, 1976.

Chancellor, V. E. *History for their Masters*. London, 1970.

Chase, Allan. *The Legacy of Malthus – The Social Costs of the New Scientific Racism*. New York: Alfred A. Knopf, 1977.

Cheltenham, Richard. 'Constitutional and Political Development in Barbados, 1946–66. PhD thesis, 1970.

Coleman, Romalis. 'Barbados and St Lucia: A Comparative Analysis of Social and Economic Development in two British West Indian Islands.' PhD thesis, Washington University, 1969.

Cox, Oliver. *Race Relations: Elements and Social Dynamics*. Detroit: Wayne State University Press, 1976.

Davis, Ioan. *Social Mobilitv and Political Change*. London: Pall Mall Press Ltd, 1970.

Davis, Kortright. *Cross and Crown in Barbados Caribbean Political Religion in the Late Nineteenth Century*. Frankfurt: Peter Lang, 1983.

Devos, Ton. *Introduction to Politics*. London: Winthrop Publishers, 1975.

Drake, St Clair. *Black Folk Here and There An Essay in History and Anthropology*. Los Angeles: Center for Afro-American Studies, University of California, 1987.

Drayton, Kathleen. 'Racism in Barbados.' *Bulletin of Eastern Caribbean Affairs* 9 no.2 (May–June 1983).

Drayton, Richard. 'Colonialism and Cultural Dependency in the Caribbean – The Case of Sugar Cane Breeding in Barbados.' IXth Annual Meeting of the Association of Caribbean Studies, London, England.

Duncan, Neville. 'Post Constructed Text of. Panel Presentation of Planter Democracy in Barbados, Movements as Subculture – A Preliminary Examination of Social and Political Protests in the Anglophone Caribbean.' n.p, 1983.

Emtage, S. E. *Growth Development and Planning in a Small Dependent Economy – The Case of Barbados*. n.p.

Fermor, Patrick Leigh. *The Traveller's Tree – A Journey through the Caribbean Islands*. London: John Murray, 1950.

Forde, G. Addington. *The 1937 Disturbances of Barbados. A Summary of the Report of the Deane Commission of Enquiry*. n.p, 1999.

Fortney, Nancy. 'The Effects of the First World War on the British West Indies.' Caribbean Societies Vol.1 Collected Seminar Papers No. 29. London: Institute of Commonwealth Studies, University of London, 1982.

Giddens, Anthony. *The Class Structure of the Advanced Societies*. London: Hutchinson and Co. Publishers, 1981.

Girvan, Norman. *Aspects of the Political Economy of Race in the Caribbean and the Americas – A Preliminary Interpretation*. Kingston: ISER, University of the West Indies, Mona, 1975.

Hamilton, Charles, and Stokeley Carmichael. *Black Power – The Politics of Liberation in America*. London: Johnathan Cape, 1967.

Harewood, Leroy. *Black Powerlessness in Barbados*. Bridgetown: Black Star Publications, 1968.

Hewitt, J. M. *Ten Years of Constitutional Development in Barbados 1944–1954*. Bridgetown: Coles Printery, 1954.

Hoetink, H. *'Race' and Colour in the Caribbean*. Washington, DC: The Woodrow Wilson International Center for Scholars, 1985.

Hoyos, F. A. *Barbados: A History from the Amerindians to Independence*. London: Macmillan Caribbean Ltd, 1978.

———. *The Rise of West Indian Democracy*. Bridgetown: Advocate Press:, 1963.

———. *Grantley Adams and the Social Revolution*. London: Macmillan Education Ltd, 1974.

Hume, C. H. 'The Public Health Movement.' In *Popular Movements 1830–1850*, edited by J. J. Ward. Hampshire: Macmillan Education Ltd, 1970.

Hunte, Keith. 'Charles Duncan O'Neal: Apostle of Freedom.' *New World Quarterly* III nos1 and II (Barbados Independence Issue).

Joseph, C. L. 'The British West Indies Regiment 1914–18.' *Journal of Caribbean History* 2 (May 1971).

Karch, Cecilia A. 'The Transformation and Consolidation of the Corporate Plantation Economy in Barbados1860–1919.' PhD thesis, Rutgers University, 1974.

Kunsman, Charles Henry. 'The Origins and Development of Political Parties in the British West Indies.' Thesis, University of California, 1974.

Kerles, Daniel. *In the Name of Eugenics – Genetics and the Uses of Human Hereditary.* Berkeley: University of California Press,

Lenin, V. I. *Selected Works Vol. 3.* Moscow: Progress Publishers, 1971.

Lewis, Arthur. *Labour in the West Indies – The Birth of a Worker's Movement.* London, 1971.

Lewis, Gordon K. *The Making of the Modern West Indies.* New York: Modern Reader Paperback, 1969.

————. 'Caribbean Society and Culture.' *Contemporary Caribbean Issues* edited by Angel Cadderon. Cruz Instituto de Estudios de Caribe, Universidad de Puerto Rico, 1979.

Lewonthin, R. C., et al. *Not in Our Genes.* New York: Pantheon Books, 1984.

Lipson, Leslie. *The Great Issues of Politics – An Introduction to Political Science* 5th edn. Englewood Cliffs: New Jersey Prentice Hall Inc, 1975.

Lowenthal, David. *West Indian Societies.* London : Oxford University Press, 1972.

Mack, Raymond. 'Race, Class and Power in Barbados.' In T*he Democratic Revolution in the West Indies* edited by Wendell Bell. Cambridge, Massachusetts: Schenkman Publishing Co. Inc, 1967.

Mackenzie, W. J. M. *Politics and Social Science.* Harmondsworth, Middlesex: Penguin Books, 1969.

Macmillan, W. M. *Warning from the West Indies – A Tract for Africa and the Empire.* Faber and Faber Ltd., London.

Malik,Kenan. *The Meaning of Race-Race, History and Culture in Western Society.* London: Macmillan, 1996.

Mark, Francis. *The History of the Barbados Workers Union.* Bridgetown: Advocate Commercial Printing, 1966.

Martin, Tony. *Marcus Garvey Hero.* Dover: The Majority Press: 1983.

————. *Race First – The Ideological and Organizational Struggles of Marcus Garvey and the Universal Negro Improvement Association.* Westport, Connecticut: Greenwood Press, 1976.

Maughan, Basil. 'Some Aspects of Barbadian Emigration to Cuba 1919–1935.' *Journal of the Barbados Museum and Historical Society* XXXVII no.3 (1985).

McLellan, David. *The Thought of Karl Marx.* New York: Harper and Row Publishers, 1971.

Miller, J. D. B. *The Nature of Politics.* London: Gerald Duckworth and Co. Ltd, 1974.

Mills, Robert. *Racism.* London and New York: Routledge, 1989.

Morris, Robert. *Charles Duncan O'Neal – Father of Democracy in Barbados.* n.p.

————. 'The Rise of the Labour Movement in Barbados from about 1920 to about 1946.' Seminar Paper 1974/75, UWI, Cave Hill.

Orum, Anthony. *Introduction to Political Sociology the Social Anatomy of the Body Politic* 2nd edn. Englewood Cliffs, New Jersey: Prentice Hall Inc., 1983.

Parris, Ronald Glenfield. 'Race, Inequality and Underdevelopment in Barbados.' PhD thesis, Yale University, 1974.

Payne, Clement. *Political Memoirs of Barbados.* n.p.

Phillips, Anthony. 'The Racial Factor in Politics 1880–1914.' Seminar Paper 1, 1973–74, UWl, Cave Hill.

Puzzo, Dante. 'Racism and the Western Tradition.' *Journal of the History of Ideas* (October–December) XXV no.4.

Raphael, D. D. *Problems of Political Philosophy.* Revised Edition. London: Macmillan Press Ltd, 1976.

Roberts, G. W. 'Emigration from the Island of Barbados.' *Social and Economic Studies* no.3 (September 1955).

Rubin, Vera. 'Culture, Politics and Race Relations.' *Social and Economic Studies* II no.4, (December 1962).

Rudé, George. *Ideology and Popular Protest.* New York: Pantheon Books, 1980.

————. *The Crowd in History 1730–1848: A Study of Popular Disturbances in France and England.* New York: John Wiley and Sons Inc., 1964.

Skeete, C. O. *The Condition of Peasant Agriculture in Barbados.* Bridgetown: Advocate Ltd, 1930.

Smith, F. B. *The People Health 1830–1910.* London: Croom Helm, 1979.

Smith, M. G. *Culture, Race and Class in the Commonwealth Caribbean.* Mona, Jamaica: Department of Extra Mural Studies, UWI, 1984.

Sniderman, Paul and Philip Tetlock. 'Reflection on American Racism.' *Journal of Social Issues* 42 no.2 (1986).

Starkey, Otis P. *The Economic Geography of Barbados.* New York: Columbia University Press, 1939.

Stone, Carl. *Class, Race and Political Behaviour in Urban Jamaica.* Kingston: ISER, UWl, Mona, 1973.

Sturge, Joseph and Thomas Harvey. *The West Indies in 1837.* London: Frank Cass and Co. Ltd, 1965.

Tawney, R. H. *Equality.* London: George Allen and Unwin Ltd, 1964.

Trollope, Anthony. *The West Indies and the Spanish Main.* New York, 1860.

Walters, Vernon. *Introductory Psychology* 3rd edn. Chicago: Rand McNally Publishing Company, 1980.

Walvin, James. 'Recurring Themes: White Images of Black Life during and after Slavery.' *Slavery and Abolition* 5 no.2 (September 1984).

————. *Passage to Britain – Immigration in British History and Politics.* Suffolk: Penguin Books, 1984.

Weber, Max. *The Theory of Social and Economic Organization.* New York: The Free Press, 1968.

Weisbord, Robert. 'British West Indian Reaction to the Italian-Ethiopian War: An Episode in Pan Africanism.' Caribbean Studies. 10 no.1 (April 1970). Instituto de Estudios del Caribe, Universidad de Puerto Rico.

Wickham, Clennel. *Pen and Ink Sketches by a Gentleman with a Fountain Pen. Herald*, 1921.

————. *Colour Question – Some Reflections on Barbados.* n.p., 1936

Will, Wilburn Marvin. 'Political Development in the Mini-State Caribbean; Focus on Barbados.' PhD thesis, Missouri University, 1974.

Wood, Robert. 'Individuals in a Rioting Crowd: A New Approach.' *Journal of Interdisciplinary History* XIV no.1 (Summer 1983).

Zahar, Renate. 'Frantz Fanon: Colonialism and Alienation.' New York: Monthly\ Review Press, 1974.

# INDEX

change, 143–44; victimisation of
members of the, 103–08; and early
working class activism, 83, 84,
89–90, 100–12;
Wood, Kenneth: political activist, 82
Wood, Major E.F.L: and sugar industry,
49–50

Yearwood, H.G.: and the habitual Idler's
Bill, 57
Young, Governor Mark: and the
Legislative Council, 27; and the
1937 strike, 135–37

www.ingramcontent.com/pod-product-compliance
Lightning Source LLC
Chambersburg PA
CBHW070911270326
41927CB00011B/2534